ADDITIONAL PRAISE FOR *THE GIFT OF GLOBAL TALENT*

"If immigration is to provide sizable economic gains to a receiving country, the place to look is high-skill. William Kerr gives a comprehensive and objective summary of what we know about its economic impact. The book is an invaluable resource."

—George J. Borjas, Harvard Kennedy School and author, *We Wanted Workers*

"America owes its economic success to its unmatched ability to attracted global talent. But technology is changing rapidly and that means the skills needed for success are changing rapidly as well. William Kerr provides a definitive road map of how America needs to reform its talent strategy and immigration policy."

—Erik Brynjolfsson, Professor at MIT and coauthor, *The Second Machine Age*

"*The Gift of Global Talent* offers key insights on how immigrant entrepreneurs spur U.S. economic growth, create American jobs, and help to further technological and scientific advancement in the U.S. It is an important addition to our national dialogue on immigration and should be required reading for policymakers."

—Bobby Franklin, President and CEO, National Venture Capital Association

"*The Gift of Global Talent* crystalizes how much the American economy benefits from skilled foreign workers. For American innovation to thrive in the twenty-first century, we must attract the best minds out there, and Kerr's excellent book teaches us how to do just that."

—Edward Glaeser, Harvard University and author, *Triumph of the City*

"William Kerr does a masterful job exploring the economic and social benefits global talent has on local communities and the impact it continues to have on their home countries. Any reader will be better equipped to understand the importance of global talent now and in the future."

—Dejian Liu, Chairman & Founder, NetDragon

"America's small businesses are under pressure when it comes to accessing the skilled workers they need to compete. William Kerr brilliantly illuminates a framework for the critical conversation that we need to have if we want small businesses to continue to drive our nation's economic success."

—Karen G. Mills, Former Administrator of the U.S. Small Business Administration and Cabinet Member under President Obama

"This is a clear-eyed exposition of how talent moves around the world and why so much lands in the United States. Chock-full of compelling data, this book shows that the economic stakes in today's overheated immigration debate couldn't be higher. This is a must-read for policy makers."

—Janet Napolitano, President of the University of California, former Secretary of Homeland Security and Governor of Arizona

"The competitive advantage of nations in today's international economy depends upon accessing top global talent. America is going down the wrong path when it comes to immigration, and political gridlock is threatening a key historical advantage. This timely and powerful book tells us how to get back on track."

—Michael Porter, University Professor, Harvard University

"If you want to understand why Boston and Silicon Valley have created such vibrant ecosystems, read this book! All of the best and brightest don't work in the U.S., and we should do everything we can to attract and keep that talent. This is the fuel for future generations of startups."

—Dharmesh Shah, Cofounder and CTO, HubSpot

"Kerr's explanation of the role of high-skilled immigration and the reforms that are needed to maintain U.S. competitiveness make this one of the most important books on policy of our time. He demonstrates knowledge and talent are now the world's most important resources."

—Vivek Wadhwa, Carnegie Mellon University and author, *The Driver in the Driverless Car*

THE GIFT OF GLOBAL TALENT

How Migration Shapes Business,
Economy & Society

William R. Kerr

STANFORD BUSINESS BOOKS

An Imprint of Stanford University Press • Stanford, California

Stanford University Press

Stanford, California

Special discounts for bulk quantities of Stanford Business Books are available to corporations, professional associations, and other organizations. For details and discount information, contact the special sales department of Stanford University Press. Tel: (650) 725-0820, Fax: (650) 725-3457

Printed in the United States of America on acid-free, archival-quality paper

Library of Congress Cataloging-in-Publication Data

Names: Kerr, William R. (William Robert), author.

Title: The gift of global talent : how migration shapes business, economy & society / William R. Kerr.

Description: Stanford, California : Stanford Business Books, an imprint of Stanford University Press, 2018. | Includes bibliographical references and index.

Identifiers: LCCN 2018009497| ISBN 9781503605022 (cloth : alk. paper) | ISBN 9781503607361 (ebook)

Subjects: LCSH: United States—Emigration and immigration—Economic aspects. | Foreign workers—United States. | Skilled labor—United States. | United States—Emigration and immigration—Government policy. | Emigration and immigration—Economic aspects.

Classification: LCC JV6471 .K47 2018 | DDC 331.6/20973—dc23

LC record available at https://lccn.loc.gov/2018009497

Typeset by Newgen in Baskerville 11.75/16

Cover design by Rob Ehle

To Saku and Sara
TGG

CONTENTS

FIGURES

PREFACE

When a business leader or politician or university president talks about global talent—often about "winning the war for talent!"—their perspective is deeply colored by their job and personal history. It is like the old story of blind men describing an "elephant" to one another. One feels the trunk and describes it to the group as a "thick snake." A second believes the elephant's leg to be a tree trunk. Others are touching a spear (its tusks), a rope (its tail), or a massive wall (its sides). Each description is correct but misses seeing the whole animal. In a similar way, it can be hard to piece together all the business, innovation, and policy angles of global talent flows. This combined perspective is the goal of this book.

My personal journey also shapes the story being told, and thus I should share a little about myself. My day job is at Harvard Business School, where my research considers high-skilled immigration and its economic consequences. I also collaborate with many global companies in nations like China, India, Finland, and Turkey. Prior to entering academia, I worked in Hong Kong at a telecom job that brought lots of travel and global teams. That was eye popping for someone who had gotten his passport only after college. Likewise was the time I got deported from Korea for some visa troubles—who knew how rigid these immigration rules really were? Given my background, the narrative ahead mixes business examples, economic theory, and policy details to tell the story from multiple vantage points.

My viewpoint does not fit neatly into tidy political or cultural buckets. I cast my first vote at age eighteen for Ross Perot, and I have sided as frequently with Democrats as with Republicans since then. Growing up in Alabama, I loved guns and accidentally shot a hole through the floor of my childhood home. But now I advocate for greater gun control. I attend an evangelical church but work in one of the most left-leaning cities in America, being most content when escaping to a cheap BBQ joint or McDonald's PlayPlace with my kids. Thus, I happily admit to being hopelessly confused on many hot button issues. But not on global talent.

America's surge to preeminence over the past 250 years is due to the promise of the "American dream" and the talent it has welcomed to its shores. This unique power is currently suffering from deep backlash against globalization and inequality. The struggle for openness is likely to last for decades, a defining issue for our time. I don't have all the answers, and this book showcases triumphs of global talent flows alongside the struggles of its victims. Both demand our attention, as talent is the global resource that we want to use most wisely.

Perhaps surprisingly, President Trump plays a rather small role in this book, despite its focus on immigration. The current hostility toward immigrants might finally break the promise of America that is held by so many talented people around the world. But America has neglected global talent for more than a decade, starting well before the 2016 election.

Some may cheer at the prospect of reduced inflows of talented immigrants, but they should not. Ceding U.S. talent leadership would hurt Middle America as much as it would harm Manhattan or Silicon Valley, as a result of lost tax revenues, weakened colleges, and more. It would diminish America, not make it whole again. This loss would also be felt beyond America's borders, as other countries cannot yet deploy global talent with the productivity and scale of the U.S. We must harness and improve global talent, not destroy it, to thrive in the century ahead.

ACKNOWLEDGMENTS

Many people helped make this book happen. Starting with the writing itself, I thank the team of Alexis Brownell, Elaine Cummings, Carl Kreitzberg, Louis Maiden, Don Maruyama, James Palano, Mark Poirot, Manjari Raman, and Shirley Sun for their invaluable assistance, ranging from looking up obscure details to challenging many of the thoughts presented. Alexis deserves a special callout for her persistent editing of each chapter to smooth out my bumpy prose. Margo Fleming was a valuable coach in the early stages, and I thank the team at Stanford University Press of Olivia Bartz, Steve Catalano, and Kate Wahl for helping to punch this book through.

Additional thanks to the many colleagues and friends for their reviews of the first draft: Daron Acemoglu, Derek Bathrick, Gilles Duranton, Alan Friedman, Ina Ganguli, Boris Groysberg, Kalle Heikkinen, Bill Lincoln, Norm Matloff, Ernest Miguelez, Tsedal Neeley, Tim Rowe, Sidar Sahin, Chad Sparber, and Su Min Sng. I am grateful for particularly in-depth reviews by Jeff Bussgang, Rob Carpenter, Mihir Desai, Rob Fairlie, Martin Kenney, Carole Kerr, Joe Kerr, Scott Kominers, Jan Rivkin, Rob Snyder, and two anonymous reviewers. These comments pushed the book much further than I could have ever taken it alone.

I also thank my many coauthors and colleagues over the past two decades. While I describe the key findings of many of their studies, early drafts became quite clunky with the names of authors here, there, and everywhere. So I ask my colleagues' forbearance as I have relegated the names of researchers to citations, and the onus is on me to convey to them in person how important their work has been. I am deeply grateful to Harvard Business School and MIT Economics, my professional homes over the past seventeen years, and to those who have supported my research: the Alfred P. Sloan Foundation, the Bank of Finland, the Ewing Marion Kauffman Foundation, the National Bureau of Economic Research, and the Smith-Richardson Foundation.

My greatest thanks go to Sari Pekkala Kerr, who is a colleague, coauthor, and (you guessed it) my wife and boss. Sari inadvertently exposed me to many idiosyncrasies of U.S. immigration law when she immigrated in the mid-2000s, after we met at MIT. Sari is now an American citizen, holding great pride in her naturalized home but also deep worries about the world ahead, like many of us. Most important, for more than a decade, Sari has put up with my own idiosyncrasies, which vastly outnumber those of the worst immigration system. For that, I owe my deepest gratitude.

A NOTE ON TERMINOLOGY

The terms in this book balance readability with precision. One could spend hours parsing the term "American" and whom it includes. I seek to navigate potentially sensitive terms but also not overburden readers with hundreds of caveats. I use the term "we" only as a narrative device, meaning you the reader and me the author. Many readers of this book will not be American, and I will thus write "America should" rather than "We should."

THE GIFT OF GLOBAL TALENT

INTRODUCTION

Why Global Talent Matters to You

WHETHER YOU ARE A STUDENT, a CEO, a programmer, an Uber driver, or a government official, and whether you live in Atlanta or Zagreb, the story of global talent is important for you and will, in many ways, shape your future.

Talented people have an impact on all aspects of our lives, from those who are inventing the next versions of our smartphones to those researching how to extend life. Some lead large companies, others craft effective government policy, and yet others teach and research. The collective power of global talent took us from horses in the nineteenth century to space shuttles in the twentieth century; from an average global life expectancy of thirty-one years in 1900 to seventy-two years today; from disease-ridden cities to powerful and safe metropolises. We certainly also got a lot of things wrong along the way, ranging from atomic bombs to malware, but even so, the progress has been substantial.

This talent moves around a lot. The teams at Apple or Siemens or the London School of Economics draw people from far and wide, accomplishing more together than they ever could in isolation. Much of the innovative power unleashed during the twentieth century came from global talent flowing to where it could be most productive and to where it had the capacity to realize its potential to change the world. Global talent has been an enormous boon to the United States and other destinations favored by high-skilled immigrants.

In the pages ahead, we explore why global talent flows matter so much, from superstar scientists to white-collar workers. There are many parts worthy of celebration, but also many parts to critique. We explore big advances in technology and some amazing start-ups, but we also see older IT workers who have lost their jobs. We study the rise of talent clusters that allow for great collaboration, but we observe many people on the outside looking in, angrily. The deep discontent that many feel toward today's economy and expanding inequality is being increasingly directed at global talent.

Sometimes discontent becomes rage. A recent issue of *Bloomberg Businessweek* had the horrible cover story "Murder in Olathe: The Shooting of Two Indian-Born Engineers Reverberates beyond Kansas."[1] The story describes how Olathe, Kansas, population 130,000, has recently fostered a strong tech community that includes Garmin, a large and successful manufacturer of GPS devices. Many immigrant tech workers have moved to Olathe and contributed to this local development. Tragically, on February 22, 2017, a fifty-one-year-old white male, enraged and yelling, "Get out of my country!" shot and killed one Indian engineer who worked for Garmin and injured another. Parallel incidents have occurred elsewhere in America, a gruesome witness to the anti-immigrant backlash that is under way in many advanced countries.

While we shudder at the terrible incident in Olathe, the same issue of the magazine was filled with many other examples of global talent, some highlighting its virtues, others bemoaning its vices. Although this magazine was not a special issue on the topic, it spoke to many ways skilled immigration influences our lives:

- In the Global Economics section, the lead story is "As Venezuela Implodes, Its Young Professionals Flee for a Chance in the U.S." The collapsed economy is leading to a substantial brain drain to America as skilled workers look for meaningful employment.

- The next article is "Cyprus' Passport to Growth: Selling EU Citizenship." A staggering 25 percent of Cyprus's gross domestic product (GDP) now comes from sales of its citizenship, which includes a European Union passport, to wealthy Russian immigrants. While this example depicts an extreme case, most countries have similar programs that offer residency to those rich enough and willing to spend.

- A bit farther down in the Technology section is an article entitled "Carmakers Are Having a Hard Time Selling Tech Talent on Detroit." As software becomes a critical input for car manufacturers, access to top talent has become a "CEO issue" rather than just an "HR issue," according to the report. The skills for running yesterday's automobile company are different from those that produce world-class software for driverless cars, and traditional companies are racing to compete.

- A later story is scary for my line of work: "A Trump Slump at U.S. B-schools, as Foreign Students Head Elsewhere." Fiery political rhetoric and uncertain future job prospects are reducing foreign applicants to U.S. professional schools. One MBA student in Toronto candidly notes: "Of course you want to be at Stanford or Columbia, but you have to place your bets. . . . Top talent is going to go where it is welcome."

- The last article is entitled "How Did I Get Here? Dara Khosrowshahi's Long Trip from Iranian Refugee to Expedia CEO." A quote from Khosrowshahi, who three months later became CEO of Uber: "What some Americans don't appreciate is how strong the brand of the American dream is around the world. I'm an example of how powerful that product is. And now, our president is trying to pull it away from people of a certain origin and religious belief. I find that very sad and very much against what our founders set out to build."

These stories highlight how the global distribution of talent affects the strength of our companies, the social fabric of our communities, and much beyond. If we truly understood this talent's power and consequences, nations would have "war rooms" focused solely on harnessing its power. What makes global talent flows so important today?

A Simple Foundation

This book builds on three simple propositions, the first of which is that talent is the world's most precious resource. Other candidates for this title, like water or oil, deserve consideration, but the power of human talent and how it is utilized is the most important. Some of our best talent, after all, is cracking the desalination of ocean water and cost-efficient solar power to replace fossil fuels. This importance of talent has to some degree always been true, ranging from the clever spark who invented the wheel to the military geniuses who won major wars. Yet for much of human history, fertile farmland, masses of labor, and heavy machinery were as important to national success. Today, the knowledge economy vaults talented individuals to the center of economic performance and the achievement of global prosperity.

The second proposition is that talent as a resource is quite movable, unlike a harbor or a coal mine. A nonstop flight from Boston to Hong Kong takes just sixteen hours, and business managers today can visit three continents in a single week. This is different from a few decades ago, when travelers eagerly recounted for years that rare trip to Africa or Japan. This mobility is also unprecedented in terms of the needed inputs for business success. Much of the economic activity at the start of the twentieth century centered on the waterways that were essential for commerce. Talent, however, can cluster anywhere, with Silicon Valley barely a spot on the map fifty years ago. In today's digital era, the control and execution of work itself is also becoming movable, such as the logistics of a harbor being managed from afar.

The final proposition is that talent is significantly shaped by the environment that surrounds it. A recent film depicts the rare genius of Srinivasa Ramanujan, a boy born in India in 1887, who achieved astounding mathematical insights without formal training before being discovered by leading European academics. We all stand in awe of self-taught minds like Ramanujan, but the development and utilization of talent works very differently. Families around the world sacrifice deeply to send their children to the very best schools in advanced economies, and the ability to put talent to work increasingly depends on interacting with other skilled minds. Ramanujan himself moved to England to collaborate on frontier research with the leading mathematician G. H. Hardy.

Our Focus on Skills

If these three propositions—talent's primacy, its mobility, and its dependence on its environment—are even roughly correct, then global talent flows are of central importance to every nation, business, and person.

This book focuses on high-skilled immigration, and principally those migrations that are employment based, such as when Apple hires Chinese programmers and brings them to Cupertino. This applies to a minority of U.S. inflows, with most immigrants instead entering for family-based objectives, such as reuniting parents with their children who have already immigrated. Employment-based immigration is of most immediate consequence in many skilled sectors of the economy, but talent can enter through any category and build up over generations—this is the "American story," in fact.

Why, then, focus on high-skilled individuals? First, the processes and policies governing these admissions are quite different from those covering family reunification or refugee objectives. Firms and universities take on prominent roles, and the organization of work in talented industries produces distinct economic outcomes. More-over, the consequences of global talent flows are different for businesses and society than general migration. An easy example is U.S. inequality, where grappling with illegal immigration would muddle our inquiry into how high-skilled immigrants have an impact on U.S. earnings.

A second rationale is the politics of high-skilled immigration reform. National polls show Americans have three times more support for the immigration of "high-skilled workers" than they do for "low-skilled workers."[2] As voters think about immigration differently depending on skill level, we will focus all our bandwidth on high-skilled inflows, and this book's policy recommendations will be exclusive to that group. But we are skipping ahead at this point, and need to commence with how global talent flows got started.

The Roots of Global Talent Flows

The first five chapters describe the global flows of skilled people, bringing together why individuals want to move, how they are employed in their new locations, and who are the gatekeepers governing their admissions.

Chapter 1 describes the landscape of global talent flows. Talented people come from many countries, especially China and India in recent years, but they consistently prioritize a few places. America has long been the preferred destination for many skilled people. The United States continues to hold a staggering "trade surplus" for talent exchanges, but its special position is weakening with time. We examine what prompts talented individuals to move halfway around the world, including the higher earnings possible in advanced economies and refuge from crises like the one under way in Venezuela.

The fact that so many talented people congregate in just a few spots seems straightforward, but how is it sustainable? If we placed much of the world's oil into Silicon Valley, we would expect its local price to plummet dramatically—yet the abundance of internet entrepreneurs does not diminish the Valley's draw for future talent. What makes this resource and the knowledge economy different? Chapter 2 introduces us to the economics of talent clusters, in which many skilled individuals work in sectors of the economy where their productivity is increased mainly by collocating with other talented workers (e.g., Hollywood actors versus your local dentist). This process allows a growing cluster of talent to become the most productive place to work, thereby encouraging even further migration. After all, where do the world's aspiring actors and actresses want to go?

These outcomes differ from those of lower-skilled immigration, where an abundance of labor reduces the attractiveness to future migrants because of capped local work opportunities. In fact, the largest brake on the talent-clustering process typically emerges from ridiculously high home prices and costs of living, which allows for smaller cities like Olathe to develop a tech presence, too. Detroit's struggles also highlight how traditional companies can find it hard to compete with the powerful interactions that talent clusters generate. Detroit was built to harness an enormous scale beneficial for automobile production, combining huge factories with an army of assembly-line workers. The skills for running these traditional businesses are different from those that produce world-class software for driverless cars, which scares Motor City. Ford fired its CEO in 2017 for moving too slowly in the race toward the driverless car, which finds Detroit's giants suddenly competing against Google and Uber.

Indeed, the influence of global talent flows is most pronounced in the U.S. tech sector, the subject of Chapter 3. Immigrants account for about a quarter of U.S. patents and entrepreneurship, and more than half of America's PhD workforce in science and engineering is foreign born. These shares have grown substantially since the 1970s, particularly with the sharp rise of Chinese and Indian immigration. A deep dive into the American tech sector uncovers why these skills and occupations align so well with global talent flows. It also shows how immigrants are reshaping the geography of innovation in America—one in every eleven U.S. patents is developed today by a Chinese or Indian inventor living in the San Francisco Bay Area.

The immigration of talented people is constrained by national regulations, and Chapter 4 describes how countries vary substantially in their openness to immigrants and the methods used to select candidates. Following Canada's example, many advanced countries built points-based systems that score potential immigrants on dimensions like education and language fluency. This approach positions the government as the primary gatekeeper, and it helps encourage diversity and select long-term talent. But a points-based approach also struggles with selecting immigrants who can fulfill critical job opportunities, leading many countries to instead delegate significant responsibilities for the selection of skilled immigrants to two other gatekeepers: firms and universities.

In contrast to Canada, in the United States companies are a central gatekeeper for talent admissions. Firms directly select high-skilled immigrants whom they want to employ, most notably by obtaining an H-1B visa for the worker. This delegation means that incoming talent is guaranteed to match with a job. But this approach also has an important consequence—the self-interested motivations that firms have when selecting new employees, good or bad, become implicitly the nation's policy toward migration of skilled workers. Some firms use immigration to unlock growth and innovation by gaining access to scarce skills, whereas others seek to minimize labor costs or to offshore work from America. Consequently, the benefits of innovation and job creation happen alongside the painful replacement of older IT workers to boost profits. We will explore the complex relationship of firms and talent flows and why some lobbyists refer to the limits on H-1B admissions as "America's national suicide."

Chapter 5 shows how universities are the second gatekeeper, as the education pathway produces the foreign graduates who firms recruit. Schools are often the entry point to advanced economies for talented people, who seek both great educations and future job opportunities, a link that the "Trump Slump for B-Schools" story highlights. Indeed, the American education sector is gigantic, and the rising inflows of international students are limiting the ability of graduates to obtain work visas. This desire by universities for foreign students shows little sign of abating, however, as they provide critical funding (international students often pay full fare) as well as the researchers who staff laboratories. Indeed, the way firms and universities shape American talent inflows is not the subject of arcane policy making but is central to how worldwide talent is allocated and the gains and losses that accrue to society.

The Consequences of Global Talent Flows

The second half of the book turns to the consequences of global talent flows for businesses and societies at large. Chapter 6 begins with talent clusters and firms. The perspective that business leaders take on global talent is deeply intertwined with the large technological advances confronting their industries. To succeed in the knowledge economy, top organizations must anticipate and identify emerging ideas, access global talent to develop and refine insights, and push the applications to all parts of vast organizations. This is a demanding set of tasks, with CEOs globally rethinking past organization charts and long-range planning documents, recognizing that the future of work must be managed differently from the past.

Top of mind for many bosses is how to access leading talent clusters, from Los Angeles to London to Shanghai, as it is easiest to catch breakthrough concepts if you are nearby when they are born. These centers foster the global start-ups that are disrupting industries as diverse as hotels, taxis, communication, and finance. More MBA students today dream of starting the next Square or Spotify than of becoming the CEO of HSBC or Walmart, which was not true a decade ago. Global integration, rapid technology cycles, and better tools for coordination are pushing incumbent firms deep into these clusters, ranging from shiny new headquarters to small innovation labs. In traditional industries, personnel choices often followed corporate strategy; now, access to talent dictates many of the strategic options available to a company.

Maintaining a corporate presence in leading talent clusters is but one of the many challenges that companies face. Even as General Electric moves its headquarters to Boston, most of its employees are elsewhere, including a majority outside of America. Chapter 7 describes these human resource challenges. Building and empowering global employee bases requires choices about which language to speak internally and how to implement collaborative team structures. Companies today also obsess about talent outside of their organization. Under mantras like "open innovation," leading firms are building platforms to reach external capabilities and ideas all around the world. Terms like "virtual access" and "porous boundaries" are more than just business buzz, as even the largest companies recognize that many people outside of their organization are working on the same ideas that they are.

Chapter 8 describes how these business linkages are accelerating the international diffusion of technologies and remaking business models. Distance matters for how quickly ideas spread, but networks and people flows matter even more. As talented people move back and forth between countries, they often transport important insights with them. This can be as simple as a graduating student who takes home a new product concept for the family business, or as complex as Rocket Internet, a large company that replicates e-commerce ideas globally and spans more than one hundred countries. Many skilled individuals further affect talent-sending countries without leaving their new homes by arranging business contacts or sharing technical insights. Thus, while global talent flows concentrate new innovations in leading talent clusters, they also act as centrifugal forces that spread the benefits back out.

These cross-border actions of businesses and migrating talent determine whether talent-sending countries experience a brain drain when their best and brightest go abroad. The economics of talent clusters have the important consequence that global talent flows are not a zero-sum game for the world. Placing talented people in environments that best utilize their skills fosters global growth, with the potential to make everybody better off. Out-migration can even benefit a talent-sending country if the overseas workers provide their home country with special insights and business linkages. The prospect of immigration also encourages students to make deep investments, which can aid talent-sending countries as many young people eyeing international opportunities never actually leave.

China and India are leading contributors of global talent, and their integration with advanced economies boosts their rapid development. The huge populations of these two countries, as well as the other nations that benefit through cross-border exchanges, suggest that global talent flows benefit a majority of people in the emerging world. Unfortunately, for many small and remote countries, the numbers don't add up, as the economic incentives for making the beneficial business linkages and similar connections are too small. These countries suffer when their talent leaves for foreign opportunities. Although talent flows raise global living standards, there are winners and losers among talent-sending countries.

If talent flows are not zero-sum in nature, should we worry about where talent locates in the advanced world? Of course we should! Consider an Indian choosing between migrating to the United States for work at Oracle or to Germany for a job at SAP, increasing her earnings substantially in either country. The non-zero-sum nature of talent flows means that it is feasible for the immigrant to benefit India sufficiently from the United States or Germany to make up for her departure. But which country she selects clearly matters for where she pays taxes, buys a home, or even commits a crime. Oracle and SAP certainly want the skilled employee, and it may even have an impact on future product-market competition between them. Global talent flows have the capacity to make the world, in aggregate, a better place while still being the subject of fierce rivalry.

But what about the broader societies of talent-receiving countries? Many citizens of the United States and countries throughout Europe are questioning whether global talent flows help them or just enrich those who are already wealthy. While globalization boosts national prosperity, the rising economic tide does not lift all boats equally. It even sinks some. Chapter 9 describes how global talent is mostly a bystander in some of the technological and competitive forces that press heavily upon middle-class workers. Yet skilled migration catalyzes the offshoring of IT services, hurting older tech workers, and global talent contributes to the rise of "superstar firms" that achieve tremendous success but employ small numbers of people. Facebook is among the world's ten most valuable companies and relies heavily on immigrant talent, but it employs only 2 percent of the workers that General Motors did during its heyday.

This tension is now bubbling over—from localized protests within talent clusters like San Francisco to widespread anger at regional economic differences that propelled Brexit and President Trump's election victory. The murder in Olathe is but one particularly tragic manifestation of a social and political outrage that is increasingly channeled toward immigrants. So, where do we go from here?

A Path Forward

The world has given the United States an exceptional gift, and the country has, in turn, been remarkably open since its founding. The U.S. is a magnet for talent, but its leadership position is fragile. Looking to the century ahead, demographic and economic trends suggest that the U.S. will lose some of the lopsided position it currently enjoys. By 2030, projections hold that nine out of ten young college graduates will live outside of the U.S.

America can remain the global talent leader despite these head winds, but it faces a critical test of leadership and requires a new approach. U.S. immigration policy has been dragging the country down for some time, and the uncertainty recently unleashed by anti-immigrant rhetoric further erodes trust.

This book's concluding chapter outlines how America can craft a better set of immigration policies for the twenty-first century and its knowledge economy. Immediate objectives are to ensure that America's scarce visas are allocated to the most promising talent, to better align the country's immigration pathways and alleviate bottlenecks like school-to-work transitions, and to build more flexibility where the current system is quite rigid. The U.S. can accomplish these objectives with modest changes to current policies like the controversial H-1B program. Polling data suggest that most Americans support these reforms, even after the bitter election.

Political change can move very slowly, and then suddenly quite fast. We often underpredict how long it takes for real change to take root but then underpredict the speed at which change spreads. The extension of marriage rights to same-sex couples took the tiniest of steps for decades in many countries, until suddenly major leaps came one after another. Immigration reforms, including H-1B revisions, have been stuck in the mud for more than a decade in America, and the future is hard to predict. Some of the specific recommendations may be enacted by the time you read this book. That would be just fine by me, as America needs to get started. The debate will continue for years to come, and we need to build a better understanding of why certain proposals should be enacted and how to monitor their performance.

But the real message of this book goes beyond tweaks to the law. America needs to restore the promise of the American dream for it to remain the magnet for global talent. The U.S. economy depends upon it. But it is not just about restoring the American dream to those abroad, as many American citizens have lost their own dreams, too. The businesses that benefit so much from global talent, especially in the U.S. tech sector, must become leaders in ensuring and demonstrating that global talent helps the average person. One-sided calls for an infinite number of visas are not going to work, and people everywhere have a lot of thinking to do about how the future of work will reshape the jobs available in society and the equality of opportunity for everyone. These companies and their leaders need to apply their drive and skills to make a dent in the universe here, too.

Part 1

THE ROOTS OF GLOBAL TALENT FLOWS

Chapter 1

TALENT ON THE MOVE

IT IS DECEMBER 10, 2016, and the darkness of the long Swedish winter pervades. A light snow falls, and yet Stockholm is alive and buzzing. Over the previous days, the exceptional scientists and researchers chosen to receive the 2016 Nobel Prizes delivered thoughtful lectures, and many dignitaries from around the world arrived for the grand awards ceremony. Tonight, King Carl XVI Gustaf of Sweden awards the Nobel Medal, the Nobel Diploma, and a nice-sized check to recipients. Following tradition, President Juan Manuel Santos of Colombia will receive the Nobel Peace Prize in a separate ceremony in Norway.

The glitz and glamour of the Nobel Prize rivals that of the Oscar. The dress for the prize ceremony is precise and inspiring: "Gentlemen are required to wear white tie and tails, while ladies should be dressed in an evening gown. This is the perfect time to dress up and look like royalty!"[1] Officials rehearse the pronunciation of names many times to avoid a blunder when delivering the award. The Nobel organization also prepares a detailed dossier with the accomplishments of the recipients and their personal backgrounds, avoiding the awkward small talk of "So, tell me, what do you do?"

The dossier makes an interesting distinction: it lists both the places of birth of recipients and where they currently work. Many of these locations are very different. Seven of the eleven prizes were awarded to people working in the U.S., with the other four awards going to Colombia, France, Japan, and the Netherlands. However, only one awardee, musician Bob Dylan, was born in the United States. Six of the eleven prizes went to global migrants working outside of their countries of origin, all of whom were working in America.

Does it always look like this at the Nobel Prize ceremony? Well, the migration aspect is quite common, and the U.S. is often the new home, as well. In 2015, for example, five of the nine awardees were living outside of their country of birth. In 2013, four of the nine U.S.-based recipients were immigrants.

The migration of very talented people to America shows up in many places. Immigrant actors and performers include Justin Bieber (Canada), Bruce Willis (Germany), Rihanna (Barbados), and Natalie Portman (Israel). Professional sports boast many immigrants, with every National Basketball Association team having an immigrant in recent seasons. Prominent business executives and entrepreneurs include Google's Sergey Brin (Russia), Pepsi's Indra Nooyi (India), and News Corporation's Rupert Murdoch (Australia). Even politics is covered, with Henry Kissinger (Germany) and Madeleine Albright (Czech Republic) becoming U.S. secretaries of state—the very face of America beyond the president. The Terminator and Governor, Arnold Schwarzenegger (Austria), could fit into several talent bins at once.

Our opening chapters paint a broad portrait of talent flows around the world, preparing us for in-depth business and policy discussions. The global migration of superstars turns out to look a lot like that of college graduates, and both groups differ in important ways from the migration of lower-skilled workers. This first chapter equips us with this background, but to move on we must first discuss what we mean by "talent."

Defining Talent

In a famous 1964 Supreme Court case regarding pornography, *Jacobellis v. Ohio*, Justice Potter Stewart concurred with the court's decision that the Constitution protected all obscenity except "hardcore pornography." Stewart then wrote: "I shall not today attempt further to define the kinds of material I understand to be embraced within that shorthand description; and perhaps I could never succeed in intelligibly doing so. But, I know it when I see it."[2] The "But, I know it when I see it" standard has since been used in everything from tacit business decisions to descriptions of love at weddings.

"Talent" is similarly easy to recognize but hard to define. It is easy to agree that Nobel Prize winners display great talent, but our focus is on a broad set of people outside of this extreme. Education is a good yardstick, as it is roughly comparable across countries and often used to screen immigrants. Yet Bob Dylan dropped out of college. The same is true for tech pioneers like Steve Jobs, Bill Gates, and Mark Zuckerberg, and for twenty-one members of the 2017 U.S. Congress.[3] Education credentials are thus helpful, but not perfect, either.

It would also be quite useful to separate innate talent from education, but these two factors become hopelessly intertwined. A promising Indian student may gain a scholarship to MIT, with that education then leading to a great job at Microsoft. But her equally promising friend may attend one of the famed Indian Institutes of Technology, later to be recruited by Microsoft after graduation. Parsing education from talent in these settings is not feasible; Microsoft likely valued both. We will instead find it more productive to consider the different pathways that talent take to reach their new home.

In the end, we use shorthand descriptions like "talent" and "skilled." This is admittedly imprecise, and yet this vagueness can be helpful when formal definitions are limiting or lead to premature conclusions. Talent is a spectrum, not a binary trait, and we want to describe as much of the terrain as possible. To get started, we will offer three complementary approaches to measuring talent. By triangulating common patterns across multiple sources, we overcome their individual shortcomings and build a rigorous foundation for the observations that follow. Moreover, the differences are fascinating to explore.

Data Sources on Global Talent Flows

Our first approach to measuring talent continues with Nobel Prize winners. This approach employs individual-level data for the Nobel Prizes in Chemistry, Medicine, and Physics, which have been awarded since 1901, and for the Nobel Prize in Economic Sciences, which has been awarded since 1969.[4] Nobel Prizes in these four fields are particularly useful for studying global talent flows, as their historical records identify countries of origin and places of work.

Second, we consider inventors. The World Intellectual Property Organization (WIPO) compiles data on patents and inventors, including inventor nationalities, from intellectual property offices around the world. This global database allows apples-to-apples comparison of immigrant invention across countries.[5] We also undertake a detailed analysis of patents granted by the U.S. Patent and Trademark Office (USPTO), which offers comparable data over a longer time span for America. This second approach provides a wider portrait of innovative activity than the extremes of the Nobel Prize.

Finally, the broadest metric of talent that we employ is possession of a college degree. A massive data project led by the Organisation for Economic Co-operation and Development (OECD), the

World Bank, and the International Migration Institute at Oxford University has recently combined and harmonized immigration records and censuses from many countries to build a systematic database on global education levels.[6] We have historically known far more about the traded physical products being shipped in cargo boats than about the people migrating in jet airplanes, which is crazy for today's knowledge economy. These Herculean data efforts are substantially closing the gap.

The most reliable data focus on immigration to twenty-nine OECD member states (we refer to this simply as "the OECD data" for this chapter).[7] These countries include most of the economically advanced nations in Europe, North America, and Asia. Inflows come from around the world and afford education-based metrics of global talent flows. To provide a sense of these data, there were about twenty-eight million college-educated immigrants residing within the OECD member states in 2010. About one-third of these immigrants were born in one OECD country and then moved to another, but the majority came from non-OECD nations. China, India, and the Philippines alone accounted for five million of these immigrants. Talent flows from non-OECD countries increased by 185 percent from 1990 to 2010, making them the largest contributor to expanding talent bases in many countries.

These three measures—Nobel Prize winners, inventors, and college graduates—provide different views of the movement of global talent, but also show some remarkable similarities. What features do they hold in common?

Patterns of Global Talent Flows

Collectively, our data sets trace out five important patterns regarding the mobility of talent. These features are quite consistent, differing only in the strength of the effects.

1. Exceptionally talented people migrate around the world much more frequently than the general population does.

Approximately 3 percent of the world's population lives outside of its country of birth, a share that has been fairly constant since the 1960s. As the world's population has increased from three billion people in 1960 to more than seven billion today, the absolute count of migrants has more than doubled. The United Nations places the world migrant count at 244 million for 2015.[8] To put this number in perspective, the global refugee count stands at twenty million. And yet, relative to other forms of international engagement, people flows are rather low. Physical goods, for example, move across borders at a relative rate that is ten times greater than that of people.[9]

Against this general backdrop of migration, talented individuals move more frequently. College-degree holders are estimated to migrate globally at three times the rate of those with secondary educations. The precise numbers here are hard to nail down, but one set of estimates suggests that 5.4 percent of college-educated workers migrate, compared with 1.8 percent of those with high school diplomas and 1.1 percent of those with lower education levels.[10]

Mobility increases with higher levels of talent. Since 1901, 31 percent of Nobel Prizes in chemistry, medicine, physics, and economic sciences have been awarded to scientists working outside of their countries of birth (203 of 661 individuals). This is about seventeen times higher than the migration rate of high school graduates.

Moving down a notch on the talent spectrum, the WIPO data estimate a 10 percent worldwide migration rate among inventors for 2000–2010.[11] More precisely, one in ten inventors active during the 2000s was a citizen of a country different from the one in which he or she was working. Since some immigrants become naturalized citizens of their new home, this measure undercounts the total global talent flow, but it is close enough. The 10 percent

	Nobel Laureates 1900-2016	WIPO inventors 2000-2010	College educated ~2010
1. Global migrants as a percentage of total group worldwide	31%	10%	5%
2. Share of global migrants moving to United States	53%	57%	41%
3. Immigrants as a share of the United States' group	33%	18%	17%

FIGURE 1.1   Global movement of talent by skill level.
Sources: Data from Nobel Prize records, Miguelez and Fink (2013), Kerr et al. (2016), and Hanson and Liu (2017).

inventor migration rate sits between the college-educated rate of 5 percent and the 31 percent rate for Nobel laureates, indicating a continuum across talent levels as shown in Figure 1.1. This is also true among inventors themselves. The top 5 percent of inventors, as measured by the impact of their work, are five times more likely to be migrants than other inventors.[12]

2. A few advanced economies, especially America, receive most of these talented migrants.

Let's begin again with the broadest measure of talent: Although OECD countries contain less than 20 percent of the world's population, these advanced economies host two-thirds of the world's college-educated migrants. America has historically grabbed more than half of these skilled immigrants who come to OECD countries, although that share declined to 41 percent by 2010. Australia, Canada, and the United Kingdom are the next-most-common destinations, combining to garner about 25 percent of talent flows.[13] By comparison, lower-skilled migration is more diffuse and flows toward a broader set of countries.

As one proceeds up the talent hierarchy, the tilt in America's favor becomes pronounced. Within the WIPO data, displayed in

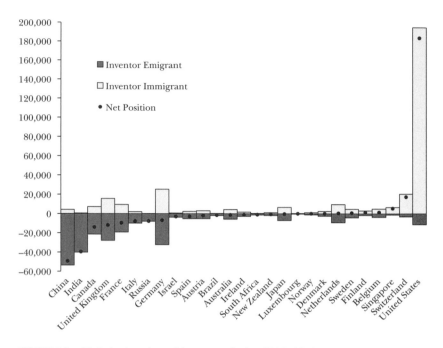

FIGURE 1.2　Global migration of inventors during 2000–2010.
Sources: Data from World Intellectual Property Organization and Miguelez and Fink (2013).

Figure 1.2, the four most prominent destinations for inventors are the U.S., Germany, Switzerland, and the U.K. These four nations collect 65 percent of immigrant inventors, and America accounts for 57 percent by itself! The U.S. pulls from everywhere. The draw is so extreme that, even though Germany and the U.K. rank among the four largest destinations for inventors, their outflows to America are even larger than their inflows and consequently they end up as net sending countries.

The Nobel Prize data are also unambiguous: America received 53 percent of all global migrants who won the Nobel Prize in the four fields of chemistry, medicine, physics, and economic sciences (107 of 203 individuals). While four American citizens were affiliated with a foreign institution when they received the award, 107 immigrants had come to a U.S. institution. Talk about a "trade imbalance." When a leading French economist lamented to me the flow of his nation's academic talent to America, he said did not know the exact share, but he was pretty sure it included "almost everyone who mattered."

3. Immigrants account for a large share of America's accumulated talent, and the size of that share grows as the level of talent rises.

Even for the world's largest economy, global talent flows matter. Immigrants account for about 17 percent of America's college-educated workforce, a significant increase from their 7 percent share in 1980.[14] Looking specifically at science and engineering, about 29 percent of the country's college-educated workforce in these areas is foreign born, and that share rises to 52 percent when we isolate those who hold doctorates.

The WIPO data also show that foreign nationals account for 18 percent of America's inventors who filed global patents during the 2000s. Furthermore, roughly one in four technologies developed in the U.S. was invented or coinvented by a foreign-born inventor (keep in mind that these numbers again underestimate the total migrant contribution).[15] Finally, since 1901, immigrants account for 33 percent of U.S.-based awardees of the Nobel Prize (107 of 330).

There is also a deep connection between talented immigrants and the commercialization of ideas that result in jobs and economic growth. Many of America's most famous brands—Goldman Sachs, DuPont, Kohl's, Nordstrom, Kraft, and Procter & Gamble, to list a few—bear the name of their immigrant founders. Advocates for immigration policy reform frequently note that about 40 percent of Fortune 500 companies in America were founded by immigrants or their children,[16] and another widely cited figure is that half of the start-up founders in Silicon Valley are immigrants. It will take a whole book to explore the good and bad implications of global talent flows for America, but for now we can conclude that the flows are substantial enough to make a difference.

4. Growth in global talent inflows is often closely timed with stronger participation of skilled natives as well.

Our first three patterns are snapshots in time; they do not convey dynamics. An important fourth pattern is that rapid rates of talent inflows are typically associated with broad-scale increases in skilled activity for countries, cities, and firms. That is, global talent tends to flow to where great opportunities exist, and this often occurs side by side with increased involvement of talented natives. This pattern is far from guaranteed in global exchanges. After all, the massive flow of Chinese textiles into American markets over the past few decades coincided with the closure of many U.S. apparel plants.

Again, an example comes from the Nobel Prize awards. Immigrant contributions to U.S. Nobel Prizes in 2016 were higher than average, but not far off the long-term trend. During the first third of the twentieth century, 13 percent of Nobel Prizes went to scientists working in America, and immigrants accounted for about one-third of those U.S.-based recipients. Since 1970, more than 65 percent of the awards have been to scientists in America, with immigrants now accounting for more than half of these recipients. In other words, both American-born and American-migrant talent are receiving record numbers of awards at the same time.

This pattern crops up again and again: find a place, a company, or an industry where there is substantial growth of immigrant talent, and you are very likely to find native talent growth as well. As immigrants have flocked to Silicon Valley for entrepreneurship, so have natives. The same holds true for bankers in London and Hong Kong, and in previous eras, other places, like Renaissance Florence, held global sway. In scientific terminology, the spatial growth rates of immigrants and natives are strongly correlated.[17] While correlations do not yet prove that talented immigrants help natives, this observation that immigrant and native fortunes tend to rise and fall together is a critical starting point.

5. Talent flows from Asia, and especially China and India, are surging.

Talent flows exist between many countries, ranging from African medical doctors working in rural America to British executives in Shanghai's skyscrapers. Some patterns are quite long standing, such as those among advanced countries or following along historical colonialization. Others are more recent. The open borders of the European Union increased talent flows among member states, and many skilled people exited the former Soviet Union after its collapse.

But within this varied landscape, the exceptional flows of talent from China and India jump out. The OECD data suggest that about 3.5 million college graduates from China and India worked in advanced economies in 2010. This represents about 20 percent of the total immigrant inflow from outside the OECD. The WIPO records also measure that 28 percent of migrating inventors during the 2000s were Chinese or Indian nationals. Potentially impressive, but these two countries represent a third of the world's population. By this benchmark, are China and India underrepresented?

Yes, they are, but the growth curve is something to behold! For much of the twentieth century, the talent within China and India was poorly utilized. The causes were sometimes of a country's own making (e.g., Mao's Cultural Revolution) and sometimes due to the outside world (e.g., Indian suppression under British colonization). Consequently, cases like Srinivasa Ramanujan's, the Indian mathematical genius we met in the introduction, were very rare, and most talent flowed only between industrializing economies. Even in the 1970s and 1980s, the global student and professional contributions from China and India were very limited.

Welcome to twenty-first-century global talent flows. China and India are still catching up, but by the 2000s, they already accounted for one in four immigrating inventors. The share of Indian workers in U.S. science and engineering rose from practically zero in the 1960s to more than 9 percent today, and India could probably double that supply again.[18] And as a window to the future, consider university students. There are more than 350,000 and 186,000 Chinese and Indian students, respectively, enrolled in U.S. universities. The two countries accounted for half of all foreign students in America during the 2016–2017 academic year; compared to the prior academic year, these student populations have grown 6.8 percent for China and 12.3 percent for India![19]

The size and traits of these talent flows, such as their bent toward science and engineering, carry big implications. The recent growth has already been exceptionally influential and disruptive for many, and the untapped capacity within these countries is even greater. A conversation about talent flows in 1975 could have glossed over these two countries, but now they are center stage.

These five points describe the basic shape of talented migration as it occurs today, and we next turn to how countries seek to grab their share.

The Global Talent Race

Our portrait of global talent flows has been rather lopsided, with the U.S. attracting many talented migrants. The chapters ahead describe how America came to this leading position and its impressive strengths. However, the U.S. has often taken its special position for granted and has done little recently to make itself more attractive. This contrasts sharply with the efforts countries are taking to become more competitive for talent. During periods when the U.S. system has been particularly frustrating, billboards like that in Figure 1.3 cropped up around Silicon Valley to advertise moving north to Canada!

As the hostility toward immigrants increases in America, Canada is doubling down with new programs like its Global Skills Strategy to lure in innovative companies. Beyond just making visas

FIGURE 1.3   Canadian immigration billboard in Silicon Valley.
Source: Google Images.

available, Canada promises employers: "A new dedicated team at Employment and Social Development Canada (ESDC) will provide all Global Talent Stream employers with streamlined, client focused service . . . [including] faster processing of your Global Talent Stream applications with a service standard of 10-business days . . . [and] personalized, high-touch assistance throughout the assessment process."[20]

Countries that have historically had lower rates of skilled immigration are also exploring how to attract talent. Some efforts are symbolic—Malaysia literally rolled out the red carpet for immigration lines at some airports to signify the importance of talented individuals (a far cry from the heavy-handed shakedown of many immigration queues!). Other countries are aggressively challenging conventional wisdom. Start-Up Chile is a program that pays foreign entrepreneurs $40,000 to stay in Chile for at least six months, requiring only that visiting entrepreneurs participate in local community events that help build Chile's start-up culture. (This book expresses all figures in U.S. dollars.) This is far from a typical use of taxpayer funds, and the program is unlikely to land the next WhatsApp. But it is helping Chile build a global business network to foreign talent.

Migration patterns are not immutable laws of nature, even with America's enormous head start. Through these and other programs, countries are seeking to close the gap bit by bit and become more attractive to talent migrating locally in their own parts of the world. Skilled worker migration is the outcome of a complex process that involves firms, universities, and national governments. Not everyone gets their first choice of country, and many countries likewise don't get their first choice of talent. To make progress, let's start with the migrants: why do they move?

The Pursuit of Opportunity

Most talent migration occurs as people seek the best opportunities for themselves (and their families or even broader community). For many, migration initially happens for education, a process we will call the "education pathway." While it is an enormous step to leave home for school abroad, many do so in pursuit of lifelong advantages—from superior academic training, degrees from prestigious schools, and better access to labor markets.

Prateek, a young Indian working in the finance industry of New York City, illustrates this pursuit. Born to a middle-class family in New Delhi, he attended an academic high school in India that had seven thousand students. He chose to pursue an undergraduate degree in the U.S. to ensure he could study his passion of computer science and avoid rote-learning styles. After casting a wide U.S. search, and convincing his parents it was a good idea, he landed at Brown University. Two summer internships later, and Prateek was further convinced he wanted to work in America permanently.

Others move later for career opportunities. Bengt Holmström, one of the two winners of the 2016 Nobel Prize in Economic Sciences, performed his early studies in Finland. He came to America initially for graduate education at Stanford in operations research, and then returned to Finland for work. Later, however, Holmström received an offer he couldn't refuse: he was invited to be an assistant professor at Northwestern University. In the emerging field of contract theory, Northwestern had no equal and boasted several professors who would go on to win Nobel Prizes. Holmström was only there for four years before moving onto Yale and later MIT, but he credits that short period as transforming his career.

Prateek and Holmström stayed, but many immigrants come on a temporary basis to get boosts in compensation, more rapid advancement, or simply a chance to prove themselves. Sons and daughters of prominent family businesses in emerging economies frequently want to show that they, too, can succeed in Dubai or Paris, even if they will later join the family firm. Sports stars and other highly compensated workers may also migrate to take advantage of lower tax rates during peak earning years. Most migrants move directly from their home country to their long-term destination, but about one in ten recent immigrants to the U.S. arrived from a third country.[21] These "transit" stays in third countries may be for schooling or work, often with the goal of ultimately reaching America.

How much can immigration boost one's career? It is hard to measure the precise opportunity that global migration provides. The average wage in India is about $300 a month, but that is not the right point of comparison for an Indian programmer working in California who earns $75,000 a year. The migrant programmer typically has a good education and strong internal motivation, such that she would be earning more than $300 a month if she were still in India.

The ideal experiment is to randomly assign the right to migrate among otherwise identical people, like the drug trials conducted by pharmaceutical companies. A treatment group gets the real drug being evaluated while a control group gets a fake placebo pill with no real medicine. The random assignment to the groups ensures that they have roughly similar observable traits (e.g., age, education) and hidden ones (e.g., belief in medicine, supportive family). Consequently, differences in group outcomes will be due to the new drug.

In one case, a rather odd lottery provided researchers with something akin to this ideal experiment for skilled migrants from India. The H-1B visa program is one of the most important pathways into the U.S. for skilled work. We describe this controversial program—a punching bag in the 2016 U.S. presidential debates— in detail throughout this book. For now, let's just focus on how its features help quantify the wage gains of global migration.

On April 1 of each year, the U.S. Citizenship and Immigration Services (USCIS) begins accepting applications for H-1B visas. Because the visa supply runs out quickly, the start of H-1B visa season makes the front page of many U.S. newspapers. Normally, applications are processed on a first-come, first-served basis, and visas are awarded until the limit is reached. When pent-up demand is high, however, it only takes a few days for the number of applications to exceed the quota. For instance, the USCIS received more than 190,000 applications for 85,000 total slots within the first five days of April 2018. When this happens, the USCIS collects visa applications for one full week, before closing applications until the following year. Then, a lottery determines who from this multitude of applicants will receive a visa.

This lottery provides a treatment-control test akin to the medical trials. One clever study accessed internal employee data from a very large Indian firm that used the H-1B program extensively to bring in skilled workers to the U.S.[22] Looking at the 2007 and 2008 lotteries, employee selection in the H-1B lottery was, in fact, random, with the lottery winners and losers looking very similar on every dimension.

But the winners took home far more than H-1B visas. The employees who won the visa lottery saw a $55,000 jump in annual earnings, compared with their counterparts in India who did not receive visas. This illustrates the size of the income gap even after controlling for the personality traits and circumstances that lead one to migrate. The earnings jump from winning this lottery isn't on par with winning Powerball, but talented people experience real gains when they reach the places that can best use their skills.

The opportunity gap measured here is only a lower bound, as the Indian programmers involved in the study were at the low end of U.S. pay scales, both for H-1B recipients and for skilled workers generally. This gap would be much larger for truly exceptional talent. Soccer stars like Neymar and Lionel Messi thrive in European leagues, and it is unlikely that Pierre Omidyar's eBay would have flourished as successfully in France. The same holds for many working on Wall Street and in top fashion design houses in Milan. We do not need to precisely quantify these earnings jumps to know that they are substantial.

Of course, migration happens for personal reasons. Talented individuals sometimes migrate to be near loved ones, perhaps early in life (true love!) or later (to be near an ailing family member). Global cities like New York, London, and Dubai also capture the imagination. My own move to Hong Kong at the age of twenty-three was simply because it was on the other side of the planet, and I could survive there knowing only English. Hong Kong lived up to its billing, but from the start I intended to come back to America.

And poignantly, in the long shadow of the most recent refugee crisis that began in 2015, many people flee from horrible conditions.[23] Support for refugees principally follows humanitarian considerations, but it does have an impact on talent distributions. More than one hundred thousand German Jewish refugees fled from Nazi Germany to America, including the likes of Albert Einstein and John von Neumann. Despite facing discrimination at times in their new home, these migrants revolutionized U.S. science and innovation. Looking at the field of chemistry, one study found that American invention increased significantly more in subfields that saw a refugee influx compared with those that did not.[24] This was one case of doing well by doing good.

Ultimately, these decisions, made separately by millions of people in their own unique ways, add up to create the major flows of talent that are reshaping our world. However, we can't stop the story at this point, because these decisions are only possible given the world that surrounds immigrants. How can a small number of places absorb these individuals?

Chapter 2

THE ECONOMICS OF TALENT CLUSTERS

MANY ASPIRING ACTORS AND ACTRESSES clamor to get to Hollywood, and global financial centers draw bankers from every nation on earth. While it is intuitive that talented people migrate for greater earnings, it is also a rather incomplete account. Many skilled professions, like doctors and architects, do not show this "clustering" behavior. What explains these differences? Why do some skilled occupations gravitate to one or two world-famous centers and others do not?

To better understand the origin and persistence of talent flows, we next delve into the economics of skilled work. We explore how a concentration of talented individuals can either improve or weaken their joint economic opportunities. This refined picture yields a better foundation for understanding the global concentration of talent flows, well beyond the choices of a single person.[1]

A Simple Foundation of Supply and Demand

The simplest economic story, perhaps familiar from Econ 101 in college, is always one of supply and demand. To make this especially tangible, let's use the example of dentists filling cavities in

Nashville, Tennessee, a city of one million people in the heart of America. Residents of Nashville have some demand for getting their cavities filled, and this demand will decline as the prices charged by local dentists rise. It is an easy decision to fill a cavity if the price is $10, but many would balk at a price of $10,000! These consumer choices add up across Nashville to create a classic downward-sloping demand curve for dental services, as shown in the left-hand panel of Figure 2.1.

Dentists want to fill more cavities when the compensation for doing so is high. It is not worth it to come in on the weekend if the price is $10 per cavity, but at $10,000, they might even skip their children's birthday parties. This results in an upward-sloping supply curve for dental services. The point (P*, Q*) at which these two curves intersect determines the wages and quantities of dental services in Nashville.

This simple graph is a foundation for thinking about the impact of changes in labor supply. The dashed line shows what happens when the supply of dentists to Nashville increases but the number of residents in Nashville stays fixed. The growing pool of dentists will perform more dental services than before, but this lowers the price that the dentists can charge for filling cavities. Consequen-

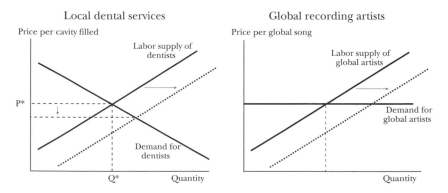

FIGURE 2.1   Impact of increased labor supply across skilled occupations in the example of Nashville's dentists versus global recording artists.

tially, some dentists will work less, and others will be less likely to take up the trade or move to Nashville.

The model describes many occupations, particularly those serving customers in a local area. For tasks that require limited training, such as mowing a lawn or driving for Uber, wages are typically governed by these simple forces of supply and demand, and workers can move quickly between occupations. If the wages for one low-skilled task become very attractive, new labor can quickly rush into the market, with Uber drivers becoming landscapers when cuts reach $100 per residence. This occupational shift lowers the wages paid to landscapers, which, in turn, makes it less likely that others will want to jump in.

The model also applies to many skilled occupations, like dentistry, family law, and accounting. Yet other skilled occupations in Nashville do not behave this way.

Selling to the World

Nashville's claim to fame is being the country music capital of the world—it even holds the moniker "Music City." It is home to the industry's biggest stars, like Tim McGraw and Faith Hill, major record labels, the guitar company Gibson, the Country Music Hall of Fame, and the Grand Ole Opry. The music industry provides more than fifty thousand jobs to Nashville and constitutes the largest concentration of music-related employment in America.[2] The title of one recent online ranking sums it all up: "Top 10 Music Cities Other Than Nashville."[3]

For those seeking to be a part of the country music industry, all roads lead to Nashville. But this seems rather odd in terms of the traditional model. If Nashville's dentists face declining salaries as more dentists flock there, how can the city be home to so many in the country music industry? And this includes not just the star singers themselves but also the songwriters, record executives, music equipment providers, and so on. While Tim and Faith are super-stars, most of the talented individuals working within Nashville's music industry have skill levels comparable to the dentists who also live there.

The fact that you have (or should have) heard of Tim and Faith hints at one ingredient that we must add to our model—an industry's ability to sell its product outside its local area, just as Nashville's music industry reaches a global audience. This greater market reach creates a setting in which wages for the music in-dustry do not necessarily fall as more country singers migrate to Nashville.

As a simplified example, if the world has an unlimited demand for country music at today's price, then the demand curve for Nashville's music industry is perfectly flat rather than downward sloping. This is illustrated in the right-hand panel of Figure 2.1. As the local industry expands and the supply of music from Nashville grows, the existing talent does not suffer reduced wages. Employ-ment expands one for one with the incoming talent, and there is nothing that dampens the incentives for others to join Nashville's country music scene.

Contrast that with the economic struggle of musicians around the world who play only at local events, ranging from weddings to dive bars. This market looks a lot like the filling of cavities—the market size is determined by the number of local residents who go out for entertainment. The fixed demand makes it quite hard to make a living through live performances, and many musicians supplement their meager incomes with jobs in other sectors of the economy.[4]

The global product reach that we see in the Music City is also evident in many other industries with talented workers. The devel-opment of blockbuster movies in Hollywood (Los Angeles), Bolly-wood (Mumbai), and even Nollywood (Lagos) relies on selling to consumers who are far away. Similarly, the financial products developed by bankers in London, New York, and Hong Kong, the internet technologies created in San Francisco, Shanghai, and Berlin, and the fashion designed in Paris, Los Angeles, and Milan permeate the lives of people all around the world, not just the residents of those cities.

Although the ability to sell products globally explains some differences in clustering behavior across skilled occupations and industries, it still does not tell the whole story. In fact, there are many examples of industries that sell products globally but do not create these talent clusters. These products usually have lower skill requirements; they range from towns in China organized around the manufacturing of a single good for export (e.g., bicycles) to call centers in India and rural parts of the U.S. that answer the phones for companies located many miles away. To further trace the additional conditions needed to generate talent clusters like Nashville, it is necessary to study the organization of work.

Adding It Up: 2 + 2 = ?

Framing the question as a playful arithmetic problem, our Nashville example has the property that 2 + 2 can equal 4, in that two existing country music professionals and two new migrants to the city can all be happily employed as the overall size of the music industry grows. However, there are many times when the ability to sell a product at great distances does not yield these favorable outcomes. In such settings, a growing concentration of talented people in the field can reduce opportunities as the greater talent supply competes for work, even though overall global demand is not affected. We might say that 2 + 2 = 3 in this scenario, as jobs don't keep pace. Why is that?

In many industries, firms combine talented individuals with other critical inputs, such as less-skilled workers and machinery. The role of high-skilled professionals in these settings is to manage the firm's resources and make the business more productive. This talent is crucial for a company's success, but firms do not gain much from having double the managing talent unless they can also double the other inputs they use in production. The same logic applies to a talented mechanical engineer who maintains the plant's machinery or the accountant who monitors the company's finances. The demand for these skilled inputs is roughly proportional to the amount of other inputs that a firm uses.[5]

These settings constitute much of the world's economy and do not lead to talent clusters. Instead, talent clusters form for occupations and industries where the most important complementary inputs to the work of skilled and talented people are . . . other skilled and talented people. For Tim and Faith to be exceptionally successful in generating their next country music hit, they need access to the very best vocal coaches, backup singers, songwriters, and producers. Other inputs are far less important. People of all skill levels surround Tim and Faith, ranging from janitorial staff to white-shoe lawyers, and state-of-the-art recording studios are expensive. But what really matters is the complementary human talent from the music industry.

This is the second condition that explains clusters like Nashville: the productivity of talent workers must be enhanced by proximity to other talented people. Think about it like baking a cake: talent is no longer one ingredient to be mixed among many, but instead it becomes practically the whole recipe. When both conditions are met, exceptionally powerful interactions emerge.

Consider industries that depend on specialized knowledge transfers and interactions, similar to the collaborations among country music artists. When the biotech industry took off during the 1970s and 1980s, the sharpest predictor for where the new industry would take root was the presence of leading researchers who held specialized knowledge in the young field. The accumulation of this star talent did not reduce the researchers' effectiveness but instead built a deep foundation for early industry success. Other inputs, like venture financing and skilled technicians, subsequently flowed to wherever this talent found an early foothold.[6]

Another example comes from ad agencies in Manhattan, where success depends on networking among talented workers in nearby firms. Manhattan's agencies supply about a quarter of all advertising in the U.S., thus clearly meeting the first condition of long-distance sales opportunities. These agencies rely on personal networking to share project work among themselves, splitting up larger jobs into parts that can be independently attacked by each firm. This collaboration and subcontracting allows ad agencies to be individually more productive than they would have been in isolation, meeting our second condition. These beneficial interactions decline rapidly with geographical distance, disappearing entirely when two firms are more than a half mile apart.[7] The implications are rather striking: to be effective as an ad agency often requires going to New York, and even to the few city blocks where most of the action is.

Industries that rely on the best matches between firms and talent are also conducive to the formation of talent clusters. For our Nashville example, some songwriters and backup singers are a better match for Tim and Faith than other local stars like Toby Keith, and vice versa. Or, think about casting in Hollywood movies. Rather than being able to select only between Brad Pitt and Johnny Depp for the lead male role in an upcoming movie, which my wife might love, Hollywood studios can screen hundreds of candidates to find the perfect match. And because there are so many studios making films, Brad and Johnny can similarly search around for the best roles for themselves. This superior matching makes for more compelling movies and thereby increases the industry's sales.

This matching occurs in less visible ways in other sectors, too. There are so many start-ups in leading tech clusters like Silicon Valley and Boston that some local CEOs concentrate on a development stage. A CEO might, for example, focus on growing a start-up from the development of its first prototype until it has sufficient market sales to pursue rapid scaling. This CEO knows how to align early manufacturing and distribution, growing the staff from three to fifty. However, once the venture achieves its product-market fit and starts to scale, the CEO hands the reins over to another professional who specializes in taking companies from fifty to five thousand employees, while the first CEO instead recycles her efforts at a new start-up with the next great prototype.

This matching in specialization is impossible without the depth of local talent that we see in leading clusters. Based in Istanbul, Peak Games is a very rapidly growing game developer that has already reached more than three hundred million users. However, despite being in Turkey's largest city and surrounded by a highly educated workforce, founder Sidar Sahin laments his difficulty in finding local workers with the specialized abilities required of the company's top talent. In his estimation, there are only a handful of cities globally that contain all the rare skills that his company needs. While most of Peak Games' employees remain in Istanbul, Sahin has turned his attention to gaining better access to these frontier cities. The abundance of start-ups in places like Silicon Valley only make them more important in the eyes of people like Sahin.[8]

We now have an idea of the ingredients necessary for global talent clusters to emerge and how they can make talented workers more productive. Returning to our simple math analogy, the gains can even make the whole greater than the sum of the parts: 2 + 2 = 5. Splitting Hollywood in ten separate miniclusters would reduce the total output achieved. Beyond this organization of work, reinforcing factors strengthen these clusters and encourage their growth via global talent.

The Ecosystem Effect

Spillovers among talented individuals create local "ecosystems" to support specialized work. In its original biological use, the term "ecosystem" describes how a complex community of animals and plants interacts. In many skilled industries, such ecosystems emerge through face-to-face interactions among residents. That extends beyond the talented professionals to also include the specialized lawyers, investors, standard-setting organizations, and similar collaborators who surround them.

People often question whether face-to-face interactions are still important, given communication advances like the internet and rapid, safe travel. If talented work is truly "weightless" and often happens in Starbucks anyway, can't that Starbucks be anywhere? Perhaps that will happen someday, but for now, new technologies are used more to facilitate work within a single company or project team rather than externally. For example, the number-one destination for emails sent from Harvard Business School is . . . Harvard Business School. These forms of weightless technology can thus reinforce the role of space and proximity as much as they diffuse it.

Ecosystems also foster a vital local culture or ethos around the work being performed. In most nations, and even in large chunks of the U.S., a business failure severely damages the long-term reputation of an entrepreneur. That is true even if the entrepreneur had a great idea and pursued it diligently, but the business simply did not work because of factors beyond his control (e.g., the technology failed to deliver on its initial promise). In addition, draconian legal procedures around bankruptcy in some countries can ruin a failed entrepreneur's personal finances and prohibit the starting of a new firm for many years. These very high costs of failures often steer entrepreneurs toward safer bets.

In Silicon Valley, by contrast, the local ethos holds that it is better to have started a new firm and failed than not to have tried at all. A failed entrepreneur maintains respect if the failure occurred for the "right" reasons, and the local culture celebrates the pursuit of audacious goals. Legally, business bankruptcy does not bring the personal financial ruin that it can elsewhere. This ethos goes beyond the entrepreneurs themselves, with financial investors and others understanding when an entrepreneur has failed for "good" reasons rather than for incompetence or misconduct. Such "experienced entrepreneurs" are highly sought after and often move on to new opportunities with the same investor. Such support allows greater daring among start-ups, which, in turn, draws even more entrepreneurs to the Valley.

Outsiders often take issue with the ethos that emerges in a specialized cluster. Many have decried Wall Street's culture, cast most infamously in Gordon Gekko's proclamation that "greed is good" in *Wall Street*. Others take offense at Hollywood's liberal attitude or Nashville's conservatism, and I am sure many readers of this book have some "feedback" they would like to give about Harvard academia. But these examples show that the more that "everybody is doing it," the easier it is to believe that "it" is the right way to do things. This makes a talent cluster a place of shared values and attracts others with those same values.

While ecosystems emerge for many professions, global talent flows are particularly associated with clusters of innovative activity and creative work. What makes these frontier economic clusters extra special?

Enhanced Innovation

Innovation requires selecting the very best ideas among many candidates. Firms and cities don't "win" by having an average idea that is better than the average idea elsewhere; instead, they win with the great ones. This is a daunting task, as entrepreneurs generate thousands of new business ideas each year, the great majority of which fail. To "google" something is now everyday lingo, but Google was a late arrival in the search-engine space. The superior algorithms behind Google ultimately won out over competitors, but it took a fight. Similarly, Dropbox is today a household name for online data storage and collaboration, but there were more than eighty competitors when the company was founded. And some Hollywood movies turn out to be big flops, but the films that do make it to our theaters are much better than the average initial script.

While companies use many strategies to find and capture the very best ideas, it's easier if they don't have to go very far to realize them. This proximity is especially valuable when emerging trends are hard to describe and most visible close to the action. Those within Silicon Valley are often able to forecast the ultimate successes of a Google or Dropbox better than outsiders because of access to the people (investors, employees, suppliers) with insight into these companies. However, clusters can sometimes lose track of some of the strongest ideas and actors emerging outside their borders—one example being the effectiveness of Donald Trump's campaign as he challenged many of the limits perceived by career politicians in Washington, DC.

Moreover, the organization of a cluster can fundamentally change to promote the selection and scaling of the very best opportunities, thereby making the cluster more innovative. Rather than awarding business through the "old boys' network," clusters can become very competitive places where the best designs are selected and implemented throughout the industry, much as Google became the dominant search engine technology. This requires a fluid labor market that rapidly reallocates employees to winning firms. Modular product features also allow companies to compete while knowing that the best candidate will ultimately be awarded the business.[9] This environment is how Google grew from its start in 1998 to more than $200 million in daily search revenue in 2017.

Beyond this concentration and vetting of ideas for innovation, the accumulated diversity of talent and inputs in a cluster enables new ideas to come together in novel ways. This was famously first put forward by Jane Jacobs, an urban theorist who wrote two of the top one hundred nonfiction books of the twentieth century, despite not having had a college degree. Jacobs emphasized how the creation of new work requires recombining existing building blocks (as well as a good dose of serendipity). The required diversity goes beyond different skills and talents, such as cutting-edge materials science or electrical engineering knowledge, to include holding different perspectives on the world. This is evident in the power of teams that unite people of different sexes, ethnic and religious backgrounds, ages, and so on.[10]

These dynamics make talent clusters special, and they reinforce the overwhelming need felt by many creative tech workers to be in the world's most innovative hot spots . . . unless they find the price tag too high.

Why We All Don't Live in Silicon Valley

While talent clusters can grow without diminishing the productivity of member firms, they do reach a size limit due to their competition for other resources. The denizens of San Francisco, Hong Kong, and Mumbai face very high real estate prices. Everybody needs some space, and the supply can be quickly maxed out, even with tall buildings and longer commutes. The same holds for the other necessities of life, with many visitors shocked by menu prices in London or taxi fares in New York.

These rising local costs will lead some individuals and firms to seek out cheaper locations, such as the promise of Olathe discussed in the introduction. The record-high prices of key talent clusters simultaneously demonstrate their growing importance and hinder their further expansion. More subtly, rising costs make it so that the hotspot is only attractive to those who can benefit the most. A chemicals manufacturer would be foolish to place their headquarters on Wall Street, given the very high costs but weak benefits for them. It only makes sense for those closely connected to the financial sector. Escalating prices yield ever sharper fidelity in those who choose to locate in the limited space.

Our range of examples also helps us differentiate talent clusters from the more general concept of economic clusters, sometimes called "agglomeration economies" in the scientific and business literature. Economic clusters emerge for reasons beyond just interactions of skilled individuals. The automobile industry in Detroit has been one of the world's most prominent clusters over the past century. While auto manufacturers have always hired talented people, other factors—like achieving economies of scale in production or the labor pooling of less-skilled factory workers, for instance—were more important reasons for Detroit. Talented workers were inputs to the production process in Detroit, but they were not a driving force behind the creation of the cluster.

As auto manufacturers race to build the software for driverless cars, they also shift toward a very different organization of work. The most important factors become the creative interactions among talented workers, which gives an advantage to Detroit's new competitors in Silicon Valley. While it is far too early to declare a winner, as the giants of Motor City have their own strengths, this example highlights the distinction between the talent clusters central to this book and the traditional clusters built upon factors like cheaper inputs for manufacturing processes. Moreover, it uncovers why large firms around the world are frightened to their core—the rules of engagement are shifting away from those of traditional industry and toward those of talent clusters.

You Are Now Free to Move About the ~~Country~~ World

While talent clusters are powerful magnets that draw people globally, existing hot spots can be rather fragile. Silicon Valley is special first and foremost because of the people there, but those people could decamp and move elsewhere. Thus, the leading center for the tech industry is free to move around in space. In practice, great universities, research labs, or even the culture of an ecosystem provide an anchor. It is very hard to replicate talent clusters in a new location—just ask the many governments around the world that have struggled to create the next Silicon Valley![11]

But Silicon Valley was an orchard before the 1950s, which is a blink of the eye in business history, and parts of its creation were serendipitous. It got its start when Fred Terman, dean of Stanford's school of engineering, had the idea to lease the land surrounding the university to tech companies. Later, semiconductor pioneer William Shockley started Shockley Semiconductor in the area because his ailing mother lived nearby, and his firm would ultimately give birth to future giants like Intel and AMD. Moreover, proximity to a great university is not an instant recipe for success. Kendall Square in Cambridge, Massachusetts, is now a premier talent spot and benefits deeply from being next door to MIT. But Kendall Square was rather sleepy a decade ago, and great centers of thought have given way throughout the ages. Detroit was the Silicon Valley of the early 1900s but now struggles to stay viable; similarly, present-day Londoners worry that Brexit might cost the city its prominent financial leadership position.

Our next chapter takes on this dynamic perspective, bringing together the global talent flows of Chapter 1 and the economics of skilled work. We look at the powerful role of high-skilled immigrants in the accelerating development of innovation and entrepreneurship in the U.S. over the past four decades.

Chapter 3

INNOVATION IN THE UNITED STATES

OVER THE PAST FORTY YEARS, high-skilled immigration and the economics of talent clusters have combined to dramatically transform America. We now take measure of what this means for U.S. innovation and entrepreneurship, using several resources related to science, technology, engineering, and mathematics (the so-called STEM fields). The American technology sector is the largest lever through which global talent flows influence the world. One prominent study calculates that half of U.S. productivity growth in recent decades is due to increases in the number of U.S. STEM workers, most of which is due to immigration.[1] As American companies compete in international markets, talent flows into places like Silicon Valley affect the lives of workers globally. A detailed investigation of this sector is, thus, far more than an illustration of the phenomenon, but instead a critical building block for our understanding.

In 2016, immigrants accounted for 16 percent of the U.S. workforce with a college education, but their share within STEM occupations was larger yet, at 29 percent.[2] These occupational statistics align with the World Intellectual Property Organization (WIPO) data, which indicate that citizens of foreign countries account for roughly a quarter of patents filed from the U.S. The comparability of these statistics foreshadows two core findings of this chapter: First, immigrants make up about a quarter of the country's innovative workforce, according to the various ways we measure the importance of immigrants in American innovation. Second, this high percentage is due to large numbers of talented immigrants going into STEM occupations rather than because of special creativity or inventiveness possessed by immigrants. While this snapshot describes conditions today, the path to this point is fascinating and important for being able to project forward. To understand that journey, join me in 1975.

Expanding U.S. Innovation

The U.S. Patent and Trademark Office (USPTO) houses complete digital records for all patents granted by the USPTO since 1975. This is a longer horizon than the WIPO data, making the USPTO data set a better resource for analyzing long-term trends.[3] And while the USPTO does not collect the immigration status of inventors, I use techniques in my research to identify the likely ethnicity of inventors according to their first and last names. The simple idea is that inventors with the surnames Gupta or Desai are more likely to be of Indian ethnicity, whereas Martinez and Rodriguez signify probable Hispanic inventors. Wang and Ming are typical Chinese names, and Tran and Nguyen are common names among Vietnamese immigrants. The approach uses several name databases originally developed for advertising purposes (read: junk mail) and algorithms built around common name patterns (surnames ending in "ovich" are very likely Russian, for example).

These tools identify the probable ethnicity for more than 99 percent of USPTO inventors. Inventors with Anglo-Saxon and European names serve as the baseline, with emphasis on how the composition of America's inventors has shifted toward ethnic groups like Chinese, Hispanic, Indian, Korean, Russian, and Vietnamese. Although this approach isn't perfect—some inventors with Anglo-Saxon names are immigrants from Canada or the United Kingdom, for instance—these series align with other data sources and perform well in quality-assurance exercises.[4]

In 1975, inventors with Anglo-Saxon and European names accounted for more than 91 percent of U.S.-based patents. Over the subsequent four decades, to 2015, this share declined to 72 percent. The drop was primarily due to the exceptional growth in U.S. inventions coming from people of Chinese and Indian ethnicity. In 1975, both groups represented about 1.5 percent of U.S. inventors. By 2015, Chinese contributions had reached an astounding 10.4 percent, with Indian contributions not far behind, at 7.3 percent. Other ethnic groups, like Korean and Hispanic inventors, have also become more important.[5]

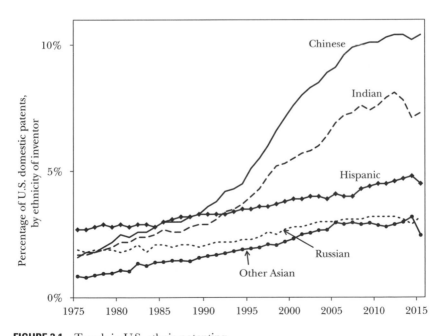

FIGURE 3.1 Trends in U.S. ethnic patenting.
Source: Data from U.S. Patent and Trademark Office. Series uses ethnic naming conventions applied to inventors based in the United States.

Figure 3.1 demonstrates the steady rise in U.S. ethnic patenting, and Appendix Figure 1 shows the overall increase in U.S. patenting during this period by ethnic groups. The rising ethnic inventor share mirrors a persistent upward march in immigrants as a share of the STEM workforce, from a 6.6 percent rate in 1960 to 29 percent today. Chinese and Indian patenting contributions accelerated in the 1990s when the two countries integrated more internationally and sent talented people abroad for education. U.S. universities and businesses were seeking immigrants for STEM work, and that increased supply was mostly welcomed in America, as we explore in detail in the chapters ahead.

Because the ethnic inventor platform builds on the individual records of millions of patents, we can segment inventors by technology field, geographic region, and company or university. The general rise in ethnic invention is present in all slices of the data, but it also shows interesting variations. Creating an "ethnic inventor" label to capture all inventors who are not of Anglo-Saxon or European descent, we observe in Figure 3.2 the importance of ethnic inventors for the expansion of advanced technologies.

The proportion of ethnic inventors varies widely across corporations. Since 2005, ethnic inventors account for more than 40 percent of patents from Google, Intel, and Oracle, compared with less than 20 percent from 3M, Boeing, and Procter & Gamble. Most large companies fall in between these extremes and follow regular patterns. Companies located in major tech clusters, or those having a computer-heavy focus, tend to have greater proportions of ethnic inventors. Defense contractors often require employees have U.S. citizenship for sensitive projects, which cuts down their immigrant inventor shares.

While our data confirm that immigrants are a large part of the STEM workforce throughout America, it is just as important to evaluate the skills that immigrants possess and how they affect the workforces they join.[6]

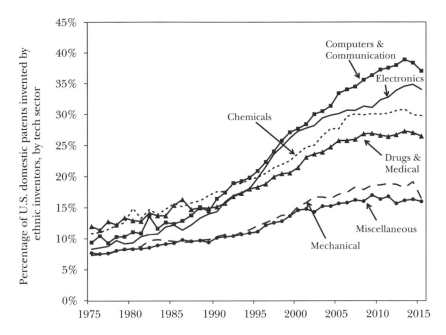

FIGURE 3.2   Trends in U.S. ethnic patenting by technology sector.
Source: Data from U.S. Patent and Trademark Office. Series show the share of a sector's inventors who do not have Anglo-Saxon or European ethnic names.

Best and Brightest?

Business leaders and policy makers care deeply about how the skills of immigrants stack relative to natives. Are immigrants the "best and brightest"? In Washington, you hear this phrase continually in debates about the merits of immigration reform. If immigrants are the "best and brightest," it is easier to justify the greater inflows to skeptical senators and the American public. But if immigrants are less productive than native scientists and engineers, the expanding role of immigrants in U.S. innovation may be a cause for concern if the immigrants are displacing better native talent.

As we saw in Chapter 1, U.S. immigrant shares rise with the level of impact: they are highest among Nobel Prize winners, followed next by inventors, and then generally lower for college graduates. Beyond the Nobel Prize, immigrants account for a disproportionate share of many top scientific awards or measures of extreme impact, including academic citations or election to the National Academy of Sciences.[7] Superstars are not controversial, however, and so we need to analyze instead the typical immigrant. How does he or she stack up against the pool of two million STEM workers in the American economy? Are immigrants more innovative and entrepreneurial than natives on average, in addition to being more present among superstars? This quality dimension turns out to be rather nuanced, far less amenable to a sound bite than the quantity side.

In a nationally representative data set, like the National Survey of College Graduates, the data show that immigrants who came to America for study or employment are more likely to file a patent, publish a scientific paper, start a company, and earn higher wages than are American-born college graduates.[8] The qualification of migrating for study or employment is important, as the same advantage does not exist among immigrants who came to America for family reunification. But the data confirm the immigrant advantage that is frequently portrayed in the press and lobbying reports.

The nuance arises because this raw advantage is explained by immigrants having different fields of study and higher levels of education than natives, on average. If we compare natives and immigrants in the same field of study and with the same education level, there is not a significant difference across the two groups. A similar pattern holds if we look at wages or the quality of patents created—the average for immigrants usually exceeds that of natives, but the differences are quickly explained by field of study and education. Entrepreneurship is the one exception, as these basic controls do not fully account for the greater start-up rate among immigrants. One study further argues for underperformance of immigrants in computer science who came to the U.S. as foreign students compared with peers of the same background.[9]

This evidence highlights two distinct ways that global talent flows have an impact on U.S. innovation. Immigration first provides America with exceptional superstars for STEM work, evident in major awards or walks around the campuses of the California Institute of Technology or Microsoft. Global migration also acts through the sheer number of STEM workers that it provides to America. While these immigrants are roughly comparable to natives in the field, they make up a sizable share of the STEM workforce. Both dimensions are important, but my bet is that the large quantity of non-superstars carries the bigger impact for the U.S. economy and the world.[10]

We can filter business and policy responses through these lenses: How should businesses access these superstars, especially as fast technology cycles heighten the competitive advantage of being at the innovative frontier? Can policies like the H-1B program be refined to yield an immigrant pool with better skill sets than current cohorts? This nuanced understanding of global talent flows provides a stronger foundation for responses to these questions. But first, let's consider an additional way that talent flows have an impact on America. We've focused so far on innovation, but what about its close cousin, entrepreneurship?

Driving U.S. Entrepreneurship, Too

Immigrant entrepreneurship is a hot topic, the subject of Silicon Valley lore and proposed legislation like the Startup Act and the Attracting and Retaining Entrepreneurs Act, which would make it easier for immigrant entrepreneurs to enter America. This focus is for good reason, as entrepreneurship fosters a dynamic and growing economy. We will use administrative data to measure the role that immigrants play in U.S. entrepreneurship, the way we did for patenting. This proves a bit harder, but a conclusion nonetheless emerges: Global talent flows have also been a substantial driver of U.S. business creation. As most job creation happens when new firms are born, this is an important way immigration affects the livelihoods of people.[11]

Some early and influential surveys measured the role of immigrant entrepreneurs in Silicon Valley, documenting that 24 percent of ventures there were run by Chinese or Indian CEOs during the 1980s and 1990s. Subsequent work expanded the geographic sample and isolated companies that received venture capital investment or went public.[12] For the most part, these surveys also suggested similar levels of immigrant contribution. These statistics are frequently cited by policy advocates in Washington, along with "poster boy" cases of entrepreneurship like Jerry Yang (Yahoo!) and Sergey Brin (Google).

New data now demonstrate the rising share of immigrants among start-up founders nationally. The U.S. Census Bureau built the Longitudinal Employer-Household Dynamics (LEHD) database through state-level unemployment insurance records. The LEHD provides individual-level employment profiles for every worker and firm in America. As the data set records who is an immigrant, it is a tremendous resource for studying global talent flows. The LEHD tracks eleven states since the early 1990s, including Texas, Florida, California, and Illinois. By modeling founders through the top initial earners in the firm, we estimate that the immigrant share of entrepreneurs increases from 17 percent in 1995 to 27 percent by 2008, as seen in Figure 3.3. This outpaces the growth of immigrants in the workforce overall, and the immigrant share is even a few percentage points higher among high-growth start-ups backed by venture capital firms.[13]

While research confirms this entrepreneurial tendency among immigrants in many settings,[14] the reason behind it is not clear. Some explanations focus on personality traits. The challenges and uncertainties of moving overseas may select for individuals with a greater tolerance for risk, which in turn leads them to be more

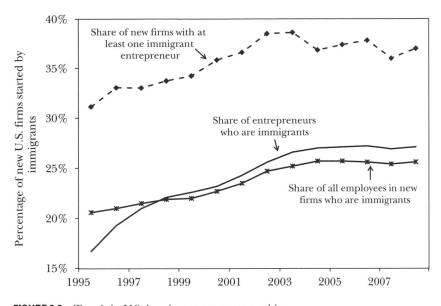

FIGURE 3.3   Trends in U.S. immigrant entrepreneurship.
Source: Data from Longitudinal Employer-Household Database. Entrepreneurs identified through top initial earners in new businesses.

willing to start new firms. Some ethnic groups also celebrate entrepreneurship as a career. Entrepreneurs need help with the many challenges of running a business, and social cohesion and tight-knit ethnic communities can provide support to founders.

Other explanations are darker, however, including one that suggests immigrants enter entrepreneurship as a result of poor opportunities for regular employment. Discrimination can play a role here, and early accounts of Silicon Valley's immigrant entrepreneurs note the career limitations they encountered at major tech firms. Similarly, if native employers are skeptical about the college and professional degrees from foreign schools, they may not provide immigrants with job offers commensurate with their true skills, leading those immigrants to pursue entrepreneurship instead. Regardless of which of these factors bears the most responsibility, the result has been a deep transformation in the places where entrepreneurship and innovation happen in America.

The Altered Geography of American Innovation

Global talent flows are reshaping the location of American innovation. Immigrants at all skill levels concentrate in "gateway" cities like Boston, Miami, New York, and San Francisco.[15] These larger cities provide greater assimilation and employment opportunities and tend to be more tolerant of foreigners. Immigrants also favor cities closer to their home countries, which was paramount in the 1700s and 1800s, given the multiple weeks needed to sail across oceans. While plane travel is now fast and safe, the seven hours and associated jetlag from New York to London remains less than half of the sixteen hours from the Big Apple to Hong Kong.

Precedent also shapes the location choices of immigrants, as the cities chosen by early migrants from a country act as a persistent gravitational pull for future ones. That is often due to personal factors like the desire of an incoming university student to be near family. Prateek, who we met in the first chapter, limited his search of U.S. schools to places with strong existing Indian communities. Prateek's sister, in turn, followed directly in his footsteps by also enrolling at Brown University.

Business considerations also play a role, with prior waves of immigrants recruiting foreign workers or providing them job information. This phenomenon exists at all skill levels, with a classic ethnographic study documenting how the job taken by an unskilled Korean immigrant was "determined by who picked them up at the airport."[16] Another example comes from taxi drivers, among whom immigrants from one country often constitute many local drivers in a city. Indeed, practically all ethnic groups in America are concentrated both spatially and in certain occupations.[17] These small features add up into recognizable patterns: Boston and New York get an extra-large dose of European inflows, Miami is home to huge numbers of Hispanic immigrants, and West Coast cities pick up many Asian influxes.

This spatial concentration means that rising immigrant STEM work disproportionately favors some U.S. cities. The trend during the 1970s and 1980s was toward the spreading out of innovative activity across America, but the 1990s acceleration of talented immigration into a handful of gateway cities stopped and reversed that diffusion. Instead, a few key U.S. clusters have become responsible for ever-larger amounts of patenting. The ten largest population centers today account for 26 percent of the U.S. population, while the patenting share of those cities is 52 percent.[18]

Delve deeper, and one sees even more stunning implications of global talent flows. In the late 1970s, about 1 in every 220 patents in America was invented, or coinvented, by a Chinese or Indian inventor residing in the San Francisco Bay Area. Today, this figure stands at a staggering one in every eleven patents! To get a sense of this effect, the innovation output of Chinese and Indian inventors in the Bay Area now exceeds the combined patenting of the bottom twenty-eight states in terms of innovation. In fact, this ethnic output exceeds the invention totals of any other state, including the big ones like New York and Massachusetts.

How is this possible? One factor is the surge in Chinese and Indian contributions, from 3 percent of U.S. patenting in 1975 to 18 percent today. But as important is the increasing spatial concentration of ethnic inventors, with the Bay Area's relative share of Chinese and Indian inventors growing fivefold over the past forty years. It is no wonder, then, that companies all around the world are trying, one way or another, to establish a research foothold there.

These trends show little sign of abating. The growing importance of ethnic invention and its concentration in key talent clusters has persisted through booms and busts, including the Great Recession, through wars and the immigration barriers that followed 9/11, and everything else since. The patterns are strongest in high-tech fields like software and semiconductors, but they are evident in most every technology.

While immigration fuels the development of major tech clusters, it also heightens the competition across them. We described earlier how the biotech industry grew up around locations where initial breakthroughs occurred. This pattern is quite general, with the "Eureka!" moment of a breakthrough usually followed by a flurry of local subsequent inventions to flesh out the advance. Immigrants tend to be more mobile than natives, and they respond faster to these opportunities. As immigrants have become a greater part of the STEM workforce, the speed at which a city can gain or lose a leading position for a technology has quickened.[19]

This rapid influx of immigrants to a city can bring benefits like more tax dollars or a higher business profile. But we might also wonder, what impact does a massive increase in the immigrant STEM workforce have for the native workers already there? If global talent flows influence U.S. innovation mainly through the quantity of people joining the STEM workforce, rather than through unique skillsets, then it is critically important to understand their effect on the quantity of native STEM workers.

The Impact of Local Wages and Employment

A classic way to analyze this question is to compare the wages of workers across cities, conceptually thinking of each city as an independent economic unit. As immigrants move into one city, what happens to wages in that city as compared to those in peer cities that did not experience the influx? In other words, as San Francisco becomes home to a large concentration of immigrant talent, does this disproportionately lower local wages or employment for natives in STEM fields compared with other large cities in America?

While intuitive, this approach has important limitations. For example, we might observe that San Francisco doubled its immigrant STEM workforce over a decade and that wages for natives in STEM work rose 15 percent at the same time. From this, a supporter of immigration would conclude that talent inflows helped domestic workers. Yet it could have been that local technology breakthroughs at Stanford were the root cause of both trends by creating a huge local demand for STEM talent. In fact, natives might have even seen faster wage growth without immigration, but this adverse effect was masked by the overall economic boom. Correlations must be viewed with a grain of salt, and economists spend years in graduate school learning to argue with one another about these issues.

The gold standard for identifying a causal connection is to study an episode where lots of immigrants were suddenly and randomly dropped into a location. If the destination is truly random, then it won't be correlated with hidden factors like Stanford's rate of scientific discovery. Because such idealized experiments have been elusive for STEM work at the city level, the next-best alternative is to mimic this concept by relying on national trends and how important they are to different locations. San Francisco and Miami have very different ethnic compositions, and we earlier noted that prior immigration waves create a pull for future immigrants. Thus, America opening the immigration flood gates to Hispanic STEM workers is more likely to provide new inventors to Miami than San Francisco, whereas the opposite is expected if the flood gates for Chinese immigrants are lifted.

Several studies measure city- or state-level effects with this approach, finding that skilled immigration has limited or even positive benefits for native wages and employment over a short horizon.[20] Over a decade or longer, the evidence becomes even stronger that high-skilled immigrants boost the fortunes of nearby natives.[21] The confidence that one places in these findings rests on certain assumptions. For example, do cities function more or less independently, or are they hopelessly interlinked? And are changes in national immigration policy really outside the influence of cities and their mayors? These assumptions do not hold perfectly true, but the important point for now is that the wages of native STEM workers hold up reasonably well in the presence of massive STEM immigration into a city.

This stability is due to the economics of talent clusters. Customer demand for innovative companies extends far and wide, and the work of inventors depends primarily on interactions with talented colleagues. These two properties allow STEM employment to expand substantially in a city with immigration without causing sharp local wage declines. Indeed, immigrant inflows have been so substantial and spatially concentrated for the tech sector that we would have observed enormous adverse effects on local wages without the economics of skilled work. This robustness does not close the door on whether immigrants harm native workers, as adverse consequences could happen outside of local areas, but it does explain how global migration helps fuel exceptional talent clusters.

Our deep dive has covered a lot of ground about the American tech sector and its connection to global talent, but so far, we have skipped a pretty big question.

Why Innovation in the United States?

This chapter began by stating that the American tech sector is the largest lever through which global talent flows influence the world, and I doubt many readers objected to the assertion. Yet now that we have explored the sector in depth, it is helpful to ask the broader questions: What is different about innovation versus other skilled disciplines? And why America?

A starting point is the recognition that skills related to STEM work are among the most transferable globally. Marketing and sales require deep local customer appreciation that can be difficult for immigrants to learn, while lawyers and accountants must master long lists of country-specific regulations. By comparison, work in STEM fields varies much less from Beijing to São Paulo, which minimizes natural barriers for talent flows. These are also fields where modest struggles in a second language are relatively easy to overcome, and there are few legal barriers or licensing restrictions, unlike in medicine or law.

The economic rise of Asia is also important. China and India account for much of the recent growth in global talent flows, and immigrants from these countries disproportionately have a STEM education or a desire to study it in school. We see this not just in America, but in many other countries as well.[22] The rapid growth of ethnic innovation in the U.S. and the outflows of talent from these Asian giants are tightly connected.

Why do these talent flows benefit America so disproportionately? Given the economics of talent clusters, other countries could have taken the lead, but several factors tilted the balance in America's direction. Wages for skilled workers are higher in the U.S. than almost anywhere else, and taxes are lower. Entrepreneurs enjoy the world's largest market, all accessible in English and with less cronyism or corruption than many other countries. Some of America's leading ecosystems further show high tolerance levels for immigrants and deep support for innovation.

Yet our picture is still incomplete. High-skilled immigration only happens with the consent of the receiving country's government, and the U.S. approach grants special power to American firms for the selection of employment-based immigrants. What are the implications of making firms into the gatekeeper? Do all countries do it this way?

Chapter 4

POINTS VERSUS FIRMS

DESPITE THE COLD MARCH DAY, the mood was warm and cheerful as Bill Gates of Microsoft testified before the U.S. Senate Committee on Health, Education, Labor, and Pensions in early 2007. The committee was chaired by Senator Ted Kennedy, a lion of the Senate for more than forty-five years, but there were to be no great surprises—Gates had delivered his testimony in writing a week earlier than expected, to many chuckles. In a town of star power, Gates could hold his own, as he was about to be named the world's richest person for the thirteenth year running.

Gates laid out three actions for improving U.S. competitiveness: better education and training for American students and workers, encouragement of more R&D, and greater high-skilled immigration. For the last point, he called out H-1B visas, noting, "I personally witness the ill effects of these [H-1B] policies on an almost daily basis at Microsoft."[1] Gates argued that expansion of the program was essential, further elaborating that Microsoft hired four employees to support each H-1B worker. "The jobs are going to exist somewhere . . . and the jobs around them are going to be created wherever those uniquely talented people are," Gates commented.

Although there was no drama that day, Gates's testimony remains quite controversial. Gates was pursuing the best interests of Microsoft, and some reactions have been bitter. A later upload of a video of the testimony to YouTube by a user named "Border-Guards" elicited comments accusing Gates of perjury and treason and suggestions that he should be beaten up in public.[2] Several American tech workers linked their job difficulties to H-1Bs, and a post after Microsoft laid off eighteen thousand workers in 2014 sarcastically commented: "So much for importing massive amounts of H1bs [to] create more jobs." A few H-1B workers chimed in with rebuttals, with one heated exchange erupting on how difficult it was to retrain American workers.

The conversation is similar a decade later. Industry leaders like Mark Zuckerberg and Mark Cuban continue to push for H-1B expansion and reform, with Cuban arguing in a hostile interview on Fox News in 2017 that the race for talent is inevitable:[3] "If American companies can't go out and hire the best talent, then those American companies are still gonna have to compete with those smarter people in the global economy, no matter what." This link between American competitiveness and immigration is a persistent theme for the tech industry. In contrast to the coal mines and seaports that anchored past industrial centers, talent in the knowledge economy can go anywhere—excepting, of course, where nations impose limits on people flows. This raises immigration policy from obscurity to central importance. Silicon Valley firms employ many immigrants, so why, then, are limits on talent inflows called "America's national suicide"?

"Give Me Your Tired, Your Extremely Vetted . . ."

The Statue of Liberty has long been associated with the iconic lines "Give me your tired, your poor, / Your huddled masses yearning to breathe free." And yet American immigration policy has never exhibited the unrestrained openness of Emma Lazarus's poem. Despite being a self-proclaimed land of immigrants, the U.S. has restricted people flows since its founding. Governments want to limit risks to citizens, and so health standards have long been mandated, including physical examinations at Ellis Island. Moreover, countries that provide substantial social benefits may worry about becoming "welfare magnets" for those simply seeking the best public programs.

Citizens further task their leaders with building employment opportunities, safeguarding their social and cultural well-being, and much beyond. This often requires navigating competing objectives, as governments seek to protect the jobs of their workers but also foster the labor market competition important for a dynamic economy. While U.S. history speaks to the long-term gain that can come from immigration, America's bitter recent debates testify to how unsettled the matter is in the short term. The tension in many other countries is even worse.

Countries make many decisions about immigration that focus on the core issues of how many people to admit, what type of immigrants to admit, and how to choose specific individuals. Most countries maintain strict control over their borders, but there are exceptions.[4] The open borders of the European Union allow labor to flow freely across member nations while restricting migration from beyond Europe. The discontent of the U.K. electorate regarding unlimited immigration shone through in Brexit voting, but there were also criticisms from those who supported European Union membership. London finance firms, for example, often decried that it was harder to bring in a PhD from America than a plumber from Poland.

America answers these questions in a distinctive way. First, America admits a lot of people. The net immigration to America of five million people during 2007–2012 is more than the net inflow to the European Union during the same period, and the relative rate of immigrants admitted per capita to the U.S. is three times higher than the EU rate.[5] In contrast to America, most large countries experience net people outflows, and few countries of any size come close to America's relative rate of admissions.

What about the types of immigrants to admit? Here again, America is unusual. Other than citizenship, the final step in U.S. immigration is permanent residency, also known as the "green card." Most green cards are used for family-based immigration.[6] While approximately one million green cards are granted every year, green cards granted for employment are subject to an annual cap of 140,000 individuals, including family members accompanying the worker. This allocation is quite different from Canada's, where most slots are for employment-based purposes.[7] Although talent can enter through any category and build up over generations (the "American story," as noted in the introduction), the emphasis on family-based selection tilts U.S. immigration toward lower-skilled groups. With that backdrop, which policies influence skilled employment specifically?

Points as the Gatekeeper

Countries differ in how they select immigrants for employment-based admission.[8] Three of the top four destination countries for skilled immigration—Canada, Australia, and the United Kingdom—emphasize points-based structures that score applicants on factors like age, education, and work experience. The formulas used to tally points are often publicly available, and the immigration site that shows Canada's structure crashed on election night as it became apparent that Donald Trump would become president.[9]

Canada was the first country to use a points-based system, beginning in 1967, in an effort to overcome prejudices and identify people most likely to succeed in the long term.[10] Today, Canada admits the majority of its skilled immigrant population through its points-based Federal Skilled Worker Program. Prospective immigrants first submit a profile through Canada's online system, which scores applicants across six categories such as work experience and adaptability. Some areas like language fluency and education have minimum standards, and an overall score of sixty-seven out of one hundred points places an applicant into the waiting pool.[11] At regular intervals during the year, the government issues invitations to apply for residency to candidates in the waiting pool, as determined by even more detailed assessments.

Several nations followed Canada and adopted elements of points-based systems, including Australia, the Czech Republic, Denmark, Hong Kong, New Zealand, Singapore, and the U.K. This approach was favored by countries seeking long-term skills development. It was also harder for small firms to recruit globally before the internet, and thus a government-run system helped attract and evaluate talent. While digital connections have lowered these barriers, points-based structures still carry advantages. The ability of immigrants to move between firms can foster better employment matches and prevent exploitation. Recent research also has found that points-based approaches help identify immigrants with top potential.[12]

Still, important limitations exist. Point structures are hard to calibrate, and it is not obvious that any chosen weighting scale is optimal—should a doctorate in art history receive more points than a two-year diploma in a technical field? The government, like all of us, has a hard time predicting market needs. It is also a big task to verify the qualifications of applicants, and backlogs can accrue when bureaus become overwhelmed.

But the biggest challenge of a points-based approach is ensuring employment of immigrants. New arrivals frequently lack local connections or knowledge of job-search channels, and overseas education and work experiences are often difficult for an employer to evaluate. Immigrants admitted through points-based systems further have no guarantee that their skills are in demand. A stylized example is a nuclear physicist who maxes out the points score but must drive a taxi to pay rent. Migration may still be the best option for the person, but the nation misses out on a better match for its needs and the tax revenue derived from higher-paid work. Faced with these challenges, countries like Canada have moved toward hybrid systems that factor in employer demand and existing job offers.[13] Nonetheless, a select few will always be subject to a "points" system.

"Give Me Your Superstars, Your Superrich"

Wole Soyinka, winner of the 1986 Nobel Prize in Literature and originally from Nigeria, left the U.S. upon Donald Trump's election, saying he had "disengaged" from America and thrown away his green card.[14] It is doubtful that Soyinka will have trouble finding a new home, and doors around the world open quickly for professional athletes, top fashion models, exceptional researchers and writers, and so on. Every nation seems to employ a very simple points-based approach for superstars: "If your award or credential is big enough, you have enough points!" In the U.S., temporary immigration of this form falls under the O-1 visa, reserved for those recognized to have extraordinary ability. There are no limits on the number of these visas, and more than fifteen thousand were awarded in 2016.

Nations everywhere also welcome those who will invest lots of money. America's EB-5 program, often called the "millionaire's visa," allows entry for those who pony up at least $1,000,000 to finance a U.S. business that will employ ten or more American workers. The investment threshold is reduced to $500,000 if the funding goes to rural or high-unemployment areas. The vast majority of the more than ten thousand EB-5 visas granted in recent years have gone to wealthy Chinese nationals.

Thus, most countries welcome those of great talent or wealth. The real differences emerge in admissions of the merely talented, where most skilled immigration lies. This group includes some hidden future superstars, but most applicants are just what they appear to be—above-average talent with solid educations. When it comes to these individuals, most countries take a different tack than Canada and use an employer-based system. Examples range from Japan and Korea in Asia to Sweden and Norway in Europe. This approach is exemplified by America, where having a job offer is the only qualification that matters. The U.S. also makes it the prerogative of the employer, not the worker, to apply for the visa, taking us back to Mr. Gates and the H-1B program.

The H-1B Visa

The primary path for skilled immigration to America is the H-1B visa. Established with the Immigration Act of 1990, this program allows American companies to temporarily employ skilled foreigners in occupations that require specialized knowledge. Many jobs fall under this heading, including computer programming, accounting, engineering, theology, consulting, and medicine. Firms argue that the difficulty to rapidly retrain American workers to fill needs in these "specialty occupations" raises the importance of access to global talent when they struggle to find domestic workers.

The H-1B visa is valid for three years and renewable once. While the expectation is that the worker will leave the U.S. when his visa expires, the H-1B also has a "dual intent" feature, which allows the firm that sponsors the immigrant to also petition for a green card on his behalf. Thus, the worker can be a temporary resident while also seeking to stay permanently.

There is an annual cap on the number of new H-1B visas, and Figure 4.1 displays its significant fluctuations. The original cap of sixty-five thousand exceeded employer demand in the early 1990s, but applications skyrocketed during the Internet tech boom and the fixing of the Y2K bug. The cap was raised to 115,000 visas during the Clinton administration, and then again to 195,000. Demand fell short of the cap during the tech recession of the early 2000s. When the expansions expired in 2004, the limit reverted to sixty-five thousand, although legislation subsequently provided an additional 20,000 visas for applicants with postgraduate degrees from American institutions. This combined structure of eighty-five thousand visas remains in 2017, a decade later, and demand has exceeded supply in every year. Including renewals, 180,057 H-1B visas were issued in 2016.[15]

As described in Chapter 1, H-1B visas are issued on a "first come, first served" basis until the cap is reached, or they are allocated by lottery when demand exceeds the annual supply in the first week of eligibility. H-1Bs can be awarded to workers migrating from abroad or to foreigners graduating from U.S. schools. In recent years, most visas, sometimes exceeding 70 percent, have been awarded for computer-related occupations. Currently, about two-thirds of H-1B recipients come from India, followed by China. The

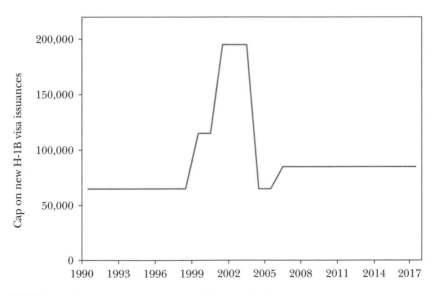

FIGURE 4.1 Evolution of H-1B visa cap for new visa issuances.

choices of firms dictate these features of the H-1B population, not legislative mandate.

The H-1B system attempts to protect American workers. The rules require that employers pay an H-1B worker the "prevailing wage" for his position, experience, and qualifications. This wage rate is benchmarked at what the firm itself pays or the local wages nearby, taking whichever is greater. Because these workers are effectively tied to their sponsoring firm, especially when a green card application is pending, the restrictions are also intended to prevent employers from abusing their relationships with foreign workers. The mean annual starting compensation for a new H-1B worker was $80,000 in 2016, but there is a substantial range, from salaries of around $60,000 to six-figure incomes.[16]

The H-1B program, and complementary pathways like the L-1 visa,[17] establish the firm as America's central gatekeeper for talent flows. The government effectively says to employers, "You tell us who you want to hire, and we will admit them to the country, subject to an annual limit and basic standards." The implications are enormous.

An employer-based approach has two powerful advantages, at least in theory. First, the immigrant has a guaranteed job upon arrival. A subtler bonus is the potential for better immigrant selection based on information that is difficult to measure. A young college graduate possessing rare expertise in a new technology might be worth far more to American companies than a very experienced worker with a PhD in an older discipline. It is impossible to capture these distinctions via points, as one cannot list all the special cases nor keep the list up to date, but employers can make these decisions on a case-by-case basis. The recruitment processes of firms also reveal insights on a person's creativity, work ethic, friendliness, and other soft features.

And yet, quoting the classic 1988 song by Poison, "every rose has its thorn." Or perhaps several of them. Placing firms in control creates important tensions, starting with the firm's relationship to the worker.

The Indentured Servants

The valuable information on applicants does not come for free, as companies incur substantial cost to interview and recruit. Understandably, Apple would be upset if its efforts to bring a talented engineer from Seoul to America were instantly undone by Google hiring the engineer away. Google would be "free riding" on Apple's search, and such poaching reduces the incentives for firms to invest in recruitment. How these dynamics play out in skilled labor markets is determined in large part by the contractual environment. Professional sports leagues tie players to teams with multiyear contracts, which incentivizes teams to pursue and develop new talent. By contrast, the market for senior business executives lacks long-term contracts beyond the "golden handcuffs" of stock-based incentives. This increases the temptation for firms to pursue known talent rather than taking the chance on new talent only to have headhunters start ringing when he or she proves a great success.[18]

The H-1B program addresses that challenge by tying employees to sponsoring firms, thereby providing incentives to pursue global talent and invest in training. The longer employment duration is especially attractive in environments like software development, where a complex multiyear project can be disrupted by employee turnover. Employee lock-in is also valuable in states like California, where employers can't enforce noncompete clauses against departing workers. Being tied to a sponsoring firm weakens a worker's negotiating position, however, if the employer demands excessive hours or is slow to offer raises.[19]

Thus, recent reforms seek to make it easier for an H-1B worker to move to another firm, but the tied relationship remains quite acute when a firm is sponsoring the worker for a green card, a process that can last many years.[20] The website Hire F-1 Students, run by a Texas law firm and nearby universities, emphasizes this to potential employers: "Due to requirements of the immigration process in the U.S., international students are required to remain with an employer for approximately 7–12 years to obtain permanent residence." The site also notes: "The international employee is not 'promising' or 'agreeing' to stay with the company for almost a decade. It is the legal system, itself, that creates this commitment to the company."[21]

Although this rigidity is one important facet of the H-1B program, the bigger story is actually its malleability.

Flexibility Versus Volatility

The "first come, first served" nature of the H-1B program allows remarkable flexibility. It is possible to have every visa be used for a single type of work, if that is what U.S. employers want. Consider how much the program's composition fluctuates over short time periods: The share of visas going to workers from India jumped from 20 percent in 1995 to about 45 percent in 1998, dipped to 28 percent in 2002, and then exploded to 71 percent in 2015. The share of visas for computer-related occupations shows similar swings.[22]

A positive view of these remarkable fluctuations emphasizes a malleability that allows the program to best match scarce talent inflows to areas that have the most current demand. Yet flexibility can also transform into undesirable volatility. Students who choose a college major based on current demand may find that heavy H-1B inflows take the air out of the labor market by the time they graduate. Volatility can also harm immigrants if they are brought to the U.S. on the basis of fleeting opportunities rather than long-term needs.

More broadly, a points-based system defines in simple formulas and on public websites the traits that a country seeks for its skilled immigrants, allowing for clear debate. By contrast, employers in the H-1B system determine U.S. immigration priorities application by application and with limited public disclosure. The overall trust that one places in big corporations like Microsoft or JPMorgan Chase thus looms heavy in H-1B debates. One comment to the BorderGuards' YouTube post begins simply with "I HATE GOOGLE!!!!"[23] This melding of immigration into corporate identities is a challenge for discussing immigration policies, and yet the rancor today is increasingly about companies most Americans have never heard of.

H-1B and Outsourcing Companies

A question that hangs over every new policy is how it will be used in practice. When debating the Immigration Act of 1990, U.S. lawmakers focused on potential uses and abuses of temporary work visas by American firms like Intel or General Motors. Yet, H-1B visas can also be used by foreign firms to facilitate outsourcing and offshoring work, with some U.S. commitments to this end even being made as part of 1995 World Trade Organization agreements on international trade in services.[24]

The flexibility of the H-1B system accommodates these uses, with far-reaching results.[25] Indian outsourcing companies like Infosys and Wipro are among the heaviest recent users, taking in more H-1B visas than Microsoft or Intel. Some American firms like IBM and Deloitte also use H-1B visas to support outsourcing projects.[26] Outsourcing companies use the visas to bring overseas workers to America to interface with clients and learn how their systems operate in preparation for sending work abroad. These workers receive lower pay and assimilate less than other H-1B holders: in 2016, the average salary for H-1B workers by outsourcing companies hovered between $70,000 and $85,000, versus about $140,000 for Apple and Facebook.[27] This substantial gap leads to the frequent suggestion that there are two types of H-1Bs, sometimes phrased as the "Infosyses" versus the "Intels."

The use of scarce visas for outsourcing operations is especially worrisome in years of high demand when the lottery is employed. The lower-skilled nature of the work allows outsourcing companies to submit many applications without caring about which ones win, while other firms may submit only a single application for a highly valued candidate with rare skills.[28] The lottery places these hard-to-find candidates at a disadvantage to the average ones. Thus, a whole business approach has been built around exploiting the inherent flexibility of the H-1B program. While attacks on the "Infosyses" are commonplace in Washington, why are the "Intels" also being called out?

Growth or Cost Minimization?

When firms decide upon which immigrants to admit, their internal economics shape the structure of talent flows.[29] Indeed, most public debate revolves around whether firms create jobs when they hire H-1B workers, as Bill Gates claimed. Firms often describe how global talent provides scarce skills that unlock innovation and growth. Critics instead suggest that firms use cheaper workers to boost profits at the expense of labor. Which is correct? In an economy with fast-growing start-ups alongside shrinking industrial giants, it is impossible to establish a generic motive for all U.S. firms. And a certain amount of normative judgment is involved—for example, how long is "too long" to wait for worker retraining? While recognizing this heterogeneity, we can still ask what happens on average.

Chapter 3 analyzed variations across cities to discern the spatial consequences of skilled immigration, and we can similarly measure whether firms that take on H-1B immigrants are simultaneously hiring or displacing native workers. While conceptually straight-

forward, the empirical challenges for identifying causal relationships are even larger than they were for cities. Firms that have great
opportunities hire workers of all varieties, while firms in trouble
shed people wholesale. Thus, raw employment data unsurprisingly
show a strong positive correlation between H-1B and native hiring.
While lobbyists happily report this to Congress, it is of limited use
as it mostly reflects the overall growth or decline of firms.

Two approaches investigate this question in a careful way.
The first uses the Longitudinal Employer-Household Dynamics
(LEHD) data set described in the previous chapter to consider how
the large ups and downs of the H-1B program, as depicted in Figure 4.1, affected firms.[30] Much as we did for cities, this technique
compares responses of very sensitive firms with their less-sensitive
peers when the H-1B program shifts substantially in size. This approach has the advantage of being comprehensive, including almost every large firm over a very long time horizon. The results
lean toward the growth narrative: The hiring of young, skilled immigrants corresponds to greater skilled native employment in that
company.[31]

The second technique uses a rare type of the H-1B lottery that
occurred in 2006 and 2007. In years when the supply of visas lasts
beyond the first week, but not for a full year, a mini-lottery determines the final few awardees from among the applications received
on the last day when the visas run out. Researchers have compared
the last-day applicants in 2006 and 2007 who obtained the final
visas with those who lost the lottery. The randomization is quite
attractive. Contradicting the optimistic view presented previously,
firms that won the lottery reduced employment of American workers in subsequent years. This accords with the narrative of cost
minimization, although the small number of firms involved in the
last-day lotteries limits precision. The lower overall H-1B demand
in these slow years may also fail to capture the hiring dynamics of
employers during the typical, vastly oversubscribed year.[32]

Both approaches have merits and flaws, and the jury remains out on total employment impact for the firm. But we might make more progress by reframing the question a bit.

Keeping Workforces Younger

Measuring overall employment of natives and immigrants may miss the heart of the issue. Prominent critics claim that tech firms use the H-1B program to keep their workforces younger.[33] As one comment on BorderGuards' YouTube post put it: "Bill Gates is just selling out American IT workers . . . when you reach 20+ years in the industry, an H1B will certainly come in with a much lower salary and work really hard for 7 years."[34]

A critique of the basic cost minimization story is that the savings from using H-1B workers are quite modest. The requirement that firms pay H-1B workers the prevailing wage within their firm or local area caps the savings achieved when replacing a twenty-five-year-old American programmer with an H-1B holder of a similar age and education. Studies find that the difference in wages of H-1B workers and comparable natives is frequently 5 percent or less.[35] A level of 5 percent would mean that an employer could save $4,000 annually on an $80,000 salary, but this would get quickly eaten up by H-1B filing fees, lawyer fees, recruitment costs, and training. Indeed, the Hire F-1 Students website warns employers that hiring international students is not a path to "sub-standard wages" and that costs may increase.[36]

But what if the twenty-five-year-old H-1B worker is replacing not a twenty-five-year-old but instead a fifty-five-year-old? The salary difference between younger and older workers can be quite substantial: a 2 percent annual wage growth compounded for thirty years takes a starting salary of $80,000 to about $145,000. It is easier to see the motivation of a firm to replace an older worker with a young one. And while age discrimination is illegal, workers can be terminated if their wages are too high for a business to support or if their skills are deemed outdated.

If this sounds too theoretical, then consider that workers over the age of forty were more than twice as likely to be laid off by Intel during its 2016 workforce reductions. Mark Kogler, a fifty-seven-year-old engineer, was one of those laid off, and his salary declined by 50 percent, to $60,000, in his next job.[37] In Mr. Kogler's case, it is unclear if the H-1B program played a role, but age was apparently a key factor. The layoffs were also complemented by buyouts and early retirement packages to shed labor costs, and the hard reality is that businesses save more per person by laying off older workers.

The LEHD analysis also documents this age dynamic in global talent flows. Although the hiring of young skilled immigrants connects with an overall increase in native skilled employment, the job growth is asymmetric. The employment of younger Americans increases, but that of older Americans stays flat. These patterns imply that older employees are at a disadvantage and are not reaping the rewards of firm growth.

Thus, the CEO who reports to Congress that "high-skilled immigration created jobs in my company and no one was laid off" could be telling the truth, as employment of older workers did not decline en masse at her firm. However, that is of little comfort to the laid-off fifty-five-year-old who is now desperate for work. This programmer sees the tech firms all around him growing and growing, but there never seems to be a job for someone over thirty. A *Bloomberg Businessweek* article from 2016, aptly entitled "We're Not Too Old for This," describes the struggle that older programmers face landing jobs in Silicon Valley. The older job applicants describe many strategies for overcoming the age gap to young tech firms, including studying up on current slang and pop culture, dyeing their hair, and even taking fashion advice from younger relatives.[38]

While the incentives are becoming clearer, why are firms replacing computer programmers? Why not the marketing department? Or CFOs and their million-dollar bonuses? The missing piece lies in differences across occupations in the importance of work experience. It is easier to substitute a younger worker for an older one when accumulated experience is less important for job performance. Data for the U.S. find that age-related substitutability is highest in science, technology, engineering, and mathematics (the STEM fields), due in part to the quick pace of change. Computer programmers are particularly vulnerable, with a substitutability four times higher than that for managers, doctors, and lawyers.[39] Technical jobs thus provide the biggest and easiest cost savings from bringing in skilled immigrants, and protective barriers like unions and occupational licensing are relatively weak in the sector.

Indeed, as American tech giants employ more immigrant talent, high-skilled natives appear to be adjusting fields. Immigrants tend to specialize in occupations demanding quantitative and analytical skills, and a rising foreign-born presence in these fields shifts native workers toward jobs that rely more on communicative skills.[40] Thus, while firms may grow their younger native workforces, they are principally doing so in non-STEM roles (e.g., sales, marketing, accounting) that are complementary to the ones favored by immigrants.

Why Innovation and the United States? Part 2

Let's now return to why global talent matters so much for tech in America. We earlier uncovered many factors that have created a large stack of logs for the innovation fire: great universities, America's position at the innovation frontier, high wages for skilled workers, and the technical bent of Indian and Chinese talent. U.S. immigration policy, however, dumps gasoline on top of these logs, sending the blaze high, and sometimes violently, into the sky.

America, perhaps by accident, uses policies that are very advantageous for the growing tech sector. Tech firms benefit from tied employment relationships, and the flexibility to adjust their workforces via short-term visas is valuable in a dynamic industry. Most important, critical occupations in the sector can be staffed with young talent. The tech industry is consistently the first in line for visa applications, because their economics benefit enormously. They depend heavily on the H-1B for their success, and thus the limits they perceive in the program are declared "America's national suicide."

Although firms are a main gatekeeper for skilled immigration, the next chapter moves upstream to consider colleges and universities, the other gatekeeper because of their influence on the student populations from which firms recruit. Dig deeper and one finds global talent is everywhere in the faculty and research staff of these institutions.

Chapter 5

THE EDUCATION PATHWAY

ANY PARTY NAMED "Prateek and Jagrit ain't getting deported!" is bound to be a rocking time. Thus, family and friends crammed themselves into a small Manhattan apartment on the Lower East Side in the summer of 2017 to celebrate that the two roommates had each won the recent H-1B lottery, the odds of which had been about one in ten. Many of the partygoers were young professionals who had graduated with Prateek and Jagrit from Brown University two years earlier. Since then, the clock for their student-worker visas had been ticking fast, and without an H-1B visa coming through, both would have had to leave America or use a backup plan to reenroll in an American school so that they could try again later. While previous shots at the lottery had failed, this time proved the charm for both.

Our picture of global talent is often an immigrant arriving from abroad, fully loaded with an education and work experience. But just as often, the person stepping off the plane looks like Prateek did when he arrived in America years earlier: a youngster full of potential and ambition but in need of lots of training before starting work. Jagrit, too, had followed this path to the U.S. from India. The education pathway is the pipeline for these global talent flows, serving as a magnet that draws them in, trains them, and then sends them out to employers. It can also be a safety net for students while they wait for scarce visas. The dependency is mutual, as universities rely on foreign students financially and to staff their research labs. Global talent is in virtually every nook and cranny of U.S. academia, making it a special laboratory to study.

A Magnet for Young Talent

Parents globally value education as one of the most important gifts that they can give to their children. Adjacent towns in America can have dramatically different home values based on the quality of public schools. Private initiatives like the Russian School of Mathematics allow for further doubling down, with words like "tiger moms" and "helicopter parents" now often used to describe the most zealous parents. Faced with weak local school systems, many parents in developing and emerging nations make heavy financial and emotional sacrifices to send their children abroad for schooling. In the Boston suburbs near me, some overseas Chinese families have even bought local homes sight unseen for access to the right high school.

Parents are especially willing to invest in very promising talent: If your daughter is apt to become the next Serena Williams, how can you get her into Florida's elite tennis programs? If her skill is in mathematics, what is the best pathway to MIT? And while today there is often a race to get the most and the best education for all kids, it was not too long ago that even wealthy families in America prioritized children showing the most promise. Sadly, poorer families around the world still face quite painful decisions on how to allocate a limited budget across the schooling of their children. Investment is sometimes made along traditional lines, such as favoring the oldest male child, but more often, parents invest the most where they see the greatest potential return.

Beyond the training, the credentials provided by schools signal an applicant's raw talent and commitment to hard work. An undergrad degree in chemical engineering indicates an ability to handle complex quantitative work and spend long nights in the lab, traits that employers may value even more than specific coursework. Elite schools have even higher signaling value, as does finishing a degree versus stopping a few credits short. Thanks to this screening, firms start with a refined pool of applicants when they come on campus for interviews. These motivations make schools in advanced economies a strong magnet for talent flows, ranging from permanent migrations to year-long exchanges. This continues well into adult education and rapidly expanding executive education programs. The best raw talent is the most likely to go overseas for training, be it the young athletic stars or the most promising executives.

We focus in this chapter on the role of universities in global talent flows, including graduate education and faculty. While a high school education is the first step for many, graduation from an elite American university is typically the end goal. More parents globally are acquiring the financial means to send kids abroad, and governments from China to Saudi Arabia offer subsidies to students attending foreign colleges in an effort to build their domestic talent while their own universities take root.[1] These forces are coming together to generate a surge of foreign students around the world, especially in America.

Training of Talent

Over one million international students attend American colleges and universities, representing about 5 percent of U.S. enrollments and a substantial increase since the 1970s. Figure 5.1 shows that China now accounts for about a third of international students in America. India, Korea, and Saudi Arabia are the next-largest sources. The foreign student population in the U.S. comprises about 439,000

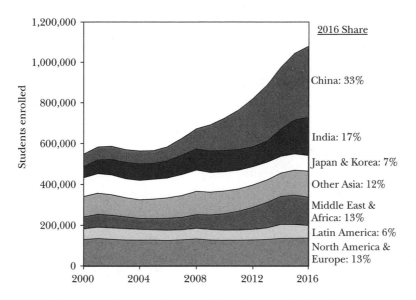

FIGURE 5.1   Foreign student enrollments in U.S. colleges and universities by country of origin.
Source: Data from *Open Doors 2017* report.

undergraduate students, 391,000 graduate students, and 249,000 non-degree-seeking students and those in training programs.[2]

The Chinese surge has been strong in undergraduate enrollments, which grew from about 8,000 in 2000 to 143,000 in 2016. Despite this surge, America's leading role in undergrad education is far from absolute. Globally, there are 4.5 million students studying outside of their home country, making America's "market share" for foreign students substantially lower than its share of overall immigrant talent. While America attracts seven times as many immigrant inventors as second-place Germany, its student inflow is only twice as large as the runner-up U.K. Many countries also have higher relative rates of foreign enrollment. Indeed, Australia has prioritized education to such an extent that it now generates more money for the country than tourism.[3] And while it is rare to find an American-born inventor or Nobel Prize winner working outside of the U.S., many American students study abroad each year.[4]

But there are also many similarities to the patterns we observed for firms, starting with the concentration of global talent. Foreign students favor large cities like New York, Boston, and Chicago, as well as some areas in the Southwest, and eight American universities hosted more than ten thousand foreign students each in 2015.[5] These places benefit the most from the $37 billion contributed to the U.S. economy by immigrant students,[6] as well as the jobs created by the ideas and technologies that universities produce.[7] One estimate suggests that international students add more to the economy of New York City than the Yankees, Mets, and Giants combined.[8] The U.K. displays a similar spatial concentration around London and Oxford. Does this concentration signify a displacement of natives by foreign students?

Universities are less flexible than Google or Goldman Sachs, which heightens the prospect that immigrants might exhaust a limited number of student slots in a program. STEM fields have received the closest analysis, and looking from the 1970s onward, immigrants did not reduce American student enrollments overall.[9] But there is some evidence that female natives may have been discouraged, which is worrisome given the long-standing challenges of increasing female STEM participation.[10] The ongoing surge in international student enrollments from China and India raises the prospect of future tightness in STEM majors, at least until departments adjust their size to keep pace with student demand.

A solid education, however, is only the first part of why many students go abroad. The introduction described the "Trump slump" at American business schools, connecting MBA enrollments to future job hopes, and we next explore just how pervasive that link is.

Access to the Labor Market

Firms recruit extensively on U.S. campuses, and many foreign students want to stay in America. This comes as a surprise for some immigrants—perhaps due to an on-campus romance or an unexpected love of Manhattan—whereas for others it was always part of the plan. Cross-border migration screens for the most talented and serious-minded students, and parents have been known to step in when teenagers fail to see the full picture. This makes universities and colleges the second big gatekeepers for U.S. skilled immigration through their admissions processes. In fact, anonymous admissions directors effectively determine much of long-term skilled immigration to America.[11]

The very best students think carefully about access to future jobs, as evidenced by international student inflows before and after the Clinton-era H-1B expansions expired.[12] Before 2004, all foreign students could bank on getting an H-1B visa at graduation, as the demand consistently fell short of the enlarged 195,000 quota. These guarantees evaporated, however, when the cap reverted to its original level of sixty-five thousand and visas ran out again. Yet prospects remained much better for students from five countries— Australia, Canada, Chile, Mexico, and Singapore—due to specific set-asides within the H-1B legislation or free-trade agreements. Students from these five "control" countries had less reason to fear that the tighter H-1B environment would harm their job prospects, compared with students from elsewhere.

What happened? In terms of student counts, undergrad enrollments from affected countries dropped by 14 percent after the expansions expired, while the five control nations had no change. Moreover, the very best students were especially apt to go elsewhere: SAT scores of applicants from affected countries declined by twenty points, on average, or about 1.5 percent. As these countries accounted for most overseas enrollments, this change in future labor market access clearly put a good-sized dent in the pool of foreign students from which U.S. colleges could select. Immigration policy thus shapes the decisions of today's incoming students through its influence on future employment opportunities, and its impact on when and how students graduate is equally large.[13]

A Holding Tank for Talent

Everyone makes decisions from time to time that take the form of "We'll figure it out when we get there," as in "Let's just get ourselves to the South by Southwest Festival, and then we'll find a place to stay." The same is true for talent seeking entry to the U.S. While barriers to the American labor market divert some students, many still come believing they can make it work once they get a foot in the door. The education pathway helps immigrants navigate challenges in obtaining employment visas and even becomes a "holding tank" when the immigration process becomes clunky.

The largest buffer is the Optional Practical Training (OPT) program, which held Prateek and Jagrit until they won the H-1B lottery. OPT lets graduates work with U.S. companies to gain practical experience for jobs connected to their majors, lasting for up to one year in most fields and three years for STEM occupations.[14] A tricky part of OPT is the narrow window allowed between graduation and the start date of the job, and foreign students often stall graduation bit by bit to ensure their jobs start within the allowable time frame. There are an unlimited number of OPT visas, with roughly 175,000 active in 2017.[15] The OPT program accounted for about 30 percent of foreign-born students entering the U.S. labor market during the 2000s,[16] and today more skilled immigrants start work via OPT than through H-1B visas or permanent residency admissions.

While OPT provides a Band-Aid for college students under the current immigration system, the setup is far from optimal. The challenge is an immigration structure that links different-sized "pipes" together. At the starting point of university admissions, there are no limits on immigrant inflow, and America issued

706,000 student and exchange visitor visas in 2015. The next pipe
is smaller and fixed in size, with eighty-five thousand potential visas
each year for school-to-work transitions. Many of the visas are won
by applicants living abroad, however, leaving fewer for foreign students graduating from U.S. schools, a fact that was especially frustrating for Prateek and Jagrit. Finally, the smallest pipe is for later
transitions to permanent residency. If most immigrants preferred
to leave America after a few years, the flow would be within the
capacity of each pipe. The reality, however, has been one of exceptional demand and bursting seams, with not everyone making it
into the next stage.[17]

While foreign students are filling up the seats of college classrooms, foreign professors have long been visible at the blackboard.
Global talent plays arguably its greatest role in the faculty of U.S.
universities, to which we turn next.

Academia's Best and Brightest

The world's top schools draw in aspiring academics with an intensity that rivals the pull of professional sports leagues for young
athletes. The U.S. awards about forty thousand doctoral degrees
annually, with the number of STEM degrees growing particularly
fast in recent years. Figure 5.2 shows that international students
earn about 40 percent of U.S. STEM doctoral degrees, a share
that spikes to more than 50 percent in engineering and computer
sciences.[18] In short, much of America's doctoral education focuses
on training global students.

If universities are the pathway for undergrads and master's students to enter the private sector, then doctoral programs are the
stepping stone to coveted U.S. academic jobs. Immigrant doctoral
students show talent that equals their native peers, even exceeding
natives in some fields, and they frequently hope to stay in America
after graduation.[19] This desire is especially true for students from

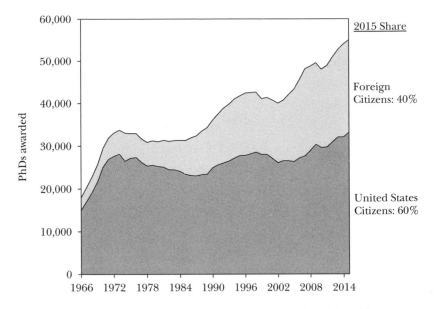

FIGURE 5.2   Doctoral degrees granted by U.S. schools by student citizenship.
Source: Data from National Science Foundation.

emerging economies, and typically nine out of ten doctoral students from China, India, and Iran have wanted to remain. Consequently, about 30 percent of the STEM PhDs working in U.S. academia today are foreign born and U.S. educated.[20] Does this make it less likely that natives become professors?

Academic research has many parallels to the economics of skilled clusters. Professors care deeply about how peers worldwide view their research, and interactions among smart and talented people are often the most important factor for academic success, outranking lab equipment and other physical resources. The tacit and emergent nature of frontier ideas means that they are best understood through rubbing shoulders with other top researchers at conferences—or even better, sitting around the cafeteria lunch table. For these reasons, doctoral students flock to select universities, despite syllabi and academic papers being available online.[21]

This sounds a lot like the economics of talent clusters, but there are important differences. Local sales matter little for business success in Hollywood or Nashville, but a substantial portion of a university's funding comes through direct student tuition and concomitant public support. Universities also raise money through channels like research grants and alumni donations, but the local nature of student-linked funding limits how concentrated universities can become. Another constraint is that faculty promotion is often determined by how much one has published in a narrow range of very competitive journals, which are slow to expand their page counts.

Thus, despite the pro-immigration stance of many faculty members, universities are among the most likely places to observe native displacement. This is visible within prominent awards. The American Economic Association awards the John Bates Clark medal annually to the top American economist under the age of forty, with U.S. citizenship being required. Yet three recent recipients were naturalized immigrants to America born in Canada, Ukraine, and India, respectively. In fact, more than half of the winners since 1995 have been foreign born, which is more than triple the 13 percent share of 1947–1994.

Awards are one thing, but what about jobs? One powerful example of displacement comes from mathematics.[22] During the Cold War, policy and economic differences between America and the Soviet Union led to mathematics research in the two countries developing distinctive flavors. The Soviets focused more on Fourier analysis, for example, but less on differential geometry. After the Soviet Union collapsed, Russia's research capabilities were severely diminished, and former emigration barriers dismantled. Consequentially, many Russian mathematicians came to America, including some of the very best. There was little impact on existing American faculty in the subfields that the Russians had neglected, but substantial displacement occurred in the areas that the Soviet Union had prioritized. Some displaced faculty simply moved to other research specialties, but others transitioned to less prestigious schools or out of academia entirely.[23]

This pattern would likely hold in many academic disciplines, and other evidence suggests that fewer natives enroll in PhD programs when global competition for spots heats up.[24] Yet reasonable people disagree about whether this is a worry. While hardship can result from natives losing academic jobs, other displaced individuals land in quite lucrative careers. Some of the displaced mathematicians ended up doing very well in finance, and many natives deterred from PhD programs end up with MBAs instead, which generates far higher average earnings.

Income, in fact, can be an awkward yardstick for measuring displacement in many talented occupations, as factors besides money influence people's choices to be scientists, politicians, musicians, social workers, doctors, preachers, and so on.[25] Even in business, which shows a sharper connection of wages and ambition, individuals often take jobs that pay less than they could otherwise earn. Why is this important? When talented natives value an occupation for nonmonetary reasons, we must decide how much weight we should give to these other incentives. Should we restrict talented immigration so that natives can work in their passion area, even if they have opportunities to earn more money elsewhere?

A second complication is that foreign faculty strengthen American universities and thereby draw in more students, allowing colleges to grow in size and number. This creates more spots for students and faculty and quickens research progress. The U.S. "mathematics pie" did not grow after the Soviet influx, but U.S. chemistry fields expanded after the Jewish emigration to America around World War II.[26] Foreign students now account for more than 60 percent of U.S. PhDs in economics, and the upward push of immigrants has expanded the field and created more opportunities for natives like myself—even if fewer of us win the John Bates Clark medal these days.

Fields as diverse as chemistry, mathematics, and economics differ in their flexibility and capacity for expansion, and this is true for professional schools as well. Business schools sell training applicable to companies globally, and there are no country-specific exams in order to practice business. Thus, great faculty can generate student demand that expands leading business schools, generating even more jobs. But the picture may be quite different in law or medicine, where students prep for country-specific exams and regulations. In the end, the overall impact of global talent flows on university faculty is nuanced, yet as we see next, its impact on financing is clear-cut.

New Sources of Revenues

Global immigration is reshaping the "business model" of universities, where administrators constantly face a budget squeeze. Education is labor intensive, and rising wages in other parts of the economy put pressure on universities competing for skilled talent.[27] Private universities do not want to overly raise their price tags, which already exceeds $60,000 annually at Harvard, and this pressure is even greater for public universities. The "fully loaded" rate at the University of Virginia (UVA), a leading public school, is $30,000 for students hailing from Virginia, while the out-of-state rate is just under $60,000. And the trend is just as steep: The average tuition for U.S. public schools has grown more than 50 percent since 2010, even controlling for inflation.[28]

Public appropriations for higher education frequently fall short of expenses. As Janet Napolitano, president of the University of California, noted in 2016, "California's situation is not unique. Nearly every state has faced this Hobson's choice, and they have all reached the same decision: Open doors to out-of-state students in order to keep the doors open to in-state students."[29] As foreign students pay full out-of-state fare, a university can hope to obtain two birds (talent and money) for one stone, financially subsidizing domestic students.[30] International students currently account for about 5 percent of the UVA student population, up from 2 percent in the early 1990s.[31] Indeed, one study estimates that a 10 percent reduction in state-level appropriations for public universities is associated with a 12 percent increase in foreign enrollment at those schools as school administrations make up for lost funds.[32] This enrollment shift is even higher at the most research-intensive schools where budget squeezes are most keenly felt.

Talent inflows also shape the types of programs offered by schools. Doctoral programs tend to offer financial support or work fellowships to graduate students, which is one reason students from poorer economies often show up in doctoral programs before master's or undergraduate programs. This financial support means that growing doctoral programs is not going to close the budget gap for U.S. schools nearly as fast as growing master's or undergraduate programs. By contrast, Finland compensates public schools well for the production of PhD students, and thus it is not surprising to see cash-strapped Finnish universities expanding doctoral programs for overseas students.

Recall how outsourcing companies found a powerful tool in the H-1B visa—some schools are using global talent in similar ways, too. Top universities and those in big cities have traditionally grabbed the most foreign students, with Harvard's incoming class now more than 20 percent foreign.[33] While the national average is much lower, online learning and part-time campus stays are tilting the field toward lower-tier and rural schools. Fort Hays State University (FHSU), located in rural Kansas, has aggressively built a "virtual campus" with an extensive international student presence. From two foreign students at the school in 1990, FHSU's foreign enrollment now exceeds six thousand, compared with its on-campus undergrad population of four thousand.[34] This is one business model that is likely to spread among remote regions of the country.

Foreign talent also staffs schools, sitting in between students and permanent faculty. The H-1B system offers universities an unlimited number of visas, not subjecting them to the cap that applies to private-sector employers. This flexibility contributes to the growing army of postdoctoral scholars (postdocs) now on U.S. campuses, where the foreign-born share stood at 48 percent in 2013, compared with 18 percent in 1973.[35] Many postdocs come to America for career opportunities after earning their doctorates overseas, especially in the life sciences and physical sciences. These workers are among the most vulnerable, given their limited career mobility and the weaker oversight for academic labor compared with industry. Universities in other countries are also competing for this talent, with the foreign-born share of European postdocs now over 40 percent.[36]

Universities are also testing how far the immigration rules can be stretched. Entrepreneurs often find U.S. immigration policy especially frustrating, as employer-sponsored visas are more suited to large companies. Launched in 2014, the Global Entrepreneur-in-Residence program at the University of Massachusetts provides a workaround in which entrepreneurs become employees of the university's Venture Development Center (VDC). Sponsored entrepreneurs must contribute eight or more hours each week to tasks ranging from student office hours to providing technical advice.[37] This modest involvement qualifies them for an H-1B visa via the university, and they can spend the rest of their time working on their start-ups! Over its first three years, the VDC has sponsored twenty-six companies that together have raised $30 million in venture investment. Other universities are starting to mimic the model, reaching ten states by 2017. Until America builds a stronger visa pathway for immigrants to private-sector firms, talent will continue to shift toward universities and their unlimited visas.[38]

Universities of Tomorrow

From students to faculty to postdocs, immigration is propelling the growth of colleges and universities everywhere. With so many people wanting admission and research jobs, schools have become as savvy as tech companies for utilizing the immigration system to their advantage. While this chapter has surfaced some downsides of global talent in American universities, the education pathway should be celebrated. It is a solid driver for the U.S. economy and enables amazing research and innovation.

Looking to the future, it is hard to know if global talent will become "too much of a good thing" for American schools. Are immigrant inflows a bubble that could pop and drain the schools that depend on them? Universities are mostly unmovable, so the University of Chicago is not going to bolt to Jakarta—it may open a campus there, but it will stay rooted in the Windy City. But we shouldn't discount the disruptive potential of online education and rapid global development, and many college presidents suffer sleepless nights worrying about the unpredictable future for global education.

My crystal ball does not reveal if this shift will happen. If virtual reality technologies become truly lifelike, future classrooms could be in the "cloud" and the faculty free to live anywhere in the world. We will later meet an entrepreneur seeking to make this happen. The exceptional pace of technology is hard to bet against, but perhaps the need to sit around the cafeteria table for research discussions will continue to reign supreme, the glue that keeps everything in place. That, too, is tough to bet against.

Part 2

THE CONSEQUENCES OF GLOBAL TALENT FLOWS

Chapter 6

TALENT CLUSTERS TO RULE THEM ALL

"MAY YOU LIVE IN INTERESTING TIMES" is a popular phrase for fancy occasions, ranging from toasts at business dinners to the political speeches of Robert Kennedy and Hillary Clinton. Wow, do we live in interesting times! Every issue of *Time* magazine, *Harvard Business Review*, or *McKinsey Quarterly* describes the latest breakthroughs— artificial intelligence, machine learning, the internet of things, blockchain, 3-D printing. Yet "interesting times" are not always enjoyable ones. Indeed, the origin of "May you live in interesting times" was a curse for one's enemies due to the insecurity, turmoil, and challenges it brings.[1]

This chapter marks a transition point in our inquiry. Part 1 of this book examined the origin of global talent flows, painting a portrait of skilled immigration and the economic conditions and policy structures that generated it. Part 2 now focuses on the consequences of global talent flows. The chapters ahead explore the implications for global businesses, talent-sending nations, and growth and inequality in America. Technology will continue to play its important role. Just as Part 1 connected global talent flows to the rise of U.S. innovation, Part 2 considers how this affects the businesses and communities around it. A small portion of us work in high-tech sectors, but we are all being deeply shaped by them and the global talent they capture.

We start with the world of business, where "interesting times" abound. If the potential of future technology is causing heartburn for university presidents, business CEOs now have ulcers. Seventy percent of CEOs reported in a 2017 PricewaterhouseCoopers (PwC) survey that they were worried about the speed of technological change, up from 58 percent two years earlier.[2] The challenges for companies are steep, as competition can bankrupt a firm much faster than a school. But challenges and opportunities can go together. Whereas universities mostly operate around fixed local campuses, businesses can go to where the talent is. If global talent is so crucial for this knowledge economy, what does a company do about it? For GE, it involved moving 160 miles down the road.

General Electric's Transformation

General Electric (GE) has been a corporate icon since its founding by legendary inventor Thomas Edison. Today, GE employs more than three hundred thousand people globally across businesses like power generation, airplane engine manufacturing, and medical imaging.[3] The internet of things provides exceptional opportunities for an industrial equipment company like GE but also an existential threat. Billions of devices, from railroad locomotives to overhead lights, will connect to one another and to the internet in the decade ahead, transforming business practice. Customers will demand new services, and firms will compete in new and unexpected ways.

To attack this opportunity, GE's leadership decided to go after new skills. As then-CEO Jeff Immelt described: "Our new jet engines have a couple hundred sensors on them providing this stream of data. We made the decision that we want to model that data on behalf of our customers and not relegate it to somebody else. That led us back into the chain of adding software talent, building a software platform. Our theory is that every industrial company is going to have to be a digital and software company. We wanted to lead that, and that's how we've invested."[4] He also stated to employees, "If you went to bed last night as an industrial company, you're going to wake up this morning as a software and analytics company."

GE first opened a one-person office in Silicon Valley for Bill Ruh, an executive recruited from Cisco.[5] From 2011 to 2013, Ruh grew his team to 150 people. Although GE employed more than eight thousand software professionals globally, 98 percent of Ruh's team were fresh hires from the Valley with new skills and ways of thinking. Initially designed to support GE's existing operations, this group grew into its own business unit, now branded GE Digital. The next step was even larger: in January 2016, GE announced the move of its long-time corporate headquarters from Fairfield, Connecticut, to Boston. GE wanted immediate access to the skills available in Boston, and it deemed them more important than the incentives offered by other contenders, including the Big Apple. When the transition is complete, GE's new headquarters will be home to eight hundred employees.[6]

The ongoing transformation of GE surfaces three tasks that companies need to accomplish in the knowledge economy: understand the frontier ideas of their sectors, access the global talent to refine and apply these ideas, and facilitate strong information flow throughout their organization. GE is placing a lot of attention on a small number of employees in places like Silicon Valley and Boston while at the same time pushing information out to many divisions and a workforce 70 percent of which exists outside of America. Let's break this complexity down into steps, starting with the talent clusters: are these places really worth all the hype?

Clusters at the Frontier

The economics of skilled work and global talent flows have favored the hyperdevelopment of places like London and Los Angeles. Do these places really matter so much more than suburban corporate labs? For a company with GE's brand and capabilities, is the tail starting to wag the dog? Admittedly, it can be hard to tell sometimes. In 2016, a German car executive described Tesla Motors as "a joke that can't be taken seriously compared to the great car companies of Germany."[7] Within a year, however, Tesla's market cap rivaled all carmakers in the world, excepting Toyota.[8] During the 2017 writing of this book, bitcoin's price fluctuated by over 2,000 percent! Future readers will know which of these valuations proved crazy, and both slipped a bit in early 2018, but many investors are betting heavily on them today. To wrap our heads around this, we need to discuss everyone's favorite: Moore's law.

Talent clusters matter because of the technological change that is disrupting many industries.[9] Our cell phones now have greater computing power than NASA's supercomputers during the space race. Intel cofounder Gordon Moore famously predicted in 1965 that the processing power of a computer chip would double every two years,[10] which has proved to be one of the greatest forecasts of all time. Through the decades that followed, this doubling rendered noticeable changes, such as the faster performance of an Intel 386 versus the 286, but these tech jumps were modest in size compared with everything else that determines business success.

Today, the size of the jumps affords staggering new capabilities. A doubling of computing power for a car in the 1990s meant the next cycle's models could have better brakes or fuel efficiency. Today, it means they may soon be driverless. You can think of it this way: a doubling of technology over the next two years means that what happens in twenty-four months is equal to everything that has ever come before it. Marc Andreessen, tech pioneer and venture capitalist, sums it up as "software is eating the world."[11]

Can this really be so? To wrap our heads around exponential change, let's look at a simple example. My son just lost his first two teeth, so our household now falls on the tooth fairy's route. Back in my day, a dime was about what one could expect for a tooth, but I have heard of families offering $10 today. Suppose that the tooth fairy, in an effort to minimize outlays, struck a deal with my son: She will pay him a dime ($0.10) for the first tooth but then continually double the amount for each future tooth. The tooth fairy spends just $0.30 for the first two teeth, and even the seventh is marked down to $6.40.

You are probably guessing that the tooth fairy comes to regret this decision, but by how much? My son has twenty baby teeth, so we have thirteen to go. Tooth No. 8 will be $12.80, No. 12 is $205, No. 16 is $3,277, and No. 20 is $52,429. Ouch! And if we want to fully map this into Moore's law for computation power, we need to keep going, as twenty-six doublings happened from 1965 to 2017. The twenty-sixth tooth alone costs the poor tooth fairy $3.4 million. Eight more doublings and the price tags get into the billions.

Let's go back to Andreessen, who says: "My own theory is that we are in the middle of a dramatic and broad technological and economic shift in which software companies are poised to take over large swathes of the economy. More and more major businesses and industries are being run on software and delivered as online services—from movies to agriculture to national defense. Many of the winners are Silicon Valley–style entrepreneurial technology companies that are invading and overturning established industry structures. . . . Why is this happening now? Six decades into the computer revolution, four decades since the invention of the microprocessor, and two decades into the rise of the modern Internet, all of the technology required to transform industries through software finally works and can be widely delivered at a global scale."

Andreessen argues that this doubling process has hit critical mass, and highly popular books like *The Second Machine Age* and *Driver in the Driverless Car* describe how crazy large the numbers could get if the doubling persists.[12] While physical limitations appear daunting for the trend to continue too far into future, optimists cite how advanced computing power and new innovations can help us overcome today's limits, as technological progress feeds upon itself. Others are more skeptical, as eighteen times as many researchers are required today to achieve this doubling compared with the 1970s.[13]

Whatever the future holds, the size of technology changes being experienced today are already big enough to influence every aspect of companies, from business models to pricing designs to location choices to organization charts. And technology will increasingly outrank other key factors in corporate decision making like market size.[14] Colloquially, companies are doomed if they hand off tech responsibilities to "two guys with ponytails" who don't have any real power or influence.

This imperative pervades every sector and extends beyond computing power: data on the web are accumulating at an even faster pace. Consequently, Goldman Sachs considers itself a technology firm, employs more engineers and programmers than the entire workforce of Twitter or LinkedIn, and has even changed its Wall Street dress code in places to accommodate tech talent.[15] Boeing and Microsoft have launched a partnership for "digital aviation," and Pitney Bowes, which introduced several key innovations in 1920 that made "snail mail" possible, is reinventing itself as a software company focused on its Commerce Cloud.[16] Regardless of industry, companies fear that "Silicon Valley is coming," to quote a 2015 letter from Jamie Dimon to shareholders of JPMorgan Chase.[17] This brings us to the land of unicorns.

Land of the Unicorns

Images of Silicon Valley revolve around start-ups and entrepreneurs, with Stanford University thrown into the mix. The same is true for Silicon Alley in New York, and for global start-up zones in cities like Tel Aviv, Bangalore, and São Paulo. Technology leaps are most visible in "unicorns," a term for start-ups valued at $1 billion or greater. Free from the many legacy considerations that slow down incumbents, these start-ups, like Uber or Blue Apron, use new capabilities enabled by technology to radically redesign our world. The aspiration to build a unicorn is now common among young global talent—more than forty unicorn founders have come from the business schools of Harvard and Stanford alone, and immigrants account for half of the founders of America's unicorns.[18]

With these splashy examples, it might be surprising to learn that America's overall rate of new business creation has been declining for decades, from above 12 percent in the 1980s to below 8 percent today as measured by U.S. Census Bureau data. Young firms also employ fewer workers.[19] This decline could be due to America's aging workforce, increases in regulation, or the rise of big-box retailers and chain restaurants. Whatever the origin, does Andreessen see something different that justifies his optimism?

Emerging evidence suggests that he does. This approach uses telltale digital signs from incorporation documents to isolate new businesses targeting rapid growth. A business named Infinity Technologies is probably thinking bigger than Billy Bob's Bicycles, as growth aspirations are tied to shorter company titles and not naming of a business after oneself. Likewise, registering in Delaware as a C corporation costs more than incorporating as a limited liability company, or LLC, in one's home state, but it also enables easier future investment into the company. Creating an index of these attributes, the quality-weighted entrepreneurship in America in 2014 was at its highest since 2000, and well above that of the 1980s. And for San Francisco (and Andreessen), it is 50 percent greater than it has ever been and still climbing. Far from a lull, it is a heyday![20]

Both accounts are correct in their own way. The first recognizes that small-business creation overall is declining, whereas the second highlights that a few talent clusters are at peak performance for game-changing entrepreneurs. You can probably guess where these rare places are: Silicon Valley accounts for 28 percent of global unicorns since 2009, and the top ten clusters jointly account for two-thirds. These clusters are split between the U.S. (Silicon Valley, New York, Los Angeles, Boston, Seattle, Chicago) and China (Beijing, Shanghai, Hangzhou), with London thrown in, too.[21] More broadly, the three largest clusters for venture capital investment— San Francisco, Boston, and New York City—grew from around 45 percent of U.S.-based venture investment in the 1990s to two-thirds since 2010.[22]

Why is this unleashed start-up energy so concentrated? Entrepreneurs can now access enormous markets quite cheaply. Whether the digital download of the *Angry Birds* app or the sale of handcrafts on Etsy, the go-to-market tool kit of smartphones, social networking platforms, search engine positioning, and e-commerce sites that emerged over the past decade is unprecedented.[23] Equally important are tools like Amazon Web Services, Dropbox, and Slack that help behind the scenes. Circa 2005, new Internet start-ups frequently required millions of dollars to buy servers, build distribution, and rent office space. Today, many entrepreneurs get going with $50,000 as a result of these tools and shared coworking spaces. These lower barriers tempt more talented people to try out their ideas,[24] and founders can aspire to bigger businesses with the greater resources and control at their fingertips.[25]

Some of these ideas turn out to be unicorns, like the founding of Airbnb in 2008. Airbnb almost magically spans every city and country (except those where regulations block it), and its platform and algorithms allowed it to scale to some three million listings in 2015 with fewer than 2,500 employees.[26] A top traditional hotel chain like Marriott, by contrast, delivers about 1.2 million rooms with around 175,000 thousand employees.[27] More of Airbnb's management also work from their San Francisco headquarters,

compared with Marriott's center in Bethesda, Maryland. New business models for global ventures, like Airbnb's, concentrate power
and decision making—and the wealth generated from them—into
a narrower set of talent clusters.[28] It also raises the importance for
global talent of being in these spots if they want to create the next
Airbnb.

Lest one think that this is an easy business, consider the reflec-
tions of one successful investor who passed on Airbnb in 2009:
"We couldn't wrap our heads around air mattresses on living room
floors as the next hotel room. . . . Others saw the amazing team
that we saw, funded them, and the rest is history."[29] Another leading venture capital firm, Bessemer Ventures, playfully provides its
"anti-portfolio" of deals it has passed on, ranging from Apple to
eBay. One hilarious entry tells of a partner sneaking out of the
home where the founders of Google were working as he could not
fathom the need for another search engine.[30]

These stories show that, while new technologies bring about
amazing opportunities, even the world's best investors struggle to
identify which ones will take off. Working in a frontier cluster raises
their prospects of being in the right place at the right time. Recognizing the irreducible uncertainty that goes along with any single
venture, these investors also build investment portfolios that include
many potential unicorns—so even if just one out of ten of their
ventures works, a handsome payday is in order. Once established,
this ecosystem becomes a magnet that further pulls in global talent,
which then reinforces the strength of the cluster. These powerful
dynamics are starting to pull others in, too.

Dismantling the Corner Office

Many industries like banks, taxis, groceries, and apparel distribu-
tors have become targets for Silicon Valley–type disruption. Companies in these industries traditionally viewed their assets as a shield

against entrants—after all, it is hard to build a new hotel chain like Marriott. Yet start-ups are increasingly flipping this logic around, instead viewing asset intensity as a good indicator of where one might make a fortune by rethinking the traditional approach. The executives of one venture told me that they wanted to make the many popular retail stores of their competitor into a "stone around their neck that would sink them"!

Consequently, leading incumbents are now also jostling for position in top talent clusters. Figure 6.1 shows the locations of corporate headquarters for the hundred largest U.S. companies in 2017, as ranked by *Fortune*, emphasizing the disproportionate influence of a few cities. In its move to Boston, GE's leadership emphasized accelerating the speed of the organization and building a more daring attitude. GE wants to continue leveraging its size and corporate strengths, but it seeks to become nimbler like a start-up.[31]

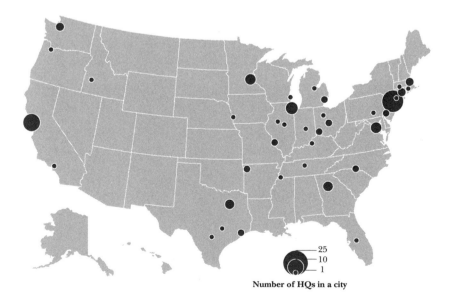

FIGURE 6.1   Locations of Fortune 100 corporate headquarters, 2017.
Source: Data from Fortune 100 rankings.

The technological forces that have increased the market reach of start-ups also provide opportunities for incumbent firms. Many established businesses have assets that will provide new value if they can be tapped for data, such as the elevator-servicing company that installs software to track real-time people flows in a building. These organizations frequently have talent and money that they can dedicate to new ventures. But big companies often face organizational traditions and rigidities that discourage change. Any successful large company is uniquely designed and equipped to do a few things quite well, which can make it very hard to introduce new ways of thinking.[32]

Many businesses are thus rethinking the proverbial corner offices of executives. These offices were established in eras when hierarchy dominated, and more barriers to reaching someone indicated greater importance. They are the exact opposite of the "open bullpens" of new competitors, which minimize distance to maximize speed and knowledge flow. Although most companies won't immediately take a sledgehammer to their office walls, they are questioning whether their traditional hierarchies and functional spaces hinder the efforts to build entrepreneurial cultures and recruit young talent.

A headquarters move is one dramatic adjustment. Packaged foods manufacturer ConAgra relocated its corporate offices from Omaha, Nebraska, to Chicago in 2016 to enable recruitment of young millennials as well as specific senior talent with experience in consumer brands.[33] While also praising the company's former home, CEO Sean Connolly stated, "Chicago is an environment that offers us access to innovation and brand-building talent."[34] He further closed a suburban Chicago facility so that more of ConAgra's executive team would be working under the same roof and intimately involved with the business. McDonalds, Kraft Heinz, and some fifty other companies have also migrated to downtown Chicago from nearby suburban locations. CEO Greg

Brown of Motorola Solutions noted that their HQ move to downtown would accelerate a change in the company's culture and enable easier recruitment of software developers and data scientists.[35]

The reconfiguration underway in the Windy City is happening in many large U.S. cities. The desire to connect with young digital talent is frequently cited, and Figure 6.2 shows the heightened level of this talent as a percentage of each cluster's college-educated workforce in 2016.[36] Companies in tech hubs frequently complain about how difficult it is to find a data scientist, but many others are envious!

The big bang of relocations also allows companies to rethink the size and composition of headquarters. When they moved their senior leadership, GE and ConAgra left many employees at their other sites, and most of Motorola Solutions' Chicago employees likewise remain in the suburbs. The new downtown offices are typically much smaller and focused on senior executives and the workforces geared toward new innovations. That makes sense, given the high rental prices and wages in the heart of Chicago, not to mention New York or Hong Kong.

This starts to look an awful lot like unicorns. Large organizations are today prioritizing key leaders close to where frontier ideas

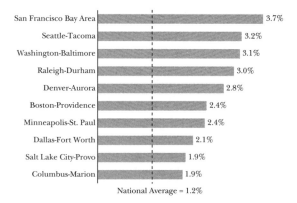

San Francisco Bay Area	3.7%
Seattle-Tacoma	3.2%
Washington-Baltimore	3.1%
Raleigh-Durham	3.0%
Denver-Aurora	2.8%
Boston-Providence	2.4%
Minneapolis-St. Paul	2.4%
Dallas-Fort Worth	2.1%
Salt Lake City-Provo	1.9%
Columbus-Marion	1.9%

National Average = 1.2%

FIGURE 6.2   Share of labor force in computer and digitally connected fields, 2016.
Source: Data from American Community Survey.

emerge, accepting that it will increase travel and communication costs for internal employees.[37] This speaks to the challenge of accurately observing the advancing frontier from a suburban office, even if leaders are well connected and willing to travel downtown. One GE executive summarized it this way: "I can walk out my door and visit four start-ups [from the new HQ]. In Fairfield, I couldn't even walk out my door and get a sandwich."[38] This difficulty is not isolated to corporate chiefs. Venture capital investors in Boston used to cluster along the Route 128 corridor that circles the city, but they have now moved downtown to better compete for deals and support their investments.

It is also hard to attract young talent to periphery campuses. Keystone Strategy is a rapidly growing consulting firm that I have worked with several times. They, too, began on Route 128, near the homes of the founders and with a nice big parking lot. In the late 2000s, they moved to Boston's last subway stop, Alewife, as a compromise with their young workers. Parking became somewhat problematic. Today, they are right smack in the center of Boston, and parking is nowhere to be found. Each move was dictated by the need to access talent. Not only is talent increasingly favoring a few cities; it wants to be right at the heart of them.[39]

Corner-office changes are also frequently linked to the adoption of flatter working structures. ConAgra and GE emphasized reducing bureaucracy in their moves, and the large European bank ING took several steps further. In 2015, ING's leaders recognized they essentially had become a technology company (a frequent conclusion in financial services today) and needed a new approach. The leaders visited many start-ups and tech firms, and even grew close to the leadership of Spotify, a unicorn for music-streaming service. In short order, ING Netherlands HQ threw out the former hierarchy, adopted an agile team structure, and renovated their building into shared workspaces. The CEO gave up his own office, too, and the company had to say goodbye to some past heroes who did not want to operate in the new way. But ING has been very happy with its newfound agility and ability to attract innovative talent.[40]

Although the placement of headquarters is a critical first step, companies only get one HQ (unless they are Amazon and can enjoy HQ2!). How do they approach the other talent clusters?

Listening Outposts Everywhere

Many companies establish small outposts in talent clusters to catch up on frontier knowledge and learn the local scuttlebutt. An Asian bank desiring greater insight into what U.S. financial technology (fintech) start-ups are accomplishing with blockchain technologies or crowdfunding can establish a presence in the Boston ecosystem; the bank listens, learns, and perhaps makes a deal or two. One study demonstrated that British firms that had an innovative presence in America grew faster than their U.K. peers when American-invented technologies in their sector took off. This was especially true when the U.S. technologies were more advanced and gave extra value to those listening carefully.[41]

Such absorption is not easy—while codified information is available via Google, real insight is harder to gather. A Japanese communications equipment manufacturer once withdrew from the U.S. market after being excluded from Federal Communications Commission hearings, because—even though transcripts were publicly available—it believed it would not observe the implicit decisions being made.[42] Absorption is also complicated by the importance today of combining ideas together in novel ways.[43] The upside is that big companies often just need a few "sparks" to reignite dormant innovation streams, which listening outposts can help gather. The challenge, though, is that the right pairings of ideas are typically hard to discern from the outset.

Much like start-ups, corporate outposts are benefiting from a decline in entry barriers. The anchor of the Boston start-up scene is CIC, formerly the Cambridge Innovation Center, which bills it-self as having "more start-ups than anywhere else on the planet." This may well be true, and start-ups located at CIC have raised billions of dollars in investment, with prominent tenants like An-droid, HubSpot, and GreatPoint Energy. Yet CIC also hosts other companies, such as the venture investors migrating in from Route 128. Large companies are attracted to the density of innovation activity, and CIC occupants have included Amazon and Apple—rumor has it that Siri was born there—but also Royal Dutch Shell, Bayer, and PwC. Requests for corporate outposts are so fre-quent that CIC has developed new types of spaces specifically for them.[44]

Access to a hot spot does not guarantee success, of course, and the facility must be staffed with people good at networking, as a closed door does not let much in. Executives must also have the right combination of technical and business savvy to recognize un-anticipated links to ideas that can best help the company. "Listen-ers" further need the power to act. Entrepreneurs are extremely busy and shun those who just want to hear what they are up to. Ex-ecutives who are able to make deals will find larger crowds around them at the watercooler.

Technological forces are pushing corporations deep into talent clusters. Many corporations are further launching venture invest-ment arms or accelerator programs to partner with start-ups. Some companies are now well positioned, while others are scrambling to catch up by sending boards and senior executive teams on ex-ploratory missions. The end result matters. In 1995, America's fifty largest companies by revenue as ranked by *Fortune* conducted 42 percent of their innovation in the ten largest U.S. patenting cit-ies, which was fewer than the 51 percent average for the country. In 2017, the figure was flipped, and the Fortune 50 worked dispro-portionately in talent clusters, with a share of 68 percent versus 58 percent nationally.

These movements will affect big companies for years to come. We already saw in Chapter 4 how technical fields show higher rates of substitution between younger and older workers, and in Chapter 3 how the locations of breakthroughs can shape future sector hot spots. If industrial and service companies are becoming technology firms, as their CEOs passionately suggest, then we have a crystal ball as to what their future will look like. These moves are also concentrating decision-making power in a handful of cities, for better or for worse.

Talent Clusters to Rule Them All

In J. R. R. Tolkien's *The Lord of the Rings*, the Dark Lord Sauron crafts the One Ring to gain dominion over Middle-earth, and many have since invoked this dark imagery to describe power too great for our own good. While the ongoing centralization of power into talent clusters is unmistakable, we are not yet at this level of concern. Collocation offers many gains, ranging from superior innovation to better corporate partnerships. Deeper executive labor markets provide for better matching of leaders to jobs, which promotes productivity and reduces boneheaded decisions. Increased diversity in leadership and talent is also to be celebrated.

Even more, the talent clusters themselves are the leading performers in this play, acting as strong magnets that can dislodge companies from their longtime corporate homes. GE's decision to move its headquarters to Boston was not a grand conspiracy but a deliberate step to expand its technological leadership. Fairfield likely wishes it was still home to GE, but one can hardly condemn GE's leadership for their efforts to transform the corporation. Most of GE's three hundred thousand workers are far away and don't really care where the bosses sit so long as the company excels.

Nonetheless, talent clusters can also cause problems. Collusion is easier, such as the antipoaching agreements that tech giants in

Silicon Valley erected among themselves in the late 2000s to prevent bidding wars for talent.[45] Additionally, studies of corporate layoffs find that employee dismissals and plant closures are more likely to happen at facilities farther away from the corporate HQ.[46] Such a pattern would concentrate layoffs in remote locations, and leaders in talent clusters might pull the trigger faster if other executives around them are doing likewise. The spatial segregation of American society is quite worrisome, and this adds to it.[47]

For now, the rising power concentrated in talent clusters remains an important trend, with the full consequences still to be seen. We should celebrate the good effects and quickly call out the bad. Still, we still have only discussed 1 percent of the workforce of huge multinational companies. These firms are scrambling to build talent bases in far-flung countries, recruit the best and brightest, and maintain information flow. Welcome to the hectic life of today's HR executive.

Chapter 7

THE NEW HR CHALLENGE

MONDAY MORNING was a sea of confusion at Rakuten, Japan's largest online retailer.[1] The cafeteria's menus, building directories, and restroom signs were all in English, having been changed over the weekend from Japanese! It was March 1, 2010, and Hiroshi Mikitani, the CEO of Rakuten, was requiring Rakuten operate exclusively in English going forward. He noted: "We held today's executive meeting in English. Many executives struggled quite a bit, but we managed to get through the entire agenda."

The decision was not met with cheers, though, as only 10 percent of Rakuten's workforce knew English. One engineer reflected: "I was simply astonished. Many Rakuten employees are 'allergic' to English and worry what they are to do." Older workers felt especially disadvantaged, and some speculated the language change was a pretense for future layoffs. The CEO of Honda curtly observed, "It's stupid for a Japanese company to only use English in Japan when the workforce is mainly Japanese." Yet Mikitani was resolute: in two years, all Rakuten employees would have to pass an English-proficiency exam, and those who failed could be docked pay, passed over for promotion, or even dismissed. Managers were responsible for their employees' progress and providing regular reports.

Mikitani's plan reflected global ambition: "Our goal is not becoming No. 1 in Japan but becoming the No. 1 Internet services company in the world. By 2050, Japanese GDP as a portion of global GDP will shrink from 12% in 2006 to 3%. As we consider the future potential growth of the Japanese market and our company, global implementation is not a nice-to-have but a must-do." Founded in 1997, Rakuten provided internet storefronts to Japanese companies, quickly growing to more than seven thousand employees by 2010. Having expanded to Taiwan and Thailand, Mikitani now sought to enter twenty-five more countries and achieve an overseas revenue share of 70 percent. He summed it up as this: "Englishnization is critical—not important, but critical. . . . You need to develop a global organization or your company will be dead in 10 years."

The transition was not easy, but Rakuten ultimately achieved an 86 percent pass rate on the English exam. The language change affected relationships at its headquarters, as Japanese speaking styles contain more embedded power relationships and signs of deference than English. The headquarters workforce became more diverse, pulling in forty-five nationalities within five years of the program adoption. This was critical for Rakuten's talent growth, given Japan's low graduation of computer scientists compared with the U.S., China, and India. As important, though, was the impact on people far away from Tokyo, as the program enhanced Rakuten's ability to recruit talent around the world, move employees between locations, and build global teams. Today, the "Our Strengths" tab on Rakuten's website prominently celebrates the move to English as part of its "diverse, dynamic and open corporate culture."[2]

Corporate headquarters and listening outposts merely scratch the surface of the opportunities and challenges for human resources (HR) that arise with global talent flows. The speed and global integration of today's business environment requires companies operate effectively across borders and reach deep into growth markets. Just as Mikitani emphasized Japan's smaller future share of the world economy, executives all over are grappling with the seismic demographic changes afoot.

The Global Footprint of Giants

The trends prompting companies to go abroad are unmistakable. By 2020, the four countries of China, India, the U.S., and Indonesia will account for about half of the world's population between eighteen and twenty-two years old. Add in nine more—Pakistan, Nigeria, Brazil, Bangladesh, Ethiopia, the Philippines, Mexico, Egypt, and Vietnam—and we reach 75 percent.[3] While these nations vary in stage of development, they showcase where new consumers and workers are coming of age. This list does not include Japan or any European nation, which are mostly shrinking in population. We have seen how the global expansion of youth pushes students toward advanced countries, but it also draws businesses abroad.

Corporations prioritize these up-and-coming places, with most CEOs in a 2017 PwC survey saying that finding the best talent trumped considerations of demographics or geography. Ignacio Galan, chairman of Iberdrola, an electric utility company spanning four continents, commented: "Up to the 19th century, the most important people were those who had liquid resources, money. In the 20th-century world, it was essentially the engineers, but in the 21st century, it is the ones who are able to manage talent. So talent is going to be the driver for the 21st century."[4] Galan's view is pervasive in corporate boardrooms. Honeywell, a large American firm famous for its engineering services and aerospace systems, uses the term "high-growth regions" instead of "emerging markets" to emphasize that these places represent the majority of the firm's new business opportunities. More than half of Honeywell's 130,000 employees are outside of the U.S.[5] Since 2011, Starwood Hotels has regularly relocated its corporate headquarters from America for month-long immersions in emerging places like China, India, and Dubai, stating "there is no substitute for witnessing firsthand this huge transformation."[6]

Many companies require that executives work in foreign regions to qualify for senior leadership positions. The Solvay Group, a multinational chemicals company based out of Belgium, has long prioritized global experience, with one executive noting he would systematically block promotion candidates for very senior positions who lacked time abroad. Solvay favors a "triple-two rule": experience in at least two of Solvay's divisions, in two functions, in two countries. It further grades the hardship of assignments, attributing the most difficulty to moves from Western Europe to very remote sites in poor countries.[7] These talent flows within multinationals are remarkable as they swim against the tide of talent moving toward advanced economies.

Yet this overseas ambition is not exclusive to companies from rich countries. The Haier Group, founded in 1984, is China's largest appliance manufacturer. As early as 1997, CEO Zhang Ruimin set out the company's "three-thirds" strategy, which dictated that one-third of revenues must come from goods made and sold in China, one-third from goods made in China and exported abroad, and one-third from goods both made and sold in international markets.[8] In the two decades that followed, Ruimin led Haier to a global market share of 10 percent.[9] China's newer tech giants of Alibaba, Baidu, Tencent, and JD.com are likewise seeking access to Western consumers and investing billions in frontier start-ups and new technologies.[10]

Cross-border expansions, whether a new plant for Haier or Tencent's opening of an artificial intelligence lab, are difficult. One challenge is just getting permission to enter. American cloud computing companies decry their inability to enter China, while the U.S. has resisted Huawei taking positions in key parts of U.S.

communications infrastructure as a result of its links to the Chinese government.[11] There was an enormous outcry in 1989 when Japanese investors purchased Rockefeller Center, and today similar touchiness exists around Chinese purchases of famous Manhattan properties.[12] The road also remains perilous even upon entry, with Mitsubishi Estate later experiencing buyer's remorse over the Rockefeller Center purchase. Much must be learned and unlearned every time a successful company enters a new location, requiring humility and extensive experimentation to boost local knowledge and customization.[13]

A common strategy revolves around market-entry teams that combine local experts with migrating individuals who understand the best practices of the parent company. While this marriage appears obvious, the subtle details vary substantially. Haier emphasizes local leadership by hiring new country managers from leading appliance firms in the markets entered, giving them extensive decision-making power. One executive reported: "We hope to have the Haier be the Haier that *they* created. For example, in the U.S., we hope that it is the Americans who build up Haier America."[14] Chinese teams play supporting roles and become more involved only as the business matures.

Rocket Internet's approach is quite different. Rocket launches e-commerce businesses in new markets, such as replicating Amazon or eBay in the Philippines, India, or Nigeria. The company was founded in 2007 in Berlin by three German brothers, the Samwers, following initial successes in replicating internet companies in Europe. As of 2016, Rocket had ventures in 110 countries that employed twenty-eight thousand people. Rocket rarely relies on local talent when first entering a new country. Early leadership usually includes Germans who have worked with Rocket elsewhere, and it hires international MBA graduates who want to return home, such as pairing an African student with a new venture in Johannesburg. Rocket starts as quickly as possible, often working out of hotel rooms and mimicking what worked elsewhere. Local staff and permanent offices are added only after initial traction is achieved.

Most companies lie in between the approaches of Haier and Rocket. During its early stages of international expansion, IKEA sent "Swedish missionaries" to create local beachheads and ensure that new IKEA stores ran smoothly until the domestic team learned the system. After some time, the daily operations in stores were turned over to locals while Swedes occupied key national positions until the market reached maturity. Following debates on how much to Americanize new U.S. operations, one manager concluded that IKEA settled on "speaking English with a Swedish accent!"[15]

These overseas expansions create strong demand for global talent as executives scramble to fulfill the international dreams of their CEOs. These actions have added up to tenfold jumps in foreign direct investment from the 1990s to 2017.[16] But I have a secret to share: these investments are shifting to be less about product sales but about something else.

Emerging Reservoirs of Talent

Rumors about Apple abound in the blogosphere, so take this one with a grain of salt: the company is currently operating a secret vehicle R&D lab in Berlin where it "employs between 15 and 20 'top class' men and women from the German automotive industry, with backgrounds in engineering, software, hardware, and sales."[17] (Shh—don't tell anyone!) Assuming this juicy rumor is true, Apple is following a long-standing pattern of using overseas R&D facilities to access technical talent with special insights for an industry. Multinationals typically devote 20 percent of their R&D to foreign countries, in sectors ranging from electronics to pharmaceuticals.[18] An outsider like Apple is more exotic than Ford or GM, but everyone in the car industry hopes to tap into Germany's expertise.

Yet companies are increasingly opening global sites purely to access talent rather than specific local knowledge. This is how Microsoft describes its Beijing lab: "By attracting the best talent from Asia and across the globe, Microsoft Research Asia has grown into a world-class research lab that constantly pushes forward the state of the art and helps to improve people's computing experiences. . . . [T]he lab conducts basic and applied research in areas central to Microsoft's long-term strategy and future computing vision."[19] In simpler terms, Microsoft Research Asia is not about adapting Windows 10 into Chinese, nor is it solely about being near to research conducted by Tsinghua University. The lab is, instead, part of Microsoft's plan to build a global research base, which also includes facilities in Redmond, Boston, New York, and Bangalore, as well as Cambridge, England.

Most every global giant boasts a similar set of places, with GE's Digital Foundries present in Silicon Valley, Boston, Paris, Shanghai, Singapore, Saudi Arabia, and Munich. Haier also maintains labs on four continents. These overseas labs rarely save money, as competition bids up the wages of top talent, and implementation is tricky.[20] But a wise rabbit has three holes, and companies want broader access to talent and protection against national restrictions on immigration. The growing importance of global talent makes this capability a must-have for multinationals.

Indeed, lovers and haters of globalization should both pause to consider this trend: By 2030, China and India are projected to be home to half of college-degree holders between the ages of twenty-five and thirty-four years old in the Organization for Economic Co-operation and Development (OECD) and G-20 nations, as seen in Figure 7.1. Half! Add in the U.S. (8 percent), Brazil (5 percent), Indonesia (5 percent), Russia (4 percent), and Saudi Arabia (3 percent), and this short list of seven countries will account for 75 percent of young college graduates.[21] This shift is incredible. In 2005, OECD countries accounted for 60 percent of

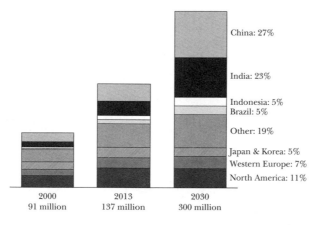

China: 27%

India: 23%

Indonesia: 5%
Brazil: 5%

Other: 19%

Japan & Korea: 5%
Western Europe: 7%
North America: 11%

| 2000 | 2013 | 2030 |
| 91 million | 137 million | 300 million |

FIGURE 7.1   Expected distribution of young college graduates in 2030 among OECD and G-20 countries.
Source: Data from Organization for Economic Cooperation and Development.

the ninety-four million young college-educated workers; in 2030, this share will have dropped to around 25 percent of an enlarged pool of three hundred million. The distributional shift will be even more extreme for innovation, with China and India expected to hold 60 percent of young STEM-degree holders in 2030.

The trends imply that large companies will soon employ most of their college-educated workers at overseas locations, which is already true in parts of Europe. It will become more commonplace for midsized companies too, absent a dramatic de-globalization. Organizations rarely operate these locations as silos but instead integrate them into cross-country teams. This is a common reason for language programs like that undertaken by Rakuten. How well do these teams work?

Global Teams and Information Flows

Cross-border teams for innovation are sprouting like weeds. Circa 1975, only 1 percent of the U.S.-based patents from large companies involved an overseas inventor, but this share exceeded

13 percent in 2018. Excluding patents that have only a single inventor, one out of five U.S.-based teams now includes an overseas member.[22] This did not happen by chance. It is quite difficult to build overseas R&D capability, and early innovations produced by research outposts tend to be weaker than the company's primary R&D centers. Collaborative global teams are stronger and close this performance gap.[23] What challenges are these teams helping to solve?

It is hard to predict what will work in a new location, and cross-border teams support learning during market entry. They are a lifeline to the mothership and even a safety valve should something go wrong. These teams further supplement local staff during early hiring and potentially in permanent ways, such as when architecture-level work is conducted in the U.S. while more-detailed developments occur abroad. Headquarters may also want to keep its best cards "closer to the vest" when entering environments where idea theft is a worry. These factors make cross-border teams more likely when a company enters an unfamiliar nation, where the traditional recipes may not work as well.[24]

The high-profile life of Kai-Fu Lee shows key roles that global talent play. Born in Taiwan, Lee came to America via the education pathway, first for high school and continuing onward to a PhD in computer science from Carnegie Mellon. After sojourns in academia, start-ups, and large corporate labs, Lee joined Microsoft in 1998 to launch the Beijing facility described earlier, moving back and forth between countries to build it up. In 2005, he was hired away by Google to launch their Chinese operations, and since 2009, Lee has run an investment company focusing on Chinese start-ups. Undoubtedly, his frequent-flier miles easily cover any travel for family vacations! Lee's colorful story illustrates a general pattern: The hiring of global talent enables investments by their employer into the talent's home countries. Skilled immigrants can strengthen a company's internal capabilities to the point that it forgoes partnerships and uses, instead, wholly owned operations for overseas entry.[25]

Cross-border teams also facilitate knowledge flow. A persistent problem for large organizations is separate pools of knowledge—not knowing what you already know—and millions of dollars have gone into knowledge management systems to bridge these gaps. Although not a panacea, cross-border teams transfer information better than exclusively foreign ones. While companies must weigh these benefits against the greater expense of collaborative teams, international expansion is placing an ever-greater premium on cohesion and common knowledge across far-flung units.

This phenomenon also affects start-ups. While entrepreneurs dream of building the next unicorn, they often can't afford the price of computer programmers in the Valley or London. They contract, instead, with developers in cheaper places like India and Estonia for early coding work, in some cases even exchanging equity ownership to minimize cash outlays. This tactic creates a global team well before the first customer is signed. As ventures gain traction and start to scale, many then bring tech development back in house to enable greater coordination. This is quite remarkable, as it flips on its head the traditional globalization narrative, in which companies went abroad only after achieving success in their home markets. By contrast, this "globalization in reverse" path starts out international before retracting to a more localized presence.[26]

Globalization and the increasing importance of teams have combined to make cross-border teams almost commonplace. The future will see even more of them, as enabling technologies like videoconferencing, Dropbox, and Slack remove existing wrinkles. Some companies are also adopting advanced technologies like Beam, a telepresence robot that allows a remote person to navigate around an office and talk to people face-to-face via a display screen.[27] Advances in virtual reality will soon push this one step further, but technology can't solve all of HR's problems.

Headaches for HR Everywhere

Show some love for your HR director at the next company gathering, as his or her responsibilities are being supersized. Global companies must support and align leadership and skilled personnel across several countries. While GE and Haier employ many workers, frictions are most common among their high-skilled talent. A factory worker in Haier's South Carolina plant is unlikely to interact much with his peer in China, but the new plant manager will.

Employment practices vary substantially across countries, and organizations must calibrate the level of consistency to impose for compensation, length of the workweek, annual vacation time, and related policies. These issues exist for top managers, but leaders make one-off compromises and are less likely to follow a standard workweek anyway. Workarounds become harder for middle management, as legal differences and cultural expectations start to bind. Sometimes, it is easy to be generous, as when Finnish game developer Supercell shocked U.S. employees by closing its Silicon Valley offices for July in accordance with Finland's summer holidays. But deeper tensions exist when the global team is designed to take advantage of differences in wage rates. While the programmer hired in Pakistan may be thrilled about his new job, there is no guarantee he won't become grumpy about being paid less than his colleagues in Paris and Hong Kong.

Questions also exist for consistency in company culture. New employees are less connected to what has come before, and integration takes time. Rapid global expansion creates difficult tensions, like selecting between a new country manager with great sales contacts and one who fits best with the company's culture. Sometimes, leaders also need to let go of past traditions. I have worked with several European companies that now have most of their employees overseas. Their leadership debates which parts of being a "Danish company" or a "Swedish company" should be preserved and which should be let go.

Global employees who collaborate frequently on tasks like product development, customer service, and operations face additional difficulties.[28] Groups of team members in multiple countries must guard against an "us versus them" mentality, which reduces trust and team effectiveness. Managers must strengthen trust across groups and avoid being perceived as playing favorites. One start-up emphasizes a "remote first" perspective, such that important actions are done only with the inclusion of remote team members. Others require that team members rotate frequently across sites.

While a whole book could be spent on these concerns, we are still only halfway done! Companies are also relying ever more on individuals who are not really their employees.

Virtual Platforms

It is not a big exaggeration for many companies to say that the employees are the firm, and vice versa. Talent creates durable assets, ranging from secret algorithms to locked-in user bases, but even virtual monopolies like Google and Facebook invest heavily in the employees that push their core technologies further.[29] Yet companies today also leverage external talent in exciting new ways, ranging from open innovation platforms to online contests to crowdsourcing. As organizational boundaries become porous, even the definition of an "employee" becomes blurred and the subject of legal debate. How are companies using these tools to meet global talent?

Ten years before Mikitani transformed Rakuten, A. G. Lafley made a large change at Procter & Gamble (P&G), the iconic maker of countless household products, from Bounty paper towels to Tide laundry detergent. Lafley worried that P&G had lost its innovative mojo. The company boasted world-class R&D, but it also had a "not invented here" mentality that rejected many valuable ideas coming from outside. P&G needed to overcome these insular tendencies to reach its aggressive growth targets.[30]

So Lafley set an ambitious goal: going forward, P&G would acquire 50 percent of its innovations from outside of its own R&D labs. For every talented P&G researcher working on a problem, the company estimated there were two hundred scientists elsewhere who were equally as knowledgeable about the issue. P&G wanted to tap into that external talent to acquire better ideas, and Lafley sought a culture that celebrated this strategy. If the firm could effectively link its 7,500 researchers to this global talent pool of 1.5 million, what kinds of cool products might emerge?

Pringles Prints, it turns out, is one example. In 2002, P&G hatched the idea of printing images onto the smooth-faced Pringles snack chip, ranging from trivia questions to pictures of a Daytona 500 race car. Achieving this simple concept would require, however, quite delicate engineering to ensure product quality and scalable production. Rather than start a multiyear process to build these capabilities internally, P&G circulated a technology brief among its global network and quickly identified a professor in Italy who had invented this exact technology for his small bakery. The collaboration that followed led to a surge in the sales of Pringles.

The success of Pringles Prints and similar products led P&G to develop a web platform called Connect + Develop, which is a prominent example of the open innovation platforms that many large companies use to access global talent. At sites like Connect + Develop, people pitch their ideas to distant organizations. As the very best innovations are orders of magnitude better than average ones, companies must cast a very wide net even when they employ thousands of scientists and engineers.

New digital intermediaries provide companies these global connections without the need for them to build expensive platforms.[31] Sites like InnoCentive and Topcoder can connect companies with some unlikely sources. Merck, a large pharmaceuticals company, ran a two-month contest to identify uses for some chemical compounds, providing access to data and promising $40,000 to the contest winner. The contest drew more than 2,500 ideas from 238 teams, translating to less than $20 per submission! But the most unexpected part is that the winning solution came from outside the life sciences. A team of computer scientists used machine learning to provide Merck with novel ideas that it might not have otherwise encountered, thus winning the contest.

The National Aeronautics and Space Administration (NASA) has also been impressed.[32] Intrigued by online contests, NASA established pilot projects in 2008 that used three for-profit platforms to seek ideas on thorny challenges, such as forecasting solar flares. People from more than eighty countries submitted ideas. NASA found that the best ideas generated by the contest were two or three times better than those developed internally, and today NASA combines internal and external talent in its research capabilities.

These examples illustrate why companies, large and small, are using external talent to help identify the very best concepts. These platforms also help validate ideas, such as using external audiences to select among logo redesigns or advertisements. Instant digital help is further available from contracting sites like Upwork and Amazon Mechanical Turk for tasks ranging from simple transcription to complex app coding. Crowdfunding is also quite active, where individuals pledge to fund a project if enough backers sign up. For the project developers, the proof of customer demand is just as important as the money raised.

A company's ability to leverage external talent will be important for future HR success, just as social networking and Google AdWords quickly became essential for marketing. The first step is rarely as dramatic as Lafley's 50 percent bombshell, and digital platforms make it easy to experiment.[33] Some early familiarity and copying of best practices will go a long way for most companies. Yet others press onward to make external collaborations a persistent part of their global talent strategy, building true hybrid organizations.

Porous Organizational Boundaries

Google's Advanced Technology and Projects (ATAP) group brings together multiple parties for breakthrough innovation, time and time again.[34] ATAP is a private-sector version of the Pentagon's Defense Advanced Research Projects Agency (DARPA), which has created amazing things like the Internet, GPS, and drones. Regina Dugan, the first female director of DARPA, initially brought the model to Motorola, and Google absorbed the capability when it acquired Motorola in 2012.[35] ATAP's model allows Google to move very fast and access outside expertise in areas where an inflection point exists for science and commercial impact. The two-year projects are very ambitious, and many fail. "It's more important to fail at something that matters than succeed at something that doesn't," Dugan explained.

Most of the staff and even team leaders for ATAP's projects are external contractors, often working far away from Google's headquarters. Collaborators are motivated by the challenges of the ventures, which have ranged from spatial awareness tablets to data security advances, and accept compensation that blends corporate and start-up approaches. ATAP contracted with more than one hundred global start-ups during its first year by using short and simple nondisclosure agreements and providing generous intellectual property rights to partners. Google is racing to beat other tech giants and is willing to give significant upside to its partners to achieve this speed.

ATAP's model is extreme, and companies vary in their focus on speed versus control and the duration of their external relationships. Having seen how quickly the internet disrupted their overnight document delivery business, United Parcel Service (UPS) wants to ensure that it is ready for 3-D printing and how it will affect the shipment of physical goods. UPS has an alliance with a start-up called Fast Radius to experiment with industrial 3-D printers in several facilities, possibly positioning themselves as tomorrow's light manufacturer. Other organizations take softer touches when threatening technologies do not fit so well within the traditional organization. Siemens and Telefónica, as well as Harvard, are experimenting with the popular accelerator model to build alliances with vibrant start-ups.[36]

The Collective Power of HR Everywhere

Companies are scrambling to keep up with the dynamic landscape of global talent. While Samsung, HSBC, and ExxonMobil are big and powerful, they are also miniscule compared with the big technological leaps accruing as a result of Moore's law, the rise of young college-educated workers in China and India (50 percent in 2030!), and the emergence of digital labor. And yet collectively HR directors wield amazing power. If they start believing Los Angeles is the place to be, others will soon follow their lead. This herding can be protective—the HR equivalent of "no one ever gets fired for buying IBM"—but it also reflects the movable nature of talent. If enough organizations favor Los Angeles, their choices will reinforce each other and render the prediction true.

Looking to 2030, I forecast that Chapter 6 and the first half of this chapter will age well, such that I won't blush too badly a decade from now. The actions of companies reflect long-standing trends. The technological imperative shows no sign of abating and likely will accelerate in importance for many traditional sectors of the economy as technology diffuses. The future is a bit cloudier for globalization. It's hard to argue against demographic trends that are boosting the importance of emerging regions, but nothing about globalization should be taken for granted in today's political and social climate.

The second half of this chapter will age much faster, however, perhaps even being embarrassing well before 2030. Many companies are prioritizing external talent and experimenting with new business models in the gig economy. We should celebrate when companies connect in new ways to critical talent, but the increased use of external talent may become problematic if it is merely to avoid hiring full-time workers. Work will be managed very differently in the future, and we need lots of experimentation and then copying of best practices on this new frontier.

The impact of global talent flows is so encompassing, however, that we must press onward to global technology diffusion and economic inequality. The actions of firms affect how global migration links to the economic advancement of countries. These implications—and perhaps more important, society's perceptions of them—feed into politics and the evolving rules of the immigration game.

Chapter 8

GLOBAL DIFFUSION REMADE

MANY RUB THEIR EYES when flying over Fuzhou, a city in southeast China. Is that the USS *Enterprise* from *Star Trek* looming below? And next to it, the Pentagon and an X-wing starfighter? Welcome to the world of D. J. Liu, one of China's leading entrepreneurs. The headquarters of his company, NetDragon, is unmistakable, as the starship measures three football fields long and five stories high. The campus also includes a working locomotive, statues of Iron Man and the Terminator, and Liu's offices: on the bridge of the *Enterprise*, behind doors marked "United Federation of Planets— Office of the President"!

Growing up in China during the Cultural Revolution, Liu absorbed his mother's entrepreneurial drive, demonstrated once when she traveled over six hundred miles alone to sell her newly invented fishing bait from door to door. The money she made allowed her to send Liu and his brother to the University of Kansas, where he studied chemistry. While in America, Liu saw the rise of the internet and began selling computer CDs. After a short stint in a cancer research lab in California, he returned home to start a company. Reflecting on his stay in America and the companies he witnessed firsthand, Liu recalls thinking: "I could do something like this. I want to build a company like Yahoo! or Broadcom."

The early start-up years were frustrating, but success came after a pivot into online gaming, ultimately culminating in the creation of the app marketplace 91 Wireless, often called the "iTunes of China" before its acquisition by Baidu. NetDragon today employs more than 4,500 people and is currently pursuing virtual reality (VR) technologies to transform global education.[1] Liu is also giving back to Fuzhou, having created a free "software university" and training programs for local entrepreneurs. Never one to think small, Liu now imagines a massive "virtual reality park" that will provide twenty thousand or more jobs, such as VR editing of wedding footage, and will position Fuzhou as the VR Silicon Valley of the world.

Liu's time abroad turned into a spectacular success for Fuzhou, but there are countless migrants who lose touch with their homelands after leaving. To this point, we have mostly focused on the individuals, universities, and firms at the heart of skilled migration, but global talent flows affect everyone. What is the impact for countries on the "sending" side of talent flows? Should they fear or embrace their best and brightest going abroad? Must this talent return, as Liu did, or can it still be a benefit from a great distance? These questions require us to study whether talent is a zero-sum game between countries.

Talent as a Zero-Sum Game?

The phrase "brain drain" has anchored the migration lingo for decades, arguing that a good Indian mind working in London is a good mind that is missing from India. This perspective holds that migration is a zero-sum game for jobs and role models, building on the importance of spatial proximity; moving talent halfway around the world surely weakens beneficial spillovers, perhaps wiping them out completely. The public finances of talent-sending countries also suffer from reduced tax revenues, potentially after significant public investment in the education of the worker who now lives abroad.[2]

Yet the zero-sum metaphor may be misguided. Talent clusters are exceptionally productive, and matching great talent with these special environments yields gains that can be potentially shared across countries. Elite universities and multinational firms, even when acting in their own self-interests, transform raw talent in ways that are often not possible without migration. Optimists speak of "brain gain" or "brain circulation" in an effort to cleverly supersede the traditional imagery. These mixed and hijacked metaphors require a step-by-step exploration.

A starting point is the ability of global talent flows to increase worldwide innovation and economic potential, a necessary condition for talent flows to not be zero-sum. From Nobel Prize winners to young students, talent thrives when placed in the right environment. When launching new internet marketplaces, there is no substitute for being in one of the leading clusters. In other fields, the gaps across advanced economies are less pronounced. One study measured the future research productivity of Fulbright scholars who were required by immigration policy to leave the U.S. after their studies. Those who ended up in other high-income countries performed as well as their peers from graduate school who remained in America, whereas those who landed in poorer economies lagged.[3]

This productivity is vital because powerful ideas are the main force behind long-term economic growth.[4] Population growth and the accumulation of machines matter, especially in the short term, and wars and environmental degradation can set us back. But long-term growth is built around innovation that allows ever greater output be derived from a given set of resources. And while we hope for a future in which anyone anywhere participates equally in advancing this knowledge frontier, this has yet to happen. These spatial differences yield a persistent link between global talent flows and worldwide advancement, and this link is strengthened with the rise of the knowledge economy.[5]

This overall global gain is a necessary condition for improvements in talent-sending countries but not a sufficient one. While a Korean scientist may be more productive in America, is Korea itself better off after that talent migrates abroad? Korea may be better off holding on to the talent, even if the worker has lower productivity in Seoul, because the work happens locally. This leads us to diffusion—or how quickly the best stuff emerging from leading clusters reaches distant locations.

A Global Tech Frontier?

Outsiders often roll their eyes at the crazy abstractions that economists make in their conceptual models. In defense of my trade, it is difficult to get a decent grip on the complex world we live in, and we should start with one such abstraction: the idea of a global technology frontier. This framing holds that people and firms everywhere draw on the same pool of knowledge, and that differences in economic performance are thus due to disparities in other factors like education levels or savings rates. This conceptual frame works well for ideas that have been around for a while, such as basic chemistry or the lightbulb, but there is surprisingly slow diffusion for even simple management practices, much less cutting-edge advances.[6]

This leads to an enriched model that can be visualized by throwing a large rock into a lake. A huge splash! And then waves roll out in all directions. The big splash is the next breakthrough in Silicon Valley, and the concentric waves describe who learns about the new technology next. Los Angeles and Seattle are expected to see it before London or Seoul. Empirical studies show this importance of distance for diffusion at every spatial scale: across floors within a building, buildings within a city, cities within a country, and countries in the world.[7] When Elon Musk achieves interplanetary colonization, it will hold true across our solar system, too!

These two models describe settings where Korea laments the migration of talent to America. In both cases, the researcher's work adds to a global set of technologies that ultimately benefit Korea, but Korea would prefer that another country provide the talent, as it does not achieve any special benefits. Even if the researcher sends most of his wages home in large remittances, it is still unlikely to tip the scales. Thus, another ingredient is necessary if brain drain is to no longer rule the day.

That addition is global networks. Although geography is important, its predictive power has limits. When a breakthrough happens in Silicon Valley, most expect to see it in Seoul before Mexico City, despite the greater distance. This could be due to Korea's more developed economy and capacity to absorb frontier advances. For example, the adoption of the latest mobile breakthrough is easier and more profitable in a nation with heavy smartphone penetration and a bevy of specialized engineers who understand the work.[8] But this is not the whole story, as many would also forecast the breakthrough to arrive in India before Mexico, despite Mexico being substantially more developed.[9] What gives India an edge?

As early as the Phoenicians and their global trading networks circa 1500 BC,[10] migrants have shaped the movements of goods, money, and ideas in ways that transcend simple distance and economic development. A country's diaspora—a term that denotes the expatriates or overseas citizens of a country—often retain special insights about their homeland, ranging from language skills to whom you can trust, which are important in business decisions. Cross-border deals are hard to protect legally, and a tight ethnic network can mitigate risks by policing itself. Altruistically, many people simply cherish their homelands and are eager to help.[11]

There are very special links today between Asian scientific talent working in Silicon Valley and leading innovation centers like Seoul, Taipei, Beijing, and Bangalore. In a survey of professional associations in the Valley, more than 80 percent of immigrant scientists and engineers reported exchanging technical information with colleagues in their home countries. Further, about half of the respondents returned home for business at least once a year, and 40 percent arranged business contracts.[12] Many members of these ethnic communities feel there is no real distance between these Asian clusters and Silicon Valley, despite the Pacific Ocean sitting in between them.

These surveys exaggerate general effects, but ethnic-based professional networks have a significant impact on global knowledge diffusion. Inventors outside of the U.S. are 50 percent more likely to cite U.S.-based members of their ethnicity, compared with others working on the same technology. These networks are providing talent-sending countries with "sneak peeks" at new innovations, and show their greatest strength in the diffusion of the newest and biggest ideas.[13] Integration also gives talent-sending countries better access to global production processes. Executives must understand the sector's trajectory and how their planned products will fit in. If a sector's industrial structure allows the best producers anywhere to win global orders, then small differences in early insights can determine success.[14]

In short, ethnic networks shape global exchanges, and tech diffusion is only one example. An African gentleman once interrupted a presentation that I was giving on this topic. He said that my research "missed the point," noting that his diaspora community had propelled his homeland to democracy, which was priceless to him. A rather hefty comment! But he was also right, and a later study connected the global diffusion of democracy from the 1950s onward to the rise in youth studying abroad in democratic nations.[15] Networks spread all types of ideas, and business models are currently in vogue.

Business Diffusion and Global Ventures

Every business school is proud of its entrepreneurs, and some of our recent business founders at Harvard Business School (HBS) illustrate the rapid dissemination that can occur via global talent flows. Anthony Tan and Tan Hooi Ling founded Grab in 2012, which today offers ride-hailing services throughout Southeast Asia, to provide safer taxi experiences in Malaysia. Two years earlier, Bom Kim dropped out of HBS to launch Coupang in Korea, inspired by Groupon and Amazon. Both companies are now worth billions of dollars. In fact, many foreign MBA students are forgoing traditional consulting or banking careers, instead heading straight to overseas flights after graduation with their business ideas in hand. What is going on here?[16]

Some businesses have an almost instantaneous global reach. Except where it is blocked by a government, Google's search platform is available everywhere as the technology operates with any browser. App stores provide similar reach for Supercell's latest game upon its global release. By contrast, many e-commerce businesses require extensive local effort. Websites must be customized for local products, neighborhood vendors recruited, and customers convinced to try the service out. An Amazon-like marketplace will look very different in places where customers use public computers at Internet cafés, pay exclusively in cash, and live beyond the reach of the postal service and perhaps even paved roads!

The best ideas to take into new global locations are often those that require lots of implementation and modification, as otherwise a "Google" is likely already there. Uber was founded before Grab, but it was not in Southeast Asia, and Grab needed a quite different business model anyway. Many users would complain if a motorcycle showed up for an Uber ride in New York, but Grab embraced the motorcycle taxis of Southeast Asia. Indeed, a Grab user in Jakarta often prefers a motorcycle and its ability to weave through gridlocked traffic! Local needs, ranging from figuring out logistics to building up customer bases, slow diffusion and give entrepreneurs a window of opportunity. Amazon's focus on China and Japan meant Korea was on the back burner, giving Kim and Coupang a head start. This effort creates long-term value for the new business as it becomes very hard to dislodge.

Global talent pervades this creation and diffusion, linking us back to Chapter 6 and talent clusters. The special advantages of frontier locations lure in many talented people and thereby increase the future discoveries emerging there. But global talent also acts as a "centrifugal force" that pushes ideas outward, whether through MBA entrepreneurs returning home or Rocket Internet's launch teams.[17] Access to young global talent drove GE to Boston, but the city also helps diffuse ideas, such as when a Thai student at Northeastern University sees a smart-connected product that is a perfect fit for the family business in Bangkok.

This duality has a strong benefit: Whereas talent clusters concentrate wealth generation in just a few places, diffusion spreads benefits back out.[18] The pace of replication is now brutally quick, often happening within six months for very high-profile ideas. Consumers benefit, but it can also harm incentives for innovators. Protections exist in some sectors, ranging from Merck's patents to Airbnb's global customer base, but other ideas are more vulnerable. The American and Chinese markets are so large that entrepreneurs will go after them even if someone else pounces on India or Brazil, but we have not seen the climax of this process of hyperdiffusion.

As global talent flows combat brain drain by linking emerging economies with frontier markets and allowing special networks and cross-border integration, talent may also choose to go back home, bringing with them educations and frontier ideas. But perhaps surprisingly, the benefit most frequently cited by development economists is still to come.

Talent Lost, Talent Regained . . . Talent Never Left?

The basketball superstar Kobe Bryant was once told growing up that "NBA players are one in a million," to which the confident young athlete responded, "Man, look, I'm going to be that one in a million."[19] It worked for Kobe, but most NBA career plans are as unsuccessful as my jump shot. Yet America's basketball talent is undoubtedly boosted because every kid tries, at least for a while, to become Kobe. In a similar and thankfully more helpful way, dreams of studying and working abroad lead to deep educational investments by students in talent-sending countries, which provides national benefits because many students never actually leave.

Although the odds of being able to migrate are much better than one in a million, they remain quite steep in many places. Some students miss the mark because of poor grades or test scores, whereas others can't make it work financially or are blocked by immigration rules. These misses come only after investments have been made. One study found that 85 percent of the best students in Tonga and Papua New Guinea considered migrating abroad, which led them to take extra courses in high school and to favor certain disciplines like science.[20]

Neighboring Fiji is an even sharper example. Following a 1987 military coup, minority Fijians of Indian descent feared their national standing and invested heavily in higher education to clear the points-based immigration hurdles set by Australia and New Zealand. Fiji's political situation stabilized in the 1990s. Yet many years later, the Indian minority group retains both higher international mobility and greater education levels than the rest of Fiji.[21]

Measuring across countries, a doubled rate of talent outflows correlates with a 20 percent increase in the domestic stock of talent, despite the talent leaving for overseas opportunities.[22] Extra investment in education can be put to better long-term use than fading sports skills, but misalignment is still a worry. STEM students may specialize in technologies that are well paid in America but in limited demand back home. This weakens the benefit to the home country for those who remain, although the preparation is still more useful than none.

Education also prompts beneficial feedback loops. Overseas entrepreneurs frequently cite a lack of skills in the workforce of their home nation as a deterrent from returning. The efforts by local talent to prepare for going abroad reduces this gap and ironically makes it more likely for the overseas talent to return or otherwise engage with their home nation. The exceptional economic opportunities in India and China are further luring second-generation immigrants back from advanced economies, as global businesses seek to staff their operations in India and China with people familiar with both the local culture and Western practices.[23]

If local education and overseas talent spark development leaps, why should a country limit itself to the return of its diaspora? China is a powerhouse in fields like financial technology (fintech) and solar power.[24] Is the future of Asia so bright that American and European talent will soon head there?

Scale and Diversity for the Future

To be attractive for global talent, emerging countries must achieve the scale and the diversity important for innovation, broadly defined. America built a large and unified market during the 1900s through heavy infrastructure investment, compulsory education, and a single national language. States retained minor policy differences, and cronyism and the "old boys' network" kept a measure of local favoritism alive. But the country's huge scale promised businesses great rewards when they created something special.

Diversity came more slowly and unevenly. The hit movie *Hidden Figures* chronicles the struggles and triumphs of three black women mathematicians who played important roles at NASA during the space race. In a poignant scene, one of the three, Mary

Jackson, is asked, "If you were a white male, would you wish to be an engineer?" Jackson replies: "I wouldn't have to. I'd already be one." Many barriers have fallen since the 1960s, and the growth of women in the labor force yielded substantial economic gains.[25] America has also made progress toward empowering minority racial groups and embracing different sexual orientations. As a result, America's leading talent clusters are quite diverse, which draws in more talent fleeing discrimination.[26] America is far from perfect, sharply illustrated by fraternity-like behavior among some Silicon Valley firms and recent xenophobic politics, but it remains more welcoming than most nations.

A handful of countries can aspire to the scale of America. China and India hold enormous internal potential, and they are knitting their nations together and fostering market development. While motivated by internal economic reasons, infrastructure projects that link rural Indian communities or the crackdowns on local corruption in China also make these countries more attractive to global talent. Other large countries face challenges for economic integration, such as Indonesia and its many islands, but the potential scale works to their long-term benefit.

Smaller economies need to build external scale and maximize the international reach for their innovators. The Nordic countries have small populations and are geographically remote, but their companies participate in the huge product markets of the European Union, placing them on a more level footing with firms in Paris or Munich. Other countries have big neighbors like Nigeria or Brazil, in which case the small nation can focus on becoming a trusted regional hub. Still others make targeted sector bets, like Singapore's Biopolis research park that seeks to draw in leading pharmaceutical and life sciences firms and researchers, offering its members the capacity to quickly reach global leaders in the sector.[27]

Diversity is often the bigger stumbling block. Countries that discriminate against women are shooting themselves in the head, not just the foot. The global migration of talented women has grown by more than 150 percent since 1990, and women now represent more than half of all skilled migrants.[28] Said differently, if you close your eyes and see a man when you hear "global talent flows," you need to update your picture! Nations should guarantee the economic and social rights of women because it is the right thing to do, pure and simple; but the bonus is better domestic and global talent that improves economic performance. In regions where countries suppress female participation, embracing women in the workforce may even be a powerful competitive differentiator.

Likewise, many countries are still learning how to integrate and leverage people from different parts of the world, a skill that should never be taken for granted. Although China has enormous scale, immigrants account for less than 0.1 percent of its population, and the country is not very open. These barriers limit its ability to become a top destination for global talent, regardless of its scale. Large global companies will send employees to China, but this talent will mostly operate within existing firms and not contribute to the formation of powerful ecosystems.[29]

The pernicious effects of xenophobia go even further than scaring away global talent. An insular culture reduces access to the insights and networks possible via diaspora, discourages return migration, and dampens the global enthusiasm of the next generation.[30] These drags harm a country's ability to attract back talent when scaling its ecosystem.[31] Breaking free is hard and requires a push for diversity that starts at the top. A good indicator is the boards of top corporations in the country: if every member looks the same, then rapid growth of diversity in professional positions is not lurking around the corner. While ideas and the occasional revolution spring forth from youth, persistent and guided leadership is needed to tip the scales for global engagement.

Guided Leadership

Finland today is a wealthy country, but it was substantially less so during the 1970s, when Bengt Holmström, the 2016 Nobel Laureate we met in Chapter 1, migrated to America. At the time, the Finnish community regretted his decision to live abroad. While it would be decades before he won the Nobel Prize, his promise was already evident in his exceptional early research. But after migrating, Holmström would publish his research in English journals, pay tax dollars to America, and spend less time teaching and mentoring Finnish students.

Yet Finland went bonkers when Holmström won the award. This celebration was because of the active interest Holmström took in his home country while living abroad. He did not return home like D. J. Liu, but the contributions he made to Finnish development were just as strong. He built many academic bridges, such as a visiting scholar program at MIT that hosts young Finns each year. The cumulative effect of this program over the decades is an almost seamless link between the Boston and Helsinki economics research communities. Other bridges included serving on the boards of Finnish universities and Nokia and commenting extensively on the Finnish economy. Holmström believes his greatest contribution has come through the sharing of best practices and tacit insights for how U.S. research universities operate, which can be difficult for outsiders to discern.[32]

Entrepreneurs in Finland also thank Holmström profusely, as the founding story of Finland's largest accelerator program recounts: "In 2008 a university professor in Helsinki told his students that becoming an entrepreneur is the worst decision you can make. At that time, the Finnish mindset wasn't an entrepreneurial one—taking risks or giving your ideas a shot wasn't respected. A group of students from Aalto University decided that it was time for a paradigm shift and embarked on a trip that would shape not only Aalto University but the whole of Finland. They decided to visit MIT and Bengt Holmström. . . . They grasped an important lesson from the professor—act on what you have learned. They decided to start Aaltoes, to create a grassroots movement around entrepreneurship."[33]

Holmström's case emphasizes the futility of trying to reach a single conclusion about brain drain. Finland lost his direct tax revenues, but the country gained overall through the high-quality work that he influenced others to do. He may have inspired fewer students in Helsinki than if he had stayed put, but he also challenged others as only an outsider could. The Aaltoes group today works with thousands of students and entrepreneurs. One of the events that began with Aaltoes, Slush, had 17,500 participants in 2016 and led to funding and collaborative deals for many Finnish companies. Slush has become so central to Europe's start-up scene that Harvard now sends a delegation to Helsinki to participate. More than anything, Holmström shows the importance of strong bonds for national progress; without them, talent-sending countries must inevitably suffer losses.

Although effective engagement depends on the goodwill of overseas talent, the leadership of talent-sending countries should also avoid ostracizing emigrants. When talent goes abroad, there is a temptation to lash out among those remaining behind. Harsh labels like "traitor" provide quick gratification, but a wiser course is to stay friendly and incorporate diaspora into as many events as possible. Countries can further lower barriers to returning talent. This may again require holding one's tongue, especially if tax incentives are necessary, but it provides the talent circulation key to long-term gains.[34]

India's prime minister Narendra Modi is particularly mindful of harnessing India's diaspora into its bid to become "the HR capital of the world." Public leaders travel extensively to meet with overseas Indians and encourage them to participate in initiatives like Digital India and Start-up India. Modi cites Mahatma Gandhi, whom Indians revere as the father of their nation, as a prime example of an overseas Indian who did not forget about his homeland. Modi encourages Indians to contribute to India's economic development, using catchy slogans to attract foreign direct investment (rebranding the FDI acronym to "First Develop India") and launching programs to bring overseas Indians to India's R&D institutions for months at a time. Over the past decade, India has granted overseas Indians greater freedom to travel, work, and invest in India, with the resulting engagement benefiting the nation.[35]

Who Decides?

Taken together, global talent flows raise world prosperity, and the resulting diffusion networks are especially beneficial for some countries. China and India are the leading contributors of global talent and experience more rapid development thanks to their integration.[36] The huge populations of these countries suggest that global talent flows benefit a majority of people in the emerging world.[37] China may well want the next ten hires in Silicon Valley to be from Shanghai, rather than Delhi or Seoul, because of the advantages it derives. Yet the picture is less rosy for most small countries due to the weak potential for collaboration, and they prefer that their talent stays home. This brain-drain picture grows especially dark for landlocked African states, tiny Caribbean islands, and other challenging places that the firms of advanced economies rarely target.

Either way, these tallies are of "academic interest," because the policies that determine global migration are made country by country. The World Trade Organization regulates the global exchange of physical products, and its voting procedures give voice to rich and poor countries. But there is no equivalent "World Talent Organization." There have been fair-minded calls to capture and distribute value from global migration to the nations that lose out, but such multilateral action is way off in the future, if it ever happens. Instead, each country must make do for itself, and small nations don't get a voice in the critical choices made by big ones like China and America.

We next turn to the implications of global talent flows for society and welfare in America. We have discussed wage benefits to immigrants and career implications for natives. But what about the lower-skilled workers in talent clusters, or those much farther away in old iron and steel towns? How does American society as whole experience these effects? This exploration is critical because in national politics everyone gets a vote, and disproportionate voice is even given to smaller places. The gains and losses across America, and the average voter's perceptions of them in Wisconsin or Tennessee, now take center stage.

Chapter 9

REVENGE OF THE NERDS

THE SIGNS WERE UNMISTAKABLE, as protesters blocked the Google buses that ferried workers from San Francisco to Mountain View: "Stop Displacement Now," "Warning: Two-Tiered System," or simply "F— Off, Google."[1] The protestors were livid about rising inequality and the general sense that techies were taking over the world. One pamphlet read: "While you guys live fat as hogs with your free 24/7 buffets, everyone else is scraping the bottom of their wallets, barely existing in this expensive world that you and your chums have helped create."

The bus protests of December 2013 were much shorter-lived than Occupy Wall Street, but they surfaced tensions that are still simmering. While "fat cat" bankers are routinely villainized, the tech industry tends to enjoy a better perception due to its world-changing innovations. Even if he was a billionaire, wouldn't we all want a few more entrepreneurs like Steve Jobs building the next Apple and Pixar?

Yet the Valley's widening gaps go far beyond free food. The buses of tech giants facilitated thirty-five thousand commutes a day in 2013, equivalent to perhaps 40 percent of those done on Caltrain, the local public commuter rail. Moreover, their palatial campuses provide dry cleaning, haircuts, gyms, and most other needs. Companies serve these benefits to keep employees productive and happy, but they also isolate talent workers. San Francisco is home to the world's most valuable companies, but the benefits are less visible than the costs for many residents.

Communities and global talent also hold different perspectives. One year after the bus protests, a viral video showed a confrontation between young professionals and locals over a soccer field in the Mission District. The twentysomethings, believed to have been techies, had reserved the field via the parks and recreation department for $27, whereas locals viewed it as first-come, first-served. When one resident explained the neighborhood's view, a young professional replied, "Who cares about the neighborhood?" Local author Rebecca Solnit commented: "No matter how lovely people are, if they're transient, if they all got there last week, there's no cultural memory. You cannot truly understand change if you don't even know that things were different."[2]

Expanding inequalities, within cities and stretching across the country, are among the most pressing business and political concerns of the twenty-first century. The Bay Area is in many ways a "best case" scenario, as San Jose and San Francisco rank as the top two U.S. cities in terms of upward mobility for someone born to a poor family.[3] The region often tops surveys of great places to live, and its firms engage in meaningful community outreach. Plus, it is always sunny and warm, as the preset Cupertino location in the iPhone's weather app continually reminds us. Yet the Bay Area struggles with rising homelessness and inequality. One sign showed San Francisco's skyline with the message "Have you seen my soul?"

Capitalism will always yield inequality. Some people have greater skills and are more productive, be it for sports, sales, academic research, or computer programming. The promise of higher income also motivates people to invest many years in education or take entrepreneurial risks. Some want to work all weekend, whereas others value their time differently. That said, inequality has become obscene, with twenty-five hedge-fund managers taking home the equivalent pay of all of America's kindergarten teachers,[4] and those born to poorer families face significant challenges. Beyond skewing today's consumption, rising inequality makes it harder to spot future talent.[5]

Discussions of inequality focus on the wealthy 1 percent (or the super-super-wealthy 0.01 percent) and the struggles of the stagnating middle class, who can't build the careers possible a few decades ago. These two forms of inequality are connected and yet distinct. We have seen that inequality of opportunity across nations is a key motivator for global talent flows, and the question now becomes how these flows impact society in advanced countries. If high-skilled immigration contributes to innovation and growth, does it also exacerbate inequality?[6]

The National Bureau of Economic Research maintains a database of economic studies, and searching paper titles for the term "inequality" yields more than one hundred hits since 2011, covering issues ranging from minimum wage to Thomas Piketty's theories. By contrast, filtering for both "inequality" and "immigration" leads to one paper from 2009, which was concerned with lower-skilled immigration from Mexico. Given this limited attention, let's proceed step by step, starting with America's wage distribution.

The Inequality of Wages

Global talent does not expand inequality through the direct earnings of immigrants. Migrants with college educations earn wages comparable to similarly skilled natives, or maybe even a bit less. The same is true at high incomes. Sergey Brin and Elon Musk are fabulously wealthy, and Chinese billionaires buy EB-5 investor visas. But these are the exceptions rather than the norm. In

2016, immigrants accounted for 16.8 percent of U.S. workers and 15.2 percent of those in the top 1 percent.[7]

Skilled immigrants also have limited impact on wage inequality in the labor market. This is intuitive given the claims that H-1B workers undercut the wages of skilled Americans, which would dampen wage inequality. A recent study estimates H-1B workers reduced the wages of native computer scientists by 3 percent to 5 percent, while also increasing the average wages by 0.2 percent to 0.3 percent through the larger supply of talent and greater innovation. These effects reduce wage gaps. Although the H-1B system causes some sector-level displacement, the study concludes it benefits America overall through boosts to the average worker's wages, lower prices of consumer goods, and increased profits for tech firms.[8]

Yet even if the direct effects are minimal, we still have a long way to go. This study did not include factors like increased automation and offshore outsourcing, and higher profits for tech firms may boost the wealth of the 1 percent. We next approach these candidates for rising inequality and ask whether talented immigrants are a driving force or simply "along for the ride."

Technology, Trade, and Inequality

Technological progress is the leading explanation for rising wage inequality. Word-processing software lowers the need for typists, and scanners at grocery stores and airports are today reducing demand for cashiers and gate agents. Robots will soon cook our burgers at fast-food restaurants, and driverless cars threaten, well, drivers everywhere. Skilled workers—stock traders displaced by algorithmic trading, for instance—also feel the heat, but technological progress since the 1970s has disproportionately reduced demand for less-skilled workers. This substitution has been strongest for "routine" jobs in which one repeats the same task again and again:

assembly lines, call-center support, even basic travel planning. These jobs are easier to automate, and robotics illustrates the quickening pace of adoption: the worldwide number of industrial robots rose from 750,000 in 2000 to 1.8 million in 2016 and is expected to soar to 2.6 million by 2019.[9]

Beyond counts of jobs, technology reshapes the required skills of workers. Long-Stanton, a metal-stamping company based in Ohio, has invested substantially in advanced machinery.[10] Output and productivity have risen continually, but the 2017 employee base is about half of its peak size a decade earlier. Yet Long-Stanton finds it ever harder to access the specialized skills that advanced processes require. The company has even used headhunters to find specialized machine toolists in recent years. This is a microcosm of American manufacturing, where output is at an all-time high in 2017, well above its level in the 1970s and far more than any other country (including China). But the sector now uses many fewer workers, and they are much more skilled on average.

Technology's transformation of work is quite scary, from drones to artificial intelligence. Yet ever since the Luddites smashed textile machinery in the 1800s, the economy has always created new and better work that complements technology.[11] Few regret the economy's transition from agriculture to industry and services during the last century, and to date, the internet has created 2.6 jobs for each one destroyed.[12] Whether this time proves different, talent flows are mostly "along for the ride" here. Immigrant inventors developed many of today's advanced technologies, but this simply reflects their prominent role in innovation and engineering disciplines overall.[13] Technology charts its own course.

The same mostly holds for global trade, the second big contributor to rising inequality. China joined the World Trade Organization in 2001, surging to become responsible for a quarter of U.S. imports. One study estimates that two million U.S. jobs were lost as a result of this competition.[14] As ethnic networks facilitate trade, are the surging inflows of Chinese talent seen throughout this book responsible?[15] Unlikely, as almost every advanced country experienced the same rise in Chinese imports, yet very few have high rates of Chinese immigration. Instead, the real link is to trade in services.

Global Migration and Offshore Outsourcing

Leo Perrero, a senior IT worker with twenty years of experience, could not believe what he was hearing.[16] It was October 2014, and his employer, Disney, was hitting record company profits. But Mr. Perrero would be unemployed in ninety days, despite receiving good performance reviews and a recent pay raise. Disney was replacing 250 IT jobs in an Orlando data center with outsourcing contracts. While half of the laid-off workers ultimately found other jobs at Disney, Mr. Perrero had a harder time, going through six months of unemployment before leaving the IT industry to start a new career. Another Disney worker, a fifty-seven-year-old with extensive IT experience, was forced into early retirement. The timing was "horrible," he later said, because his wife had recently had a medical emergency with expensive bills.

Many became outraged that the laid-off workers were forced to train their replacements as a condition for receiving severance pay. The *New York Times* quoted a worker as saying, "I just couldn't believe they could fly people in to sit at our desks and take over our jobs exactly." Worsening the public relations disaster, presidential candidates soon began outdoing each other in condemnation. During one speech, Donald Trump said: "Can you believe that? You get laid off and then they won't give you your severance pay unless you train the people that are replacing you. I mean, that's actually demeaning maybe more than anything else."[17]

The Disney experience is one of many examples connecting global talent flows to the offshore outsourcing of routine technical work from America. Half or more of the largest H-1B employers are foreign outsourcing companies,[18] whose clients include well-known U.S. businesses like Fossil, Pfizer, Harley-Davidson, and Cargill. Infosys alone sponsored four times as many visas as Microsoft and Google combined in 2016. H-1B visas are so important to these outsourcing firms that their stock prices declined as campaign rhetoric intensified and President Trump ultimately took office.

Pulling back temporarily, it is important to build from the ground up on this topic, starting with clear definitions. "Offshoring" refers to transferring work from domestic facilities to an overseas location, whereas "outsourcing" is defined as a company contracting with a vendor to perform certain tasks. Neither is necessarily evil and, in fact, both often can be quite helpful. Many companies rely on outside vendors to provide the food in the cafeteria and clean the building, as specialized vendors can provide better services and lower costs. This division of labor sometimes accomplishes more work with fewer people and can be an important step toward greater productivity. Yet the Disney case also shows the darker side. Disney's IT workers did not have a say when their bosses made the outsourcing decision, and workers in skilled and technical occupations tend to experience prolonged transitions given the specialized nature of their work.[19]

In addition, many of these IT jobs are ultimately going overseas. The economic implications of offshoring are quite debated. One might argue that it makes American firms like Disney more competitive through lower IT costs, which could potentially lead to firm growth. Some policy advocates further contend that even more IT offshore outsourcing is necessary for U.S. competitiveness in the era of digitization.[20] Yet if corporations simply stockpile the cash savings, it is unlikely that jobs will be restored any time soon.[21] Either way, Mr. Perrero, and others like him, suffer painful dislocation.

Outsourcing and offshoring likely scare American workers more than any other job-related threat. In a 2016 Pew Center poll, more than 80 percent of respondents thought that overseas outsourcing hurt U.S. workers. The level of concern was similar for trade, with other factors like automation scoring much lower.[22] Studies also estimate that between 25 percent and 50 percent of current U.S. jobs could be moved abroad in years to come.[23] This fear routinely surfaces in presidential races, such as Barack Obama's attacks on Mitt Romney's career at Bain Capital or John Kerry's accusations that George W. Bush was weak on offshore outsourcing.[24]

Global talent flows are not "along for the ride" on this one. Indian outsourcing companies make easy targets for H-1B critics, and their staffing practices have landed them the undesirable moniker of "body shops." However, while reforms can better allocate H-1B visas, they won't push back the offshoring tide. The root incentives to move routine IT tasks abroad are driven by cheap overseas technical workers and reliable data networks. The H-1B visa is a catalyst for the transition, but offshore outsourcing would continue in its absence.

A rather weird story about "Bob" (not his real name) at Verizon illustrates this global pressure.[25] Bob was a computer programmer, seen daily staring diligently at his computer monitor. Then, in 2013, Verizon discovered that Bob was mostly just surfing the internet. How was he able to do his work, which the company consistently described as the "best in the building"? It turned out that Bob had outsourced his own job to a Chinese firm, paying them less than a fifth of his six-figure Verizon salary. Bob was quickly terminated, and it appears he used the same scam with other employers. You may celebrate or hate Bob, but either way, his story shows how global wage differentials for technical work will pervade corporate decisions, with or without H-1Bs. In some cases, global outsourcing is also just a stepping stone to automation—such as overseas call centers segueing into interactive voice response systems—making the jobs even harder to hold on to.

Scary polls aside, job losses from offshore outsourcing are lower than that from automation or Chinese imports.[26] Exposure mostly shifts American workers into weaker occupations with modest wage declines. The more alarming result is an increase in the likelihood of unemployment by 1 percent, from a baseline of around 4 percent. Much like the Disney case, the pain is especially acute for workers who struggle to find jobs, whereas others adjust with minor consequences.[27]

Beyond IT outsourcing, an ongoing debate centers on the degree to which America should leverage global connections. Commentators, including Intel cofounder Andy Grove, have decried the offshoring of key parts of production, as short-term cost savings may inadvertently weaken the country's capacity for innovation and scaling new products.[28] Others instead highlight how global production chains allow leading U.S. centers to focus on creative and design work.[29] As this debate continues, it is important to consider the nuanced role of global talent, which both contributes to U.S. capabilities and enables the foreign operations of American companies.

There is no tidy way to close this section. Offshore outsourcing causes pain to displaced workers, including lost homes and broken careers, and global talent helps enable it. But it also yields cheaper products and higher share prices. Unfortunately, the next factor is just as messy and requires us to first rewind the tape a bit.

Broken Promises and Superstar Firms

In the decades after World War II, large U.S. businesses developed a powerful social contract with their workers, characterized by job security, health care and pension benefits, and mostly consistent wage increases.[30] Global competition and engagement were limited because of the heavy rebuilding in Europe and Japan after the war. This era was far from perfect, with problems ranging from gender and racial discrimination to large regulatory barriers that stifled innovation and kept prices high. Business and labor were also in bed together mostly to keep the government away, with brutal strikes and tumultuous contract negotiations being common.

But the connection was profound—people thought of themselves as lifelong employees of a corporation, and leadership felt a heavy responsibility to them. Companies often described themselves as a "family," and this spilled over into communities, too. Kodak once delayed the adoption of some new technologies until workers familiar with the older ones could retire. It is remarkable by today's standards that Kodak leadership made this decision, forgoing some profits, and that it operated in an environment where it was even possible to do so.

The 1970s and 1980s marked a turning point, as firms began to downsize and restructure, shedding less profitable tasks and layers of bureaucracy. The social contract weakened in the face of overseas competition, threats of hostile takeovers, and management theories to "maximize shareholder value." Lest one think that replacement of expensive older workers or distasteful requests to "train your replacement" began with the H-1B program, these earlier corporate layoffs exhibit many parallels, with the slight distinction that yesterday's companies sought local youth versus looking globally.

The new corporate approach favors talented workers. When Jack Welch became CEO of General Electric in 1981, he emphasized promoting talented workers faster and giving them greater compensation. Prior guarantees of lifetime employment ended, and GE's workers have become ever more skilled since then. As companies prioritize talent and winning in the marketplace, they often describe themselves as sports teams. This metaphor is far reaching: Even in the most nationalistic cities around the world, foreign players are lauded if the home team wins, and struggling veterans are quickly dismissed.

These business transformations dwarf the latest 250-person H-1B scandal. As companies race around the world to acquire talent and compete for new markets, bonds to older employees fade. Young talent carries few ties to a corporation's past, much like the soccer field in the Mission District, and implicit guarantees made in earlier periods to employees are often broken.[31] A new CEO, brought on by the board of directors to push a digitization agenda, may come from a radically different industry and purposefully overturn the older ways of doing things.

As with offshore outsourcing, global talent is not the only root cause of these corporate transformations, as the social contract began changing before the largest talent inflows. Yet high-skilled immigration deepens and perpetuates these transformations. As companies create greater opportunities and rewards for talent, they become even more attractive for tomorrow's best and brightest, who don't want to sit at the bottom of a rigid corporate ladder, be it in Paris or Tokyo. More incoming talent reinforces the sports team mentality, and a new corporate ethos takes hold. Pretty soon, everyone is moving their headquarters downtown to recruit young talent, and the transformation supersizes itself yet again.

Although talent benefits a lot from this pattern, the other big winners are the owners and executives of firms, which is not too surprising since they make the decisions. Some of the resulting gain goes into record corporate profits, and a big chunk into skyrocketing executive pay, which now stands near 275 times that of the average worker.[32] This ratio was just 25 times in the 1970s, when the transformation began in earnest, and none other than Plato argued that it should never exceed fivefold. Sometimes, crazy pay is justifiable for singular talent, but many large bonuses have little link to an executive's actions.[33] Particularly worrisome are huge pay raises for executives as their firm sheds long-term workers, often while the company is very profitable.[34] Putting it bluntly, a sad truth is that young global talent is quite useful for transferring retirement savings from older workers to the pockets of the already rich.

But as promised, the situation is messy, and the moral high ground is not always clear. Executives at older firms compete with younger rivals stocked with aggressive talent and no legacy obligations. Some have described the giants of Detroit as "pension plans with showrooms," but few consumers choose Ford over Tesla out of respect for Ford's pension commitments. Elon Musk describes working for Tesla as being in the Special Forces, noting: "That has pluses and minuses. It's cool to be Special Forces, but it also means you're working your ass off. It's not for everyone."[35]

Tesla is not alone, and "superstar firms" can now dominate sectors without many employees. Google has more than 80,000 workers, which is sizable, but also approximately a tenth of General Motors' 1979 peak of 853,000. Facebook serves more than 2 billion customers with just 27,000 employees, and Mark Zuckerberg and Sheryl Sandberg are very cautious to not let it balloon in size— like Google did![36] Running global platforms with so few people is truly remarkable, and other superstar firms include non-tech companies like Goldman Sachs and GlaxoSmithKline.[37] These firms grace the covers of business magazines and inspire entrepreneurs everywhere, and they focus first and foremost on attracting global talent.[38]

The pervasive outsourcing of noncore activities makes these comparisons of today's employee counts with yesterday's giants a bit of an apples-and-oranges exercise, given how many operations used to happen in-house. Game developer Supercell generates a staggering $2 billion in revenues with just two hundred employees.[39] Yet Supercell also contracts out more than one thousand jobs in player support roles. Supercell even decorates the vendors' offices to look like Supercell's headquarters to encourage cultural ties.

Although these jobs connected to superstar firms are welcome, outside vendors rarely offer salaries or benefits that match the company where the contractors work each day. Employees at these vendors can also struggle to advance beyond their current occupation. American business history celebrates stories like Gail Evans, who worked her way up from being a janitor at Eastman Kodak to retiring as the company's chief technology officer, with Kodak even helping with her college tuition along the way. Even if few people rose as far as Evans did, the integrated nature of yesterday's companies at least allowed hardworking employees to advance closer to where their talent could be best used. This path is blocked for many today.[40]

My conjecture (and it remains to be rigorously shown) is that superstar firms are the real link between global talent and the rise of the 1 percent wealth and middle-class stagnation, with H-1Bs and offshore outsourcing being just one controversial aspect. These forms of inequality began for different reasons and are propelled by other factors besides global talent, but superstar firms and high-skilled immigration are a perfect match. The world's best talent wants to be at Apple or McKinsey, and these superstar firms are designed to make them unbelievably productive. Together they generate exceptional results and reshape the corporate world. Looking in from the outside, the bus protests in San Francisco showed the local anger at these companies, and the victory of Donald Trump was, in part, a regional backlash.

Revenge Upon the Nerds

Global talent is sprinkled unevenly across America, creating regional winners and losers. Studies estimate that each new knowledge worker in a city creates five supporting non-technical jobs, an economic spillover that is triple the rate of manufacturing. These are good jobs, with average wages for the lower-skilled workers being higher than elsewhere in the country.[41]

In principle, high-skilled immigration can benefit rural areas, as local employers might find it easiest to attract an overseas worker desperate to come to America. Thus, we find many examples like the burgeoning tech sector in Olathe, Kansas, where international talent contributes to a local community. And while Silicon Valley had the highest number of H-1B requests per capita, the second-place city in 2010–2011 was Columbus, Indiana, a small town of forty-five thousand. Columbus is the headquarters of Cummins, a huge engine manufacturer that relies on foreign talent.[42] In addition, the price of buying a green card via an EB-5 visa is 50 percent lower if the investment is made in a rural area.[43]

Yet despite these occasional incursions into the heartland, global talent overwhelmingly favors centers like New York, Washington, San Francisco, and Los Angeles, which together account for more than one-third of recent H-1B applications. These places absorb many of the benefits of high-skilled immigrants, too.[44] This is sometimes termed a "Matthew effect" for U.S. cities, named after the parable of the talents in the Bible:[45] "For whoever has, will be given more, and they will have an abundance. Whoever does not have, even what they have will be taken from them." Global talent flows yield the sharpest productivity gains and job growth to cities that are already doing well.[46]

Some are complacent about the Matthew effect because of tax and redistribution policies. New York City absorbs more global talent than anywhere else, and the Big Apple contributes billions more in state taxes to New York than it receives in benefits, with the surplus being redistributed to poorer and rural parts of the state.[47] Similarly, fifteen states pay more in federal taxes than they receive in benefits, and these states are also the ones that typically receive the most global talent.[48] But government transfers don't make up for lost jobs, and people are insulted by suggestions they aren't pulling their weight.

The provocative book *Coming Apart* describes the long journey of America toward social isolation of elites: talented individuals are ever more likely to live near each other, go to the same schools, and marry each other. While elitism and wealth are correlated, they are also distinct. Elitism is more about holding advanced degrees and making extraordinarily complex Starbucks orders rather than pure income. This distinction helps explain why Donald Trump won many poor and rural voters, and why disgruntled voters also struck back in the U.K. against London's elite. The electorate in smaller regions and rural places hold disproportionate influence in many political systems, and their mounting anger came through with force.

Reflecting on the elections, political commentator Fareed Zakaria uses four *C*s to characterize pivotal factors:[49]

- Capitalism: those benefiting versus those left behind
- Culture: an older, white population's fears about lost national identity
- Class: hatred for know-it-all urban elites
- Communication: Twitter, social networking, and all that

Supporters of global talent flows, including the immigrants themselves, must recognize that the broader public does not see high-skilled immigration as a slam dunk success. In fact, using Zakaria's framework, global talent has the rare potential to offend on three dimensions at once: capitalism, culture, and class. Angry voters may even take the rosy statements of lobbyists—such as 50 percent of America's PhDs being immigrants—as evidence of the problem, not an effective retort. Given this tension, where does America, and places like London, go next?

CONCLUSIONS

Fragile U.S. Leadership

"Let them in! Let them in!" Thousands gathered at JFK Airport to demand the release of two Iraqi travelers. A day earlier, on January 27, 2017, President Donald Trump had closed America's borders to individuals from seven predominantly Muslim countries. The next day, protests sprang up everywhere. Senator Elizabeth Warren proclaimed by megaphone to a crowd at Boston's Logan Airport: "We will not turn away children. We will not turn away families. We will not turn away people who try to help Americans." Thousands more gathered in front of the White House, some chanting "Hey, hey, ho, ho, Muslim ban has got to go," and one poster read: "Immigration Made America Great."[1]

The outcry from the business world was especially strong, as CEOs of Fortune 500 companies like Apple and Coca-Cola voiced opposition, and more than one hundred businesses signed an amicus brief to stop the policy. Airbnb and Uber offered their services to those affected, and Starbucks pledged to hire ten thousand refugees worldwide. In the coming month, companies such as Anheuser-Busch would use their airtime during the Super Bowl to support immigration and diversity, paying up to $5 million for thirty seconds.

Many were upset at the coarse nature of the travel ban. One of the JFK detainees had worked with the U.S. government during the war in Iraq. So, too, had Fuad Sharef, who was escorted off a plane from Cairo with his family despite having undergone two years of vetting. The Sharefs had sold their house and most of their belongings and spent thousands of dollars on airfare. In another case, Dr. Suha Abushamma of the Cleveland Clinic was not allowed back into America after her vacation. When Dr. Abushamma was ultimately admitted, Senator Sherrod Brown of Ohio noted: "We cannot forget the many other doctors, scientists, students and families fleeing violence and persecution who remain in limbo. . . . [T]he chaos, confusion and cruelty caused by this order has only made America less safe."[2]

Not surprisingly, other nations made a grab for the talent. Canada's prime minister Justin Trudeau announced that Canada would welcome refugees, and a deputy prime minister of Turkey tweeted, "We'd happily welcome global talent not allowed back into #USA." Many of America's strongest allies voiced disapproval. Domestically, fierce legal challenges in multiple states led to the order being blocked in court, with the administration later issuing a narrower ban that was upheld by the Supreme Court.

In the firestorm of the moment, many worried about driving away rare talents like Maryam Mirzakhani, who came to the U.S. from Iran and won the Fields Medal in 2014, the equivalent to the Nobel Prize for mathematics. (Mirzakhani sadly passed away later in 2017 at a young age after battling cancer.) Others noted that Steve Jobs's father was a Syrian immigrant. But as days turned into months, the real concern became the enormous blow dealt to the confidence that talent placed in America—not just from the specific countries affected by the travel ban but globally. Even if American immigration policy was frustrating, it was generally predictable, which is essential for individuals making life-changing decisions.

The world has given the U.S. a unique gift and responsibility in the global talent that comes to its shores. America's leadership is a consequence of wise choices and its founding openness to new people, along with a bit of luck. Top talent has been one of America's greatest strengths, but this leadership should not be taken for granted. It is not that America should fear the continued advancement of education and skills abroad, as we all benefit from more global minds devising ways to improve our lives. But much as the U.S. benefits from the dollar's status as the world's reserve currency, America should cherish and protect its position at the center of global talent flows.

Asian Future, American Implosion?

Critics of business and economics books have easy pickings in the predictions that authors make. Once one gets beyond a self-evident thesis like "leadership is good," it is very easy to go exceptionally wrong, and fast. We focus too much on how current trends project forward, without recognizing the large changes that a couple of decades can bring. Go back to the 1980s, and few books predict the collapse of the Soviet Union, rising income inequality, and the internet revolution, and rarely is global talent emphasized. The forecasts are not entirely wrong, as discussions of computing progress and globalization abound. But the right points of emphasis are hard to discern, such as when Japan's economic might during the 1980s obscured China's emerging potential.[3] Yet having noted the perils of forecasting, allow me to engage in this fool's errand.

While America will receive a disproportionate share of global talent for some time to come, it will lose some of the staggering imbalances it currently enjoys. The overseas development of global talent and the emerging opportunities abroad are simply too profound. The worldwide number of twenty-five- to thirty-four-year-olds with college educations will double by 2030, and the U.S. will be home to fewer than one in ten of them. This talent growth will reinforce burgeoning local universities and further draw in global corporations seeking young customers and employees. As students see the distinctiveness of a foreign degree earned in the U.S. weaken, they may soon deem it better to stay home.[4] Looking among the superstars, immigrants to America will likely continue to win a disproportionate share of Nobel Prizes, but given the scientific capabilities being built abroad, this lopsidedness will also shrink over time. These changes will collectively loosen America's exceptional position.

Indeed, the race for talent will intensify despite the current pushback against globalization.[5] Rapidly aging populations and public fiscal imbalances in most advanced countries—as well as in China, because of its past one-child policy—increase demand for younger skilled workers.[6] Rising living standards make it easier for countries to draw talent home or compete for individuals from elsewhere. Many graduates also hold global career ambitions, sometimes evaluating job offers across three continents. North America is home to just 5 percent of the world's population, and many opportunities are sprouting up in emerging nations that are rapidly growing.

Yet America has every reason to continue as the world's talent leader in the century ahead. London is a very special place and holds extraordinary influence, even though it and the United Kingdom are not the global fulcrum that they were during the British Empire. It faces the future of Brexit, but London is a difficult city to bet against. Looking ahead, America is in an even better position. Its continent-sized scale, strong business foundation, exceptional universities, openness and diversity, and entrepreneurial spirit will help it maintain world-leading positions for its cities. America remains unique in its capacity to harness global talent in the workplace and provide it with so many different lifestyles, from Miami to Seattle, and everywhere in between.[7] Other countries have a long way to go before they match these features, making it America's race to lose!

But there is a risk that America will fumble the gift of global talent. This could happen slowly, as America turns inward and gradually loses its special luster. The strength of America's talent clusters, and the enormous challenges facing any country seeking to replicate that scale and global inclusiveness, suggest that the U.S. might be able to coast for a while before anything dramatic happens. Yet America's reliance on global talent makes a major exodus possible, should immigrants decide to leave. The unforgiving pace of technology also suggests that America should not rest on its laurels. Either way, the result is one that I hope can be avoided.

A first step for America is to pull back from its current hostility toward immigrants. We saw in Chapter 5 how beliefs about future access to the U.S. labor market shape foreign enrollments in American universities, especially among very top students. The changes in confidence associated with the ups and downs of H-1B quotas in the early 2000s may have seemed large at the time, and U.S. immigration policy has consistently poked potential immigrants in the eye. But today's rhetoric and erosion of trust are much more damaging. What can be done to make things better?

Making the Policy Sausage

America's leadership in global talent depends on getting many things right. The U.S. must foster a business environment that attracts global talent, including tackling issues like traditional infrastructure provisions, modern communications investments, effective tax policy, and solid education for the skills needed in today's economy.[8] On some of these, especially K–12 education, America lags its peers and needs to redouble its efforts. While recognizing these many factors, let's focus directly on the immigration policies that have the most immediate impact for high-skilled flows.

There are many considerations that should factor into these other policies, and cheerleading for better roads or broadband internet risks obscuring the core and sometimes painful choices that exist for people flows.

The difficult truth about immigration is that, in the short run, there is almost always someone who would be better off if the immigrant did not come.[9] This is true at all education and skill levels, ranging from foreign students to H-1B visa holders to world-class academics. Sometimes this pain is very slight, such as when a student ends up with her second choice of undergraduate major or when an executive is passed over for a coveted job. Yet other times the pain is severe, as in layoffs of older workers who never again establish solid employment. This turbulence is because more people are competing for slowly adjusting resources. Using scarce talent as a catalyst for company growth can produce all-around gains, but the reality is that visas are just as likely to be used to minimize costs.

In theoretical models, subsequent economic expansion alleviates these short-term losses and provides better employment to everyone. Reality is much more varied, however, and those who are displaced at vulnerable career stages may never regain the bright futures they once had. This job loss may have been inevitable, such as when a struggling company is unable to support a worker much longer regardless of talent flows, but there are also cases in which a firm can afford a worker's salary but chooses greater profits. While policy leaders should not protect every occupational passion or permanently lock in jobs, they should be diligent in anticipating when people's worlds get turned upside down.

As the benefits of immigration exceed the costs to those who are displaced, one can theoretically transfer some of the benefits to displaced workers, making everyone whole again. Government initiatives attempt to do this through financial assistance and worker retraining, such as the programs provided by the Department of Labor for H-1B-affected industries.[10] Yet these sincere efforts do not reach everyone and can be weakened by bureaucracy. Even as you read this book, it is likely that some of the laid-off IT workers from Disney are still struggling.

Thus, immigration policy must weigh economywide gains against losses for some existing U.S. workers. People will disagree about these trade-offs just as much as they disagree on tax rates and redistribution. For some, any job disruption due to immigration is too much; for others, immigration should be harnessed to maximize U.S. competitiveness and overall prosperity. Although there is no silver bullet for these ideological differences, the poor state of America's immigration policy leaves some quite feasible actions that many can agree to. These early wins could seed America's ability to have a national conversation on global talent.

As we discuss policy, it is important to separate distasteful practices from questions of legality. "Train your replacement" stories foster popular anger at the H-1B program, but they are less useful for crafting policy unless one wishes to outlaw the practice of tying severance payments to replacement training. Such a labor regulation might be justified, but it should apply equally to replacement by immigrants or natives. The media, politicians, and industry watchdogs are shining ever-brighter lights on offensive practices, and perhaps the fear of future public relations disasters will lead to better treatment of laid-off employees. Unfortunately, firms might also adjust to the scandals by dismissing workers immediately, with less severance pay and greater pain for those losing their jobs. Either way, let's focus on the underlying illnesses rather than on symptoms as we discuss how to get more out of existing programs.

Improving Immigration Pathways

Immigration reforms, including H-1B revisions, have been stuck for more than a decade, and the future is hard to predict. Yet, even after the divisive election, national polls indicate a common ground. Figure 10.1 shows that 65 percent of those surveyed in 2017 agreed that high-skilled immigration should be increased, compared with about a quarter of respondents who suggested that it be decreased.[11] Breakouts of the overall response, as shown in the appendix, highlight that this support holds across age groups, ethnicities, income levels, and regions. This relatively consistent support has also been shown in academic studies,[12] and it is not present for lower-skilled immigration.

Drilling down on the controversial H-1B program, Americans mostly conclude that the program should be kept at the same size, showing the gap between views on H-1B workers specifically versus the general label of "high-skilled immigrants." While more people believe that the H-1B program helps the economy than hurts it, this is not because they believe that Americans could not perform the jobs conducted by H-1B workers. Thus, although a slam-dunk consensus does not emerge from the polling data, effective reform

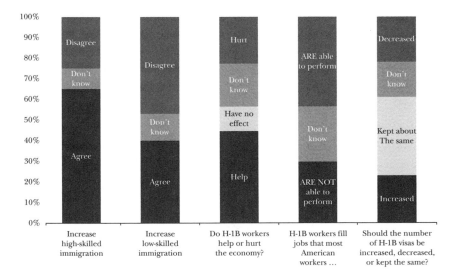

FIGURE 10.1 Registered voter attitudes toward high-skilled immigration and H-1B visa program.
Source: Data from Politico & Morning Consult Poll, 2017.

appears possible if America can increase the skill level of H-1B admissions. How could this be accomplished?

Better Selection with Any Visa

The allocation of H-1B visas is very inefficient, with the lottery system being used in the years with the greatest visa demand— precisely when U.S. employers want to be most careful in their selections! The system implicitly favors applications for lower-skilled workers, such as those made by outsourcing companies, and it does not allow companies to prioritize among their candidates. This is silly: if the country has a dire need for data analysts, the system should direct precious visas toward people with these skills.

Many of these ills could be mitigated through simple wage ranking of applications. Rather than having a mad scramble in the first week, a longer horizon of a month could be used to collect applications. Applicants could then be ordered, with selection proceeding down the wage rankings until the visa supply is used up. To the extent that applications are withdrawn (e.g., the immigrant goes elsewhere, the company shuts down), marginal applicants could be admitted from a waiting list.[13]

There are reasonable objections to wage ranking—most important, a person's salary does not capture his or her full contribution to society. Indeed, America might value the altruistic social worker striving to rebuild U.S. cities more than those engaged in much higher-paid work. While this counterargument is important, wage ranking accomplishes a tremendous amount in a very straightforward manner, which is important politically and for effective implementation. It might be useful to install occupational and regional maximums alongside wage ranking, so that all the visas are not all gobbled up by expensive coastal cities and very high-priced sectors.

Immigrant entrepreneurs also deserve special policy attention—even though they are widely celebrated, American policies are stacked against them. Proposals like the Startup Act and the Attracting and Retaining Entrepreneurs Act argue for easier admission pathways for entrepreneurs starting high-growth, job-creating companies backed by reputable venture capital firms. These are the types of spillovers we most want to encourage, but the employer-based nature of U.S. policy creates substantial gaps in the pathways of entrepreneurs into America. Many countries have programs to attract globally mobile entrepreneurs, often taking direct aim at those frustrated with the U.S. system, and so America should act fast.[14]

Taken a step further, the H-1B system is quite erratic with its April 1 filings and October 1 start dates. A quarterly system, which allocates one-fourth of the same number of visas throughout the year and has a shorter time lag until work start could help both workers and firms. America would be less likely to lose top talents who find themselves off cycle and don't want to wait a year or more after narrowly missing the filing deadline. I cherish many memories of the first year and a half as Sari and I began dating, but her departure to Toronto for fourteen months while she waited for her H-1B visa to be granted and start does not make the list. While the expenses and days apart added up, we had it quite easy compared with many others, and there is no rationale for such a lurching time schedule.

To complement wage ranking and to preserve scarce visas for the best uses, America should also raise the H-1B minimum wage from $60,000 to a higher figure like $100,000, perhaps with a few lower thresholds for occupations like social work or entrepreneurship. This minimum level can be designed with automatic adjustments for future years that are based on inflation or changes in average U.S. wages. If a higher minimum wage causes demand to fall short of supply at times, unused visas can be saved and reintroduced when supply becomes again constrained, with visas that sit too long simply expiring. There are downsides to wage floors, such as their mismatch to innovative jobs that may be better served with heavy equity incentives, but minimum wages can provide strong assurances to the public that visas are being put toward best uses.

These suggestions will foster a better selection of immigrants with whatever number of visas that exist. The sponsorship of high-skilled immigrants by employers has laudable features, and America should hold onto its best parts. But the system surrounding firms needs to be more carefully thought out considering the challenges we have discussed in this book. More broadly, America's employment-based visas are only a modest share of an immigration framework that prioritizes family reunification. With a view toward comprehensive immigration reform and a more skilled inflow, I generally favor further tilting U.S. immigration toward employment-based purposes, although the average skill level of family-based admissions has grown a lot recently and may soon close much of the gap in employment-oriented visas.[15]

Better Seat at the Table for Immigrants

Worker immobility and poor negotiating power are responsible for many abuses in labor markets. The H-1B program inhibits mobility, creating the so-called indentured servants. An employer-based system relies on firms benefiting from their costly search and recruitment efforts, and this incentive should be maintained. But the system is playing with fire and risks exploitation if the lock-in is too great. Workers are vulnerable during certain stages of the green-card applications, being scared to change employers (or even travel internationally to visit ailing family members). Faster processing and better assurance that job changes won't damage an applicant's chances after early processing steps are complete would be helpful.

As an even more radical consideration, why should a worker not have the right to apply for a green card directly? It seems unnatural that all the power rests in the employer's hands. In the initial screening of workers, there are a lot of advantages by using firms to prioritize skills and select candidates on soft information that the government can't see. But it is less obvious that firms play a special role in permanent residency decisions. Worker-initiated requests would undergo appropriate vetting, but this adjustment would make the employment pathway genuinely dual intent for workers and firms. This attractive prospect could lure in stronger immigrants and reduce exploitation. I support safeguards that protect H-1B workers, and none is as potent as giving workers the capacity to move when conditions are lacking or exploitative.

Better Pathways That Don't Create Bottlenecks

We have visualized skilled immigration pathways as pipes of different sizes that fit together poorly, with various workarounds holding together seams that are about to burst. America needs a better system that removes such bottlenecks. In a perfect world, the U.S. would establish a nonpolitical technical group to monitor and adjust immigration policies on a regular basis to optimize talent inflows, much as Australia and Canada attempt to do. The reality of American politics, however, rules out for now such "immigration engineering," partly because of the potential impact of immigration on the relative strength of the Democrats versus Republicans. Consequentially, simpler and self-adjusting proposals work better.

A starting point is to index H-1B admissions to economic conditions. Decades-long political battles to set a fixed cap are counterproductive, and any chosen quota will not reflect a growing economy for long. America should first raise the cap from its present level of eighty-five thousand to reflect the growth over the past decade, and then index future visa increases to population growth or to the national employment growth for skilled workers. When combined with wage ranking and higher minimum salaries for H-1B workers, such indexing would accommodate sector growth in a more secure way. The public does not favor increasing the H-1B program as it currently stands, but the nationwide mood is supportive of higher admissions if the immigrant inflow becomes more skilled.

The education pathway also requires close attention. America's colleges and universities are a great boon, but they are turning out ever-larger cohorts of foreign graduates seeking access to the U.S. labor market. A frequent call to action from lobbyists is to "staple a green card" to advanced science and engineering degrees from U.S. schools. This proposal is attractive, as it alleviates an ever-worsening school-to-work bottleneck for one important group. But the proposal is also unsatisfactory in how it endows university admissions officers and faculty with the power to make permanent immigration decisions on behalf of America. While I hold no great love for bureaucracy, I favor decisions about green cards being made by the government rather than by unelected universities.

Even if the "staple policy" were limited to accredited schools, the incentives for gaining permanent residency are so strong that severe abuse would likely follow. There have been serious proposals, like Blueseeds, to build large ships parked off the California coast to provide access to Silicon Valley to those who cannot obtain an H-1B. While mostly living and working at sea, residents of Blueseeds could come ashore temporarily as tourists for business meetings. Not kidding, this proposal was serious! We have seen how universities create part-time employment workarounds for entrepreneurs who can't get an H-1B visa, and how cash-strapped schools love foreign master's students who pay full fare. This intensity suggests many unintended consequences from the staple policy: imagine the pressuring and cajoling of faculty when a student is just one passing grade away from a green card.[16]

Although I struggle with this aspect of the staple proposal, I am quite sympathetic to its underlying motivations. America needs policies that reflect and harness the many foreign students who want to stay for work. One possibility is to give graduating foreign students an automatic right to work temporarily in America. This duration could be in proportion to years of education in America or schooling levels. These students-turned-workers would then need to secure an H-1B visa, which would require a solid job, and they could pursue green cards just like everyone else.[17] This plan can achieve the benefits of the staple proposal while also reducing risks and including more fields than just science and engineering.

Better Conversation and Information

Hard facts and findings are scarce in the U.S. immigration debate, with sharp ideologies and rosy or scandalous anecdotes more common. Careful empirical studies will not eliminate angry rhetoric, as reasonable people can disagree over trade-offs, but more accurate measurements would seed common understanding. One advantage of points-based systems is that they make issues explicit, such as the extra points that younger workers can earn as compared with older workers. Citizens in these countries can legitimately disagree about the weight assigned to youth, but at least they know the terms of the debate.

America invested substantially in building the required knowledge for the space race—whistling "Twinkle, Twinkle, Little Star" and gazing through older telescopes was not going to cut it! Yet in the emerging global talent race, the U.S. collects insufficient information and even buries its head in the sand when topics become politically sensitive. In 2017, the Trump administration released several data elements on H-1B wages that were quickly gobbled up by immigration researchers and reporters. Much more can be done. Let's shine a big data spotlight on global talent and learn as much as we can.[18] Some individuals will always dismiss studies that contradict their opinions, but others listen and also hunger for facts. And really, what downside is there? Can the situation get any worse than it is today?

Taking it one step further, if firms and universities are to remain the central gatekeepers, America should expect more disclosure from them. Public companies provide accounting information to investors, and reports on the use of skilled visas and the employment conditions of guest workers could be similarly required. These data would help researchers, and investors could consider these topics in their portfolio selection. It is encouraging that some firms are already considering how to provide some of these insights. This takes us beyond refinements to today's program to the bigger questions for the decades ahead.

Restoring U.S. Leadership

There is a dubious professor tactic of posing "walk-away questions" at the end of class to present big issues that one does not yet have good answers to—dubious because no one is tricked. Many such opportunities abound for global talent flows. To begin, the gains from high-skilled immigration to America mostly go to sponsoring firms, and these paydays can be profound. Eight of the ten most valuable public companies at the start of 2018 are American firms, with Apple, Alphabet/Google, Amazon, and Microsoft leading the list. Facebook is sixth, and the two non-U.S. companies are Alibaba and Tencent. Twenty years ago, in 1997, only six of the top ten companies were American, and the tech presence consisted of just Microsoft and Intel.[19]

Global talent has played an important role in this astonishing ascent of the West Coast tech industry. Surely some of this surplus can be shared more broadly without dampening incentives for new entrepreneurs and innovation. Although individual taxes are painful to pay, having a modestly higher marginal tax rate when earning millions and millions of dollars annually does not seem too awful of a price. And while being careful to avoid the perils of socialism, ideas like creating passive national mutual funds to share market gains deserve consideration. As a thought experiment, what if the hiring of an H-1B worker came with the contribution of

0.0001 percent of the firm's stock returns over the ensuing five to ten years to a fund for restoring America's community colleges? You can add or subtract a zero after the decimal point as you wish, but make the trade-off meaningful. America is awfully good at granting stock options to executives, and claiming a small share of the upside generated from global talent for national use seems reasonable. America's key national resource—preferential access to new immigrant talent—is currently being handed out for free.

If this comes across as wild-eyed crazy talk to tech executives, then the challenge to them is to provide a more compelling case for global talent flows. Simple statistics like the share of Silicon Valley entrepreneurs or inventors who are immigrants are music to the ears of many of us living in talent clusters, but they are not as convincing in Olathe or Orlando. Middle America holds a decisive vote in much of U.S. policy, and convincing them requires a more extensive playbook than one-sided calls for unlimited H-1B visas. If the tech industry engages in a battle of extremes, "steamroll or be steamrolled," as one person described it to me, I fear it will often lose the electoral math. The Valley celebrates building products with massive scale that touch millions, and its future depends on "denting the universe" here, too.

More broadly, many workers are being left behind in today's economy, from those with weaker starting jobs or limited salary growth to those with poor pathways for reengagement when turbulence strikes. While the construction of new educational, labor, and social institutions for the twenty-first century goes well beyond high-skilled immigration—including quick expansions of earned-income tax credits or calls for universal basic income—these issues should be considered together. Superstar firms dominate the *Fortune* valuation rankings, but they don't provide the jobs that the major companies of the previous century did, and most jobs at Walmart and Uber are not a foundation for a middle-class life. While heavy labor regulations are not the answer, we face a world where profits often take priority, skills become obsolete quickly, and people are living longer. This environment is rife for class- and age-based struggle, and the economic and political turbulence ahead will be rougher than what we have just experienced. The pace of Moore's law means that the cumulative computing technology that was in place on November 8, 2016, when Donald Trump won the U.S. presidency, will account for only 25 percent or so of what will exist on November 3, 2020, when the next election occurs.

Although the future of work is quite uncertain, the solution is not to squash the trends that appear to threaten today's jobs. One story highlights the Luddite fallacy in focusing just on job counts: Milton Friedman, a Nobel Prize winner in economic sciences, observed a canal project in Asia and asked why the workers had shovels instead of modern tractors and earthmovers. The government bureaucrat responded: "You don't understand. This is a jobs program." Friedman remarked: "Oh, I thought you were trying to build a canal. If it's jobs you want, then you should give these workers spoons, not shovels."[20]

How will we manage the future of work? It's a great walk-away question that deserves our utmost attention and goes well beyond this book. While prior fears of jobless futures have proved unfounded, perhaps this time is different. But even if we don't know exactly what the jobs of tomorrow will be, I believe they will be found nearby to the talented people leading these advances. We should welcome and harness global talent, not push it away.

APPENDIX

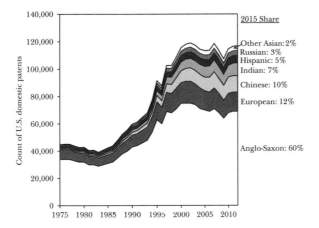

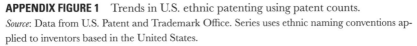

APPENDIX FIGURE 1 Trends in U.S. ethnic patenting using patent counts.
Source: Data from U.S. Patent and Trademark Office. Series uses ethnic naming conventions applied to inventors based in the United States.

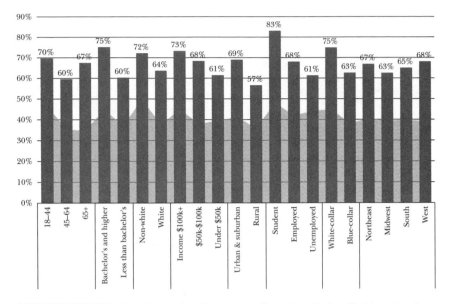

APPENDIX FIGURE 2   Breakouts of poll responses. Bars show high-skilled immigration support and shaded area displays low-skilled immigration support.
Source: Data from Politico & Morning Consult Poll, 2017.

NOTES

Introduction

1. Article titles and quotes are from *Bloomberg Businessweek*, May 15–21, 2017.

2. In an August 2017 poll, 42 percent of respondents said the U.S. admitted too many "low-skilled workers," versus 12 percent who said too few. By contrast, 36 percent of respondents felt the U.S. admitted too few "high-skilled workers," versus 15 percent who said too many. At both skill levels, about half of respondents thought the level was about right or had no opinion. Politico & Morning Consult, "National Tracking Poll #170803 February 03-06, 2017: Crosstabulation Results," August 2017, https://www.politico.com/f/?id=0000015d-c4ae -d494-a77f-e6be72bd0000.

Chapter 1

1. "The Dress Code at the Nobel Banquet," Nobelprize.org, https://www .nobelprize.org/ceremonies/dresscode/.

2. *Jacobellis v. Ohio*, 378 U.S. 184 (1964), at 197.

3. Philip Bump, "Nearly Everyone in Congress Has a College Degree: Most Americans Don't," *Washington Post*, February 2, 2017, https://www.washington post.com/news/politics/wp/2017/02/02/nearly-everyone-in-congress-has-a -college-degree-most-americans-dont/.

4. This work draws from Sari Kerr, William Kerr, Çaglar Özden, and Christopher Parsons, "Global Talent Flows," *Journal of Economic Perspectives* 30, no. 4 (Fall 2016): 83–106. The official name of the economics prize is the Sveriges Riksbank Prize in Economic Sciences in Memory of Alfred Nobel. Nobel statistics cover through the 2016 awards.

5. This work draws from Ernest Miguelez and Carsten Fink, "Measuring the International Mobility of Inventors: A New Database" (WIPO Economic Research Working Paper No. 8, World Intellectual Property Organization, Geneva, 2013).

6. The work of Çaglar Özden and Christopher Parsons provides the best entry point into these projects. While there are quite-skilled workers with vocational

training and apprenticeship models, our current ability to compare countries and follow migration on these dimensions is much weaker.

7. This work draws from S. Kerr et al., "Global Talent Flows," and Sari Kerr, William Kerr, Çaglar Özden, and Christopher Parsons, "High-Skilled Migration and Agglomeration," *Annual Review of Economics* 9 (2017): 201–34.

8. "244 Million International Migrants Living Abroad Worldwide, New UN Statistics Reveal," Sustainable Development Goals, United Nations, January 12, 2016, http://www.un.org/sustainabledevelopment/blog/2016/01/244-million -international-migrants-living-abroad-worldwide-new-un-statistics-reveal/.

9. Exports represent about 30 percent of global GDP. World Bank, "Exports of Goods and Services (% of GDP)," World Bank Open Data, http://data .worldbank.org/indicator/NE.EXP.GNFS.ZS.

10. Miguelez and Fink, "Measuring the International Mobility of Inventors"; Michel Beine, Frédéric Docquier, and Hillel Rapoport, "Measuring International Skilled Migration: A New Database Controlling for Age of Entry," *World Bank Economic Review* 21, no. 2 (May 2007): 249–54; and Frédéric Docquier and Abdeslam Marfouk, "International Migration by Educational Attainment (1990–2000)," in *International Migration, Remittances and The Brain Drain*, ed. Çaglar Özden and Maurice Schiff (New York: Palgrave Macmillan, 2006), 151–99.

11. Miguelez and Fink, "Measuring the International Mobility of Inventors."

12. Ufuk Akcigit, Salome Baslandze, and Stefanie Stantcheva, "Taxation and the International Migration of Inventors," *American Economic Review* 106, no. 10 (October 2016): 2930–81.

13. S. Kerr et al., "Global Talent Flows."

14. Calculations from the 2016 American Community Survey. See also Gordon Hanson and Chen Liu, "High-Skilled Immigration and the Comparative Advantage of Foreign Born Workers Across U.S. Occupations," in *High-Skilled Migration to the United States and Its Economic Consequences*, ed. Gordon Hanson, William Kerr, and Sarah Turner (Chicago: University of Chicago Press, 2018).

15. Vivek Wadhwa, Guillermina Jasso, Ben Rissing, Gary Gereffi, and Richard Freeman, "Intellectual Property, the Immigration Backlog, and a Reverse Brain-Drain: America's New Immigrant Entrepreneurs, Part III," Kauffman Foundation Report, August 2007, http://www.kauffman.org/what-we -do/research/immigration-and-the-american-economy/intellectual-property -the-immigration-backlog-and-a-reverse-braindrain; Vivek Wadhwa, AnnaLee Saxenian, Ben Rissing, and Gary Gereffi, "America's New Immigrant Entrepreneurs," Kauffman Foundation Report, January 2007, http://www.kauffman .org/what-we-do/research/immigration-and-the-american-economy/americas -new-immigrant-entrepreneurs.

16. Partnership for a New American Economy, "The 'New American' Fortune 500," June 2011, http://www.newamericaneconomy.org/sites/all/themes/pnae/img/new-american-fortune-500-june-2011.pdf.

17. Jennifer Hunt and Marjolaine Gauthier-Loiselle, "How Much Does Immigration Boost Innovation?" *American Economic Journal: Macroeconomics* 2, no. 2 (April 2010): 31–56; William Kerr and William Lincoln, "The Supply Side of Innovation: H-1B Visa Reforms and U.S. Ethnic Invention," *Journal of Labor Economics* 28, no. 3 (July 2010): 473–508.

18. Hanson and Liu, "High-Skilled Immigration."

19. Institute of International Education, *2017 Open Doors Report on International Educational Exchange* (New York: Institute of International Education, 2017).

20. Government of Canada, "Global Skills Strategy," Employment and Social Development Canada, https://www.canada.ca/en/employment-social-development/campaigns/global-skills-strategy.html; and Government of Canada, "Hire a Top Foreign Talent Through the Global Talent Stream," Employment and Social Development Canada, https://www.canada.ca/en/employment-social-development/services/foreign-workers/global-talent.html.

21. Erhan Artuç and Çaglar Özden, "Transit Migration: All Roads Lead to America" (Working Paper No. 7880, World Bank Group, Washington, DC, 2016).

22. Michael Clemens, "Why Do Programmers Earn More in Houston Than Hyderabad? Evidence from Randomized Processing of U.S. Visas," *American Economic Review Papers & Proceedings* 103, no. 3 (May 2013): 198–202.

23. Christian Dustmann, Francesco Fasani, Tommaso Frattini, Luigi Minale, and Uta Schonberg, "On the Economics and Politics of Refugee Migration," *Economic Policy* 32, no. 91 (July 2017): 497–550.

24. Petra Moser, Alessandra Voena, and Fabian Waldinger, "German Jewish Émigrés and U.S. Invention," *American Economic Review* 104, no. 10 (October 2014): 3222–55.

Chapter 2

1. This work interfaces with many related studies about cities and the geography of work: Edward Glaeser, *Triumph of the City* (London: Macmillan, 2011); Enrico Moretti, *The New Geography of Jobs* (Boston: Houghton Mifflin Harcourt, 2012); and Richard Florida, *Cities and the Creative Class* (New York: Routledge, 2007).

2. Garrett Harper, Chris Cotton, and Zandra Benefield, "Nashville Music Industry: Impact, Contribution and Cluster Analysis," Music City Music Council, Nashville Area Chamber of Commerce, 2013, http://www.nashville.gov/Portals/0/SiteContent/MayorsOffice/EcDev/docs/NashvilleMusicIndustryStudy.pdf.

3. "Top 10 Music Cities Other Than Nashville," Music from the Row, July 22, 2015, http://www.musicfromtherow.com/home/top-10-music-cities-other -than-nashville.

4. The legal profession is a second example. Major cities have lawyers who serve the needs of global clients, and those lawyers often locate together in the same high-rent office buildings. They must learn not to talk about their cases in the elevators, but otherwise, the presence of other top law firms in the same building is an aid to their work. In contrast, local attorneys who serve the personal and business needs of neighborhoods compete for the same fixed base of customers.

5. This setup suggests that talent should flow toward regions where it is relatively scarce. In fact, taken to the extreme, this logic predicts that talent should migrate out of the U.S. and into emerging countries, where less-skilled workers are in abundance. This is a form of the "Lucas" paradox, named after Nobel Laureate Robert Lucas, who posed the question of why capital doesn't flow to developing countries. In practice, we don't see this for reasons like fewer non-labor inputs (e.g., machinery) in emerging countries or suboptimal legal systems or financial markets.

6. Lynne Zucker, Michael Darby, and Marilynn Brewer, "Intellectual Human Capital and the Birth of U.S. Biotechnology Enterprises," *American Economic Review* 88, no. 1 (March 1998): 290–306.

7. Mohammad Arzaghi and J. Vernon Henderson, "Networking off Madison Avenue," *Review of Economic Studies* 75, no. 4 (October 2008): 1011–38.

8. William Kerr and Gamze Yucagolu, "Peak Games: Hiring Priorities in Times of Rapid Growth (A)," Harvard Business School Case No. 818-083 (Boston: Harvard Business Publishing, 2018).

9. Bruce Fallick, Charles Fleischman, and James Rebitzer, "Job-Hopping in Silicon Valley: Some Evidence Concerning the Microfoundations of a High-Technology Cluster," *Review of Economics and Statistics* 88, no. 3 (August 2006): 472–81.

10. Jane Jacobs, *The Economy of Cities* (New York: Vintage Books, 1969); Gilles Duranton and Diego Puga, "Nursery Cities: Urban Diversity, Process Innovation, and the Life Cycle of Products," *American Economic Review* 91, no. 5 (December 2001), 1454–77; and Jeffrey Lin, "Technological Adaptation, Cities, and New Work," *Review of Economics and Statistics* 93, no. 2 (May 2011): 554–74.

11. Josh Lerner, *Boulevard of Broken Dreams: Why Public Efforts to Boost Entrepreneurship and Venture Capital Have Failed and What to Do About It* (Princeton, NJ: Princeton University Press, 2009).

Chapter 3

1. Chad Jones, "Sources of U.S. Economic Growth in a World of Ideas," *American Economic Review* 92, no. 1 (January 2002): 220–39.

2. Calculations from the U.S. Census Bureau's American Community Survey and from Gordon Hanson and Chen Liu, "High-Skilled Immigration and the Comparative Advantage of Foreign Born Workers across U.S. Occupations," in *High-Skilled Migration to the United States and Its Economic Consequences*, ed. Gordon Hanson, William Kerr, and Sarah Turner (Chicago: University of Chicago Press, 2018).

3. The WIPO dataset is restricted to patents filed globally under the Patent Cooperation Treaty, and the extra expenses associated with this filing leads some inventors to skip this step.

4. William Kerr, "The Ethnic Composition of U.S. Inventors" (HBS Working Paper No. 08-006, Harvard Business School, Boston, 2007).

5. Patent applications go through a multiyear review before they are granted. Our focus on the year of patent application dates an invention as closely as possible to its creation.

6. Although the role of immigrants for invention in America has received the most attention, studies of Europe find many parallels: Max Nathan, "The Wider Economic Impacts of High-Skilled Migrants: A Survey of the Literature for Receiving Countries," *IZA Journal of Migration* 3, no. 4 (February 2014): https://doi.org/10.1186/2193-9039-3-4; and Max Nathan, "Same Difference? Minority Ethnic Inventors, Diversity and Innovation in the UK," *Journal of Economic Geography* 15, no. 1 (January 2015): 129–68.

7. Paula Stephan and Sharon Levin, "Exceptional Contributions to U.S. Science by the Foreign-Born and Foreign-Educated," *Population Research and Policy Review* 20, nos. 1–2 (April 2001): 59–79.

8. This discussion pulls extensively from Jennifer Hunt and Marjolaine Gauthier-Loiselle, "How Much Does Immigration Boost Innovation?," *American Economic Journal: Macroeconomics* 2, no. 2 (April 2010): 31–56; Jennifer Hunt, "Which Immigrants Are Most Innovative and Entrepreneurial? Distinctions by Entry Visa," *Journal of Labor Economics* 29, no. 3 (July 2011): 417–57; and Jennifer Hunt, "Are Immigrants the Most Skilled U.S. Computer and Engineering Workers?" *Journal of Labor Economics* 33, no. S1 (pt. 2, July 2015): S39–S77.

9. Norman Matloff, "Are Foreign Students the 'Best and Brightest'? Data and Implications for Immigration Policy" (Economic Policy Institute Briefing Paper No. 356, Economic Policy Institute, Washington, DC, 2013). Matloff argues that an internal brain drain exists from STEM work as a result of immigrants displacing better-qualified natives.

10. As the U.S. has more than two million STEM workers, the exceptional tail of superstars does not move overall group averages very much, at least in terms of wages or productivity.

11. John Haltiwanger, Ron Jarmin, and Javier Miranda, "Who Creates Jobs? Small versus Large versus Young," *Review of Economics and Statistics* 95, no. 2 (May 2013): 347–61.

12. AnnaLee Saxenian and Vivek Wadhwa are prominent voices on immigrant entrepreneurship: AnnaLee Saxenian, *Silicon Valley's New Immigrant Entrepreneurs* (San Francisco: Public Policy Institute of California, 1999); Vivek Wadhwa, AnnaLee Saxenian, Ben Rissing, and Gary Gereffi, "America's New Immigrant Entrepreneurs," Kauffman Foundation Report, January 2007, http://www.kauffman.org/what-we-do/research/immigration-and-the-american-economy/americas-new-immigrant-entrepreneurs; and Stuart Anderson and Michaela Platzer, "American Made: The Impact of Immigrant Entrepreneurs and Professionals on U.S. Competitiveness" (Arlington, VA: National Venture Capital Association, 2006).

13. By coincidence, the eleven states include immigrant-heavy areas like Florida and California. A larger sample of twenty-eight states over the period 2002–2008 finds similar growth rates and suggests the national average for 2008 might be closer to 25 percent, still higher than immigrants in the workforce overall. Sari Kerr and William Kerr, "Immigrant Entrepreneurship," in *Measuring Entrepreneurial Businesses: Current Knowledge and Challenges*, ed. John Haltiwanger, Erik Hurst, Javier Miranda, and Antoinette Schoar (Chicago: University of Chicago Press, 2017), 187–249.

14. Hunt, "Which Immigrants are Most Innovative and Entrepreneurial?"; and Robert Fairlie and Magnus Lofstrom, "Immigration and Entrepreneurship," in *Handbook on the Economics of International Migration*, ed. Barry Chiswick and Paul Miller (Oxford: North-Holland, 2014), 877–911.

15. Kerr, "Ethnic Composition of U.S. Inventors."

16. John Lie and Nancy Abelmann, *Blue Dreams: Korean Americans and the Los Angeles Riots* (Cambridge, MA: Harvard University Press, 1991).

17. William Kerr and Martin Mandorff, "Social Networks, Ethnicity, and Entrepreneurship" (Working Paper No. 21597, National Bureau of Economic Research, Cambridge, MA, 2015); and Robert Fairlie and Bruce Meyer, "Ethnic and Racial Self-Employment Differences and Possible Explanations," *Journal of Human Resources* 31, no. 4 (Autumn 1996): 757–93.

18. Casting a wider net, urban areas of the U.S. are home to 80 percent and 95 percent of population and invention, respectively. Nate Berg, "U.S. Urban Population Is Up . . . But What Does 'Urban' Really Mean?," CityLab, *Atlantic Monthly*, March 26, 2012, https://www.citylab.com/equity/2012/03/us-urban-population-what-does-urban-really-mean/1589/. Ethnic invention is a prominent contributor to this spikiness. While 46 percent of inventors with Anglo-Saxon or European heritage are in the ten largest patenting cities, this share is 67 percent for ethnic inventors.

19. William Kerr, "Breakthrough Inventions and Migrating Clusters of Innovation," *Journal of Urban Economics* 67, no. 1 (January 2010): 46–60; George

Borjas, "Does Immigration Grease the Wheels of the Labor Market?," *Brookings Papers on Economic Activity* 32, no. 1 (2001): 69–119; and Gilles Duranton, "Urban Evolutions: The Fast, the Slow, and the Still," *American Economic Review* 97, no. 1 (January 2007): 197–221.

20. William Kerr and William Lincoln, "The Supply Side of Innovation: H-1B Visa Reforms and U.S. Ethnic Invention," *Journal of Labor Economics* 28, no. 3 (July 2010): 473–508; Giovanni Peri, Kevin Shih, and Chad Sparber, "STEM Workers, H-1B Visas and Productivity in U.S. Cities," *Journal of Labor Economics* 33, no. S1 (pt. 2, July 2015): S225–S255.

21. Hunt and Gauthier-Loiselle, "How Much Does Immigration Boost Innovation?"

22. Hanson and Liu, "High-Skilled Immigration."

Chapter 4

1. Computerworld, "Gates Testimony Before Senate Panel," March 7, 2007, https://www.computerworld.com/article/2543810/it-careers/gates-testimony-before-senate-panel.html?page=2; and Microsoft Corporation, "Bill Gates: U.S. Senate Committee Hearing on Strengthening American Competitiveness," March 7, 2007, https://news.microsoft.com/speeches/bill-gates-u-s-senate-committee-hearing-on-strengthening-american-competitiveness/.

2. "Bill Gates Asks Senate for Infinite Number of H 1B Visas," YouTube video, posted by "BorderGuards," July 14, 2009, https://www.youtube.com/watch?v=vg0wCam2oDc.

3. Fox News, "Cuban: Trump's Review of H-1B Visa: Bad for America Overall," YouTube video, posted by Fox News, April 18, 2017, https://www.youtube.com/watch?v=_CgxaE1Fe0c.

4. Michael Clemens, *The Walls of Nations* (New York: Columbia University Press, forthcoming) provides a provocative thesis about these choices. A large literature looks at how policy is shaped. Examples include Anna Maria Mayda, "Who Is Against Immigration? A Cross-Country Investigation of Individual Attitudes Toward Immigrants," *Review of Economics and Statistics* 88, no. 3 (August 2006): 510–30; Anna Maria Mayda, Giovanni Facchini, and Prachi Mishra, "Do Interest Groups Affect US Immigration Policy?" *Journal of International Economics* 85, no. 1 (September 2011): 114–28.

5. Calculated with data derived from World Bank Open Data (https://data.worldbank.org/indicator/SM.POP.NETM). "List of Countries by Net Migration Rate," Wikipedia, last modified June 26, 2017, 8:37, https://en.wikipedia.org/wiki/List_of_countries_by_net_migration_rate.

6. These admissions reunite immediate family members (e.g., spouses, parents, and children) or admit extended relatives. There is no annual limit on green

cards for immediate family members of American citizens, and up to 480,000 additional visas are provided annually for extended family. Smaller numbers of visas are issued for other purposes, such as refugee and humanitarian concerns.

7. Annalisa Nash Fernandez, "Canada's Immigration Policies Are Just as Warped as America's—But in a Whole Different Way," Quartz Media, March 15, 2007, https://qz.com/932244/american-versus-canadian-immigration-policies-are-not-actually-that-dissimilar-yet-the-us-is-cast-as-the-devil/.

8. This discussion of points-based structure draws on several resources, with many conceptual perspectives shared across reports: National Academies of Sciences, Engineering, and Medicine, *Immigration Policy and the Search for Skilled Workers: Summary of a Workshop* (Washington, DC: National Academies Press, 2015), http://www.nap.edu/20145; Jonathan Chaloff and Georges Lemaître, "Managing Highly-Skilled Labour Migration: A Comparative Analysis of Migration Policies and Challenges in OECD Countries" (OECD Social, Employment And Migration Working Paper No. 79, OECD Publishing, Paris, 2009); Madeleine Sumption, "Top 10 of 2014—Issue #9: The Points System Is Dead, Long Live the Points System," *Migration Information Source*, December 10, 2014, http://www.migrationpolicy.org/article/top-10-2014-issue-9-points-system-dead-long-live-points-system; Australian Department of Immigration and Border Protection, *2015–16 Migration Programme Report*, 2016, https://www.border.gov.au/ReportsandPublications/Documents/statistics/2015-16-migration-programme-report.pdf; and Sari Kerr, William Kerr, Çaglar Özden, and Christopher Parsons, "Global Talent Flows," *Journal of Economic Perspectives* 30, no. 4 (Fall 2016): 83–106.

9. Rachel Cao, "Canadian Immigration Website Crashes on Election Night," CNBC, November 9, 2016, http://www.cnbc.com/2016/11/09/canadian-immigration-website-crashes-on-election-night.html.

10. "No Country for Old Men," *The Economist*, January 8, 2015, https://www.economist.com/news/americas/21638191-canada-used-prize-immigrants-who-would-make-good-citizens-now-people-job-offers-have.

11. "How Express Entry Works," Immigration and Citizenship, Government of Canada, http://www.cic.gc.ca/english/express-entry/index.asp.

12. National Academies, "Search for Skilled Workers"; and Mathias Czaika and Christopher Parsons, "The Gravity of High-Skilled Migration Policies," *Demography* 54, no. 2 (2017): 603–30.

13. National Academies, "Search for Skilled Workers"; Sumption, "Points System Is Dead"; and Erika Consterdine, "How the Coalition Effectively Scrapped Points-Based Immigration," Comment & Analysis, Politics.co.uk, March 25, 2015, http://www.politics.co.uk/comment-analysis/2015/03/25/how-the-coalition-effectively-scrapped-points-based-immigrat.

14. Joshua Fatzick, "Nigerian Nobel Prize Winner Upholds Promise to Leave US After Trump's Win," VOA, December 1, 2016, https://www.voanews .com/a/wole-soyinka-trump-nobel-prize-nigeria/3619304.html.

15. The second expansion also legislated that nonprofit research institutes, including colleges and universities, were no longer subject to the cap and that renewals of H-1B visas do not count against the cap. These two expansions still hold in 2017. The original system had an H-1A visa for foreign nurses, which later even morphed into the H-1C, but these categories are no longer in use.

16. Neil Ruiz and Jens Manuel Krogstad, "Salaries Have Risen for High-Skilled Foreign Workers in U.S. on H-1B Visas," *FactTank* (blog), Pew Research Center, August 16, 2017, http://www.pewresearch.org/fact-tank/2017/08/16/ salaries-have-risen-for-high-skilled-foreign-workers-in-u-s-on-h-1b-visas/.

17. While less visible in the media, the L-1 visa is quite important, with 79,306 visas issued in 2016 (including renewals). This visa allows for temporary migration of employees in multinational companies that have offices in the U.S. and abroad. To qualify, a worker must have been employed by the company abroad for at least one of the previous three years before coming to America. The maximum stay is seven years, and the L-1 visa also offers the dual-intent feature. Analysis of the L-1 visa can be found in Stephen Yeaple, "The Innovation Activities of Multinational Enterprises and the Demand for Skilled Worker, Non-Immigrant Visas," in *High-Skilled Migration to the United States and Its Economic Consequences*, ed. Gordon Hanson, William Kerr, and Sarah Turner (Chicago: University of Chicago Press, 2018). The TN visa, created under the North American Free Trade Agreement, covers Canadian and Mexican citizens. These workers must have a job offer with a U.S. firm before applying and are restricted to a set of occupations that typically require a bachelor's degree.

18. Marko Terviö, "Superstars and Mediocrities: Market Failure in the Discovery of Talent," *Review of Economic Studies* 76, no. 2 (2009): 829–50.

19. Although the "prevailing wage" requirement imposes some salary floor, a firm may purposefully classify an H-1B holder under an occupation beneath his true ability or job (e.g., "software programmer" instead of "systems engineer"). YouTube videos capture lawyers describing how to work around the system: "Secret Video Immigration (lawyers teach companies how to steal jobs from USA workers)," YouTube video, posted by "Mrhulot101," February 16, 2012, https://www.youtube.com/watch?v=vuY9Krvmv8I.

20. Jennifer Hunt, "How Restricted Is the Job Mobility of Skilled Temporary Work Visa Holders?" (Working Paper No. 23529, National Bureau of Economics Research, Cambridge, MA, 2017). Hunt finds that mobility is reduced by about 20 percent when waiting for green-card processing. See also Briggs Depew, Peter Norlander, and Todd Sorensen, "Inter-Firm Mobility and Return

Migration Patterns of Skilled Guest Workers," *Journal of Population Economics* 30, no. 2 (April 2017): 681–721.

21. Hire F-1 Students, December 18, 2017, http://hiref-1students.com/.

22. Sari Kerr, William Kerr, and William Lincoln, "Firms and the Economics of Skilled Immigration," *Innovation Policy and the Economy* 15, no. 1 (2015): 115–52.

23. "Bill Gates Asks Senate for Infinite Number of H 1B Visas."

24. Legal observers debate the implications of these World Trade Organization (WTO) agreements. In 2016, India filed a complaint with the WTO over changes made to H-1B visa fees that disproportionately affected Indian firms. Other proposed changes to the H-1B program might be similarly challenged.

25. Ron Hira, "The H-1B and L-1 Visa Programs: Out of Control" (Briefing Paper, Economic Policy Institute, Washington, DC, 2010).

26. Haeyoun Park, "How Outsourcing Companies Are Gaming the Visa System," *New York Times*, November 6, 2015, https://www.nytimes.com/interactive/2015/11/06/us/outsourcing-companies-dominate-h1b-visas.html?_r=0.

27. Ruiz and Krogstad, "Salaries Have Risen."

28. Sam Harnett, "Using H-1B Visas to Help Outsource IT Work Draws Criticism, Scrutiny," All Tech Considered, *NPR*, February 13, 2017, http://www.npr.org/sections/alltechconsidered/2017/02/13/514990545/using-h-1b-visas-to-help-outsource-it-work-draws-criticism-scrutiny.

29. The motives of firms feature in points-based systems, too. If Canadian employers stop wanting to hire chemical engineers, for example, it is likely that inflows of these workers will dwindle. What makes the employer-based system hyperefficient, for better or for worse, is that it is not conducted within a labor market but instead through direct employer hiring.

30. Sari Kerr, William Kerr, and William Lincoln, "Skilled Immigration and the Employment Structures of U.S. Firms," *Journal of Labor Economics* 33, no. S1 (pt. 2, July 2015): S109–S145; Anirban Ghosh, Anna Maria Mayda, and Francesc Ortega, "The Impact of Skilled Migration on Firm-Level Productivity: An Investigation of Publicly Traded U.S. Firms" (Discussion Paper No. 8684, Institute for the Study of Labor, Bonn, Germany, 2017).

31. Similarly, the reduction of H-1B visas in fiscal year 2004 did not lead to an increase in hiring of native workers at for-profit firms that subsequently faced limits on H-1B employment compared to nonprofit institutions that were unaffected. Anna Maria Mayda, Francesc Ortega, Giovanni Peri, Kevin Shih, and Chad Sparber, "The Effect of the H-1B Quota on Employment and Selection of Foreign-Born Labor" (Working Paper No. 23902, National Bureau of Economics Research, Cambridge, MA, 2017).

32. Kirk Doran, Alex Gelber, and Adam Isen, "The Effects of High-Skilled Immigration Policy on Firms: Evidence from Visa Lotteries" (Working Paper No. 20668, National Bureau of Economics Research, Cambridge, MA, 2015).

33. Norman Matloff, "On the Need for Reform of the H-1B Non-Immigrant Work Visa in Computer-Related Occupations," *University of Michigan Journal of Law Reform* 36, no. 4 (Summer 2003): 815–914.

34. "Bill Gates Asks Senate for Infinite Number of H 1B Visas."

35. William Kerr, "U.S. High-Skilled Immigration, Innovation, and Entrepreneurship: Empirical Approaches and Evidence," in *The International Mobility of Talent and Innovation: New Evidence and Policy Implications,* ed. Carsten Fink and Ernest Miguelez (Cambridge: Cambridge University Press, 2017), 193–221.

36. Hire F-1 Students.

37. Mike Rogoway, "Intel Layoffs Skew Older, Spotlighting Plight of Aging Workers," *Oregonian,* June 6, 2016, http://www.oregonlive.com/silicon-forest/index.ssf/2016/06/intel_layoffs_skew_older_spotl.html.

38. "We're Not Too Old For This," *Bloomberg Businessweek,* September 12–18, 2016.

39. Kerr, Kerr and Lincoln, "Employment Structures of U.S. Firms."

40. Giovanni Peri and Chad Sparber, "Highly-Educated Immigrants and Native Occupational Choice," *Industrial Relations* 50, no. 3 (July 2011): 385–411.

Chapter 5

1. The growth in foreign students is primarily due to emerging nations producing ever-larger total numbers of students, with China catching up from the suppression under Mao that ended in the late 1970s. John Bound, Sarah Turner, and Patrick Walsh, "Internationalization of U.S. Doctorate Education," in *Science and Engineering Careers in the United States: An Analysis of Markets and Employment,* ed. Richard Freeman and Daniel Goroff (Chicago: University of Chicago Press, 2009), 59–97. India also lifted in 1996 its earlier $500 cap on foreign exchange that its citizens could take from the country, which had previously limited students and tourism.

2. Institute of International Education, *2017 Open Doors Report on International Educational Exchange* (New York: Institute of International Education, 2017); and "How International Students Are Changing U.S. Colleges," WSJ Graphics, *Wall Street Journal,* http://graphics.wsj.com/international-students/.

3. British Council, "The Shape of Things to Come: Higher Education Global Trends and Emerging Opportunities to 2020," *Going Global Report,* 2012, https://www.britishcouncil.org/sites/default/files/the_shape_of_things_to_come_-_higher_education_global_trends_and_emerging_opportunities_to_2020.pdf; and Line Verbik and Veronica Lasanowski, *International Student*

Mobility: Patterns and Trends (London: Observatory on Borderless Higher Education, 2007), http://www.obhe.ac.uk/documents/2007/Reports/International _Student_Mobility_Patterns_and_Trends.

4. The inflow-to-outflow ratio for U.S. inventors is 17:1 in the WIPO data and 27:1 among Nobel Prize winners, but 3:1 for student flows.

5. These eight schools were Arizona State University, Columbia University, New York University, Northeastern University, Purdue University West Lafayette, University of California Los Angeles, University of Illinois Urbana–Champaign, and University of Southern California.

6. "NAFSA International Student Economic Value Tool," NAFSA: Association of International Educators and Commerce Department, http://www .nafsa.org/Policy_and_Advocacy/Policy_Resources/Policy_Trends_and_Data/ NAFSA_International_Student_Economic_Value_Tool/.

7. Naomi Hausman, "University Innovation and Local Economic Growth" (unpublished manuscript, 2017).

8. Tamar Lewin, "Study: Foreign Students Added to Economy," *New York Times*, November 12, 2007, http://www.nytimes.com/2007/11/12/us/ 12international.html.

9. STEM majors account for about one-third of U.S. undergraduates. Pia Orrenius and Madeline Zavodny, "Does Immigration Affect Whether US Natives Major in Science and Engineering?" *Journal of Labor Economics* 33, no. S1 (pt. 2, July 2015): S79–S108.

10. One leading hypothesis is that women are more likely to choose a STEM major after beginning their studies rather than having decided on it beforehand, and thus may be more easily swayed to follow another path. Immigration does not affect the number of women pursuing graduate STEM degrees. Yu Xie and Kimberlee Shauman, *Women in Science: Career Processes and Outcomes* (Cambridge, MA: Harvard University Press, 2003).

11. About 45 percent of new H-1B visas issued in 2014 went to applicants already present in the U.S., many of whom were foreign students making school-to-work transitions.

12. Takao Kato and Chad Sparber, "Quotas and Quality: The Effect of H-1B Visa Restrictions on the Pool of Prospective Undergraduate Students from Abroad," *Review of Economics and Statistics* 95, no. 1 (March 2013): 109–26; and Kevin Shih, "Labor Market Openness, H-1B Visa Policy, and the Scale of International Student Enrollment in the United States," *Economic Inquiry* 54, no. 1 (2016): 121–38. See also Mark Rosenzweig, Douglas Irwin, and Jeffrey Williamson, "Global Wage Differences and International Student Flows [with Comments and Discussion]," *Brookings Trade Forum* (2006): 57–86.

13. A 2017 survey finds 59 percent of prospective business school students intend to apply to a program outside of their country of residence, with future

employment opportunities being a top reason. Graduate Management Admission Council, *mba.com Prospective Students Survey Report 2017* (Reston, VA: Graduate Management Admission Council, 2017).

14. The OPT program is open to students on an F visa who have completed at least nine months' study toward their degree. The OPT can give a student a head start on employment before an H-1B visa starts, or it can serve as a buffer while entering H-1B lotteries.

15. Institute of International Education, "2017 Open Doors Report."

16. John Bound, Murat Demirci, Gaurav Khanna, and Sarah Turner, "Finishing Degrees and Finding Jobs: U.S. Higher Education and the Flow of Foreign IT Workers," *Innovation Policy and the Economy* 15, no. 1 (2015): 27–72.

17. More broadly, the economics of temporary migrations differ substantially from permanent ones. Christian Dustmann and Joseph-Simon Görlach, "The Economics of Temporary Migrations," *Journal of Economic Literature* 54, no. 1 (January 2016): 98–136.

18. National Science Board, *Science and Engineering Indicators 2016* (Arlington, VA: National Science Foundation, 2016), 2–7.

19. Gnanaraj Chellaraj, Keith Maskus, and Aaditya Mattoo, "The Contribution of Skilled Immigrations and International Graduate Students to U.S. Innovation," *Review of International Economics* 16, no. 3 (August 2008): 444–62; Shiferaw Gurmu, Grant Black, and Paula Stephan, "The Knowledge Production Function for University Patenting," *Economic Inquiry* 48, no. 1 (January 2010): 192–213; Patrick Gaulé and Mario Piacentini, "Chinese Graduate Students and U.S. Scientific Productivity," *Review of Economics and Statistics* 95, no. 2 (May 2013): 698–701; Eric Stuen, Ahmed Mobarak, and Keith Maskus, "Skilled Immigration and Innovation: Evidence from Enrollment Fluctuations in U.S. Doctoral Programs," *Economic Journal* 122, no. 565 (December 2012): 1143–76; Paula Stephan, "The I's Have It: Immigration and Innovation, the Perspective from Academe," *Innovation Policy and the Economy* 10, no. 1 (2010): 83–128; and Jeffrey Grogger and Gordon Hanson, "Attracting Talent: Location Choices of Foreign-Born PhDs in the United States," *Journal of Labor Economics* 33, no. S1 (pt. 2, July 2015): S5–S38.

20. National Science Board, *Science and Engineering Indicators*, 5–68.

21. The strength of these personal interactions is evident in the impact on collaborators when a superstar researcher unexpectedly dies. Pierre Azoulay, Joshua Graff Zivin, and Jialan Wang, "Superstar Extinction," *Quarterly Journal of Economics* 125, no. 2 (May 2010): 549–89.

22. George Borjas and Kirk Doran, "The Collapse of the Soviet Union and the Productivity of American Mathematicians," *Quarterly Journal of Economics* 127, no. 3 (August 2012): 1143–1203; George Borjas and Kirk Doran, "Cognitive Mobility: Native Responses to Supply Shocks in the Space of Ideas," *Journal of Labor Economics* 33, no. S1 (2015): S109–S145.

23. Another study documented better access for American researchers to mathematics knowledge developed in the Soviet Union following this Russian immigration. Ina Ganguli, "Immigration and Ideas: What Did Russian Scientists 'Bring' to the United States?" *Journal of Labor Economics* 33, no. S1 (pt. 2, July 2015): S257–S288.

24. George Borjas, "Immigration in High-Skill Labor Markets: The Impact of Foreign Students on the Earnings of Doctorates" (Working Paper No. 12085, National Bureau of Economic Research, Cambridge, MA, 2006).

25. Scott Stern, "Do Scientists Pay to be Scientists?" *Management Science* 50, no. 6 (June 2004): 835–53.

26. Petra Moser, Alessandra Voena, and Fabian Waldinger, "German Jewish Émigrés and U.S. Invention," *American Economic Review* 104, no. 10 (October 2014): 3222–55.

27. This phenomenon is called Baumol's cost disease, after William Baumol, who first discerned it in the arts.

28. National Science Board, *Science and Engineering Indicators*, 2–4; and "Higher Education: State Funding Trends and Policies on Affordability," Report to the Chairman, Committee on Health, Education, Labor, and Pensions, United States Senate (Report GAO-15-151, U.S. Government Accountability Office, Washington, DC, 2014).

29. Janet Napolitano to Elaine Howle (California State auditor), public letter, March 8, 2016, http://universityofcalifornia.edu/sites/default/files/Howle -Elaine-030816.pdf; and John Bound, Breno Braga, Gaurav Khanna, and Sarah Turner, "A Passage to America: University Funding and International Students" (Working Paper No. 22981, National Bureau of Economic Research, Cambridge, MA, 2016).

30. Kevin Shih, "Do International Students Crowd-Out or Cross-Subsidize Americans in Higher Education?" *Journal of Public Economics* 156 (2017): 170–84.

31. "University of Virginia Overview," CollegeData, http://www .collegedata.com/cs/data/college/college_pg01_tmpl.jhtml?schoolId=1571; "E02: Fall Headcount Enrollment (1992 thru Current Year)," SCHEV Research, State Council of Higher Education for Virginia, http://research.schev.edu/ enrollment/E2_Report.asp.

32. Bound et al., "Passage to America."

33. "International Students at Harvard," Harvard Worldwide, http:// worldwide.harvard.edu/node/1826; Kelli Bird and Sarah Turner, "Colleges in the United States: Foreign Student Demand and Higher Education Supply in the U.S." (EdPolicyWorks Working Paper Series No. 23, University of Virginia, Charlottesville, 2014).

34. Fort Hayes State University Virtual College, http://www.fhsu.edu/virtual college/.

35. National Science Board, *Science and Engineering Indicators*, 5–80.

36. Paula Stephan, Giuseppe Scellato, and Chiara Franzoni, "International Competition for PhDs and Postdoctoral Scholars: What Does (and Does Not) Matter," *Innovation Policy and the Economy* 15, no. 1 (2015): 73–113.

37. "Global Entrepreneur-in-Residence Program," Venture Development Center, University of Massachusetts at Boston, http://blogs.umb.edu/vdc/geir/; and Natasha Mascarenhas, "UMass Supports an H-1B Loophole for Entrepreneurs," *BostInno, AmericanInno*, April 27, 2017, http://bostinno.streetwise.co/2017/04/27/university-of-massachusetts-geir-program-supports-foreign-entrepreneurs-through-h-1b-visas/.

38. Catalina Amuedo-Dorantes and Delia Furtado, "Settling for Academia? H-1B Visas and the Career Choices of Foreign-born U.S. Graduates," *Journal of Human Resources* (forthcoming).

Chapter 6

1. The connection of globalization and technology are recently emphasized in Thomas Friedman, *Thank You for Being Late: An Optimist's Guide to Thriving in the Age of Accelerations* (New York: Farrar, Straus & Giroux, 2016).

2. "20th CEO Survey: US Key Findings," 20th CEO Survey, PwC, http://www.pwc.com/gx/en/ceo-agenda/ceosurvey/2017/us.

3. John Micklethwait, "Jeff Immelt on Dealing With Trump and Globalization," *Bloomberg Businessweek*, February 9, 2017, https://www.bloomberg.com/news/articles/2017-02-09/jeff-immelt-on-dealing-with-trump-and-globalization.

4. Micklethwait, "Jeff Immelt." In June 2017, Immelt began the handover of CEO leadership to his successor, John Flannery.

5. Karim Lakhani, Marco Iansiti, and Kerry Herman, "GE and the Industrial Internet," Harvard Business School Case 614-032 (Boston: Harvard Business Publishing, 2015).

6. Jon Chesto, "GE Is Huge, but Its Future Headquarters Will Be Anything But," *Boston Globe*, March 12, 2016, https://www.bostonglobe.com/business/2016/03/11/huge-but-its-future-headquarters-will-anything-but/INqV8GezulQDnQI1tKBxFJ/story.html.

7. Erik Kirschbaum, "German Automakers Who Once Laughed off Elon Musk Are Now Starting to Worry," *Los Angeles Times*, April 19, 2016, http://www.latimes.com/business/autos/la-fi-hy-0419-tesla-germany-20160419-story.html.

8. Zoltan Ban, "Tesla Set to Become Second Biggest Global Carmaker By Market Cap Next Year," *Seeking Alpha*, April 12, 2017, https://seekingalpha.com/article/4062035-tesla-set-become-second-biggest-global-carmaker-market-cap-next-year.

9. Richard Florida has been an influential and long-time observer of talent clusters. His early work, like *Rise of the Creative Class* (2002) and *Cities and the Creative Class* (2007), emphasize connections between technology and talent, and he continues these themes in his *CityLab* blog posts.

10. Moore's precise prediction was that the number of transistors that fit on a standard affordable computer chip—which determines how fast that chip processes information—would double every two years.

11. Marc Andreessen, "Why Software Is Eating the World," Andreessen Horowitz, August 2011, http://a16z.com/2016/08/20/why-software-is-eating-the-world/.

12. Erik Brynjolfsson and Andrew McAfee, *The Second Machine Age: Work, Progress and Prosperity in a Time of Brilliant Technologies* (New York: W. W. Norton & Company, 2014); Alex Salkever and Vivek Wadhwa, *The Driver in the Driverless Car: How Our Technology Choices Will Create the Future* (Oakland, CA: Berrett-Koehler Publishers, 2017).

13. Nicholas Bloom, Charles Jones, John Van Reenen, and Michael Webb, "Are Ideas Getting Harder to Find?" (Working Paper No. 23782, National Bureau of Economic Research, Cambridge, MA, 2017).

14. The Maldives became an independent country in 1965, at the time that Moore's law began. Had its initial population of 102,723 followed Moore's law, the Maldives would be home to 3.5 trillion people today, vaulting it to the sole concern for any company.

15. Jonathan Marino, "Goldman Sachs Is a Tech Company," *Business Insider UK*, April 12, 2015, http://uk.businessinsider.com/goldman-sachs-has-more-engineers-than-facebook-2015-4?r=US&IR=T; and Courtney Connley, "Goldman Sachs is Changing One Key Policy to Attract Tech Talent," CNBC, July 17, 2017, https://www.cnbc.com/2017/07/17/goldman-sachs-is-changing-its-dress-code-to-attract-tech-talent.html.

16. Todd McKinnon, "6 Companies That Give Real Meaning to 'Digital Transformation,'" *Inc.*, January 12, 2017, https://www.inc.com/todd-mckinnon/is-digital-transformation-the-real-deal-these-6-companies-think-so.html.

17. Alyson Shontell, "Jamie Dimon: Silicon Valley Startups Are Coming to Eat Wall Street's Lunch," *Business Insider*, April 10, 2015, http://www.businessinsider.com/jamie-dimon-shareholder-letter-and-silicon-valley-2015-4?r=UK&IR=T.

18. Nathan Allen, "B-Schools with the Most 'Unicorn' Founders," *Poets & Quants*, March 3, 2017, http://poetsandquants.com/2017/03/03/b-schools-unicorn-founders/; Yoree Koh, "Study: Immigrants Founded 51% of U.S. Billion-Dollar Startups," *Digits* (blog), March 17, 2016, https://blogs.wsj

.com/digits/2016/03/17/study-immigrants-founded-51-of-u-s-billion-dollar
-startups/.

19. Ryan Decker, John Haltiwanger, Ron Jarmin, and Javier Miranda, "The
Role of Entrepreneurship in US Job Creating and Economic Dynamism," *Journal of Economic Perspectives* 28, no. 3 (Summer 2014): 3–24.

20. Jorge Guzman and Scott Stern, "The State of American Entrepreneurship: New Estimates of the Quantity and Quality of Entrepreneurship for 15 US
States, 1988–2014" (Working Paper No. 22095, National Bureau of Economic
Research, Cambridge, MA, 2016).

21. "The Global Unicorn Club," CBInsights, https://www.cbinsights.com/
research-unicorn-companies; https://www.cbinsights.com/research-unicorn
-exits.

22. Calculations from Thomson One.

23. Michael Malone, Salim Ismail, Peter Diamandis, and Yuri Van Geest,
*Exponential Organizations: Why New Organizations are Ten Times Better, Faster, and
Cheaper Than Yours (and What to Do About It)* (New York: Diversion Books, 2014).

24. In parallel, new approaches to start-up management promote lean testing and experimentation. Eric Ries, *The Lean Startup: How Today's Entrepreneurs
Use Continuous Innovation to Create Radically Successful Businesses* (New York: Crown
Business Publishing, 2011); and William Kerr, Ramana Nanda, and Matthew
Rhodes-Kropf, "Entrepreneurship as Experimentation," *Journal of Economic Perspectives* 28, no. 3 (Summer 2014): 25–48.

25. Robert Lucas, "On the Size Distribution of Business Firms," *Bell Journal
of Economics* 9, no. 2 (Autumn 1978): 508–23.

26. Craig Smith, "98 Amazing Airbnb Statistics and Facts (July 2017),"
Digital Company Statistics, DMR, http://expandedramblings.com/index.php/
airbnb-statistics/5/.

27. Marriott International (2018), Form 10-K, http://investor.shareholder
.com/MAR/secfiling.cfm?filingID=1628280-18-1756&CIK=1048286.

28. William Kerr, "Entrepreneurship Reading: Launching Global Ventures," Core Curriculum Readings Series, Harvard Business Publishing 5277
(Boston: Harvard Business Publishing, 2015).

29. Fred Wilson, "Airbnb," AVC, March 16, 2011, http://www.avc.com/
a_vc/2011/03/airbnb.html.

30. "The Anti-Portfolio," Bessemer Venture Partners, http://www.bvp
.com/portfolio/antiportfolio.

31. Technology trends can compete with each other. Communication advances often push firms to centralize decision making, as leaders can better influence events throughout a distributed company and receive feedback in real time.
Advances in information access often work in the opposite direction, and today

an iPad can deliver abundant data to any employee in real time. Nicholas Bloom, Luis Garicano, Raffaella Sadun, and John Van Reenen, "The Distinct Effects of Information Technology and Communication Technology on Firm Organization," *Management Science* 60, no. 12 (December 2014): 2859–85.

32. Clay Christensen, *The Innovator's Dilemma: When New Technologies Cause Great Firms to Fall* (Boston: Harvard Business School Press, 1997); Lynda Applegate and William Kerr, "Leading Breakthrough Innovation in Established Companies," Core Curriculum Readings Series, Harvard Business Publishing 5272 (Boston: Harvard Business Publishing, 2016); Charles O'Reilly and Michael Tushman, *Lead and Disrupt: How to Solve the Innovator's Dilemma* (Palo Alto, CA: Stanford University Press, 2016).

33. Lee Schafer, "ConAgra's Move from Omaha to Chicago Shows That Big Cities Still Reign," *StarTribune*, October 10, 2015, http://www.startribune .com/conagra-s-move-from-omaha-to-chicago-shows-that-big-cities-still-reign/ 331826751/.

34. Barbara Soderlin, "After 'Agonizing Debate,' ConAgra Moving HQ to Chicago, Cutting 1,000 Omaha Jobs," *World Herald*, October 2, 2015, http://www.omaha.com/money/after-agonizing-debate-conagra-moving-hq -to-chicago-cutting-omaha/article_40ef4148-6798-11e5-8f93-9bea8a0abeb2. html.

35. Patti Waldmeir, "Companies Follow Millennials to Downtown Chicago," *Financial Times*, December 16, 2016, https://www.ft.com/content/16f45e6a-acf6 -11e6-ba7d-76378e4fef24?mhq5j=e2.

36. Calculations from 2016 American Community Survey using individuals outside of group quarters. Included occupations: 1000: Computer Scientists and Systems Analysts, 1010: Computer Programmers, 1020: Software Developers, Applications and Systems Software, 1050: Computer Support Specialists, 1060: Database Administrators, and 1100: Network and Computer Systems Administrators. Geographical units are Combined Statistical Areas, and Figure 6.2 focuses on those with more than 1 million population.

37. This trade-off of internal and external linkages is studied in Juan Alcacer and Mercedes Delgado, "Spatial Organization of Firms and Location Choices Through the Value Chain," *Management Science* 62, no. 11 (November 2016): 3213–34.

38. Thomas Gryta, "What's Behind GE's Move From the Connecticut Suburbs to Boston," *Wall Street Journal*, May 15, 2017, https://www.wsj.com/articles/ why-ge-is-moving-from-the-connecticut-suburbs-to-boston-1494987300.

39. One study estimates that the population of young college-educated workers grew 20 percent from 2010 to 2014 for the twenty largest U.S. cities, compared with overall population growth of 5 percent. See Pete Saunders, "The Demographics Behind GE's HQ Move to Boston: Young Talent Is on the Move,"

Forbes, April 19, 2016, https://www.forbes.com/sites/petesaunders1/2016/04/19/business-goes-where-talent-flows/#3a4135734f3e.

40. William Kerr, Federica Gabriel, and Emer Moloney, "Transformation at ING (A): Agile," Harvard Business School Case 818-077 (Boston: Harvard Business Publishing, 2018); and Peter Jacobs and Bart Schlatmann, "ING's Agile Transformation," interview by Deepak Mahadevan, *McKinsey Quarterly* (January 2017), http://www.mckinsey.com/industries/financial-services/our-insights/ings-agile-transformation?cid=other-emi-ttn-mkq-mck-oth-1704.

41. Rachel Griffith, Rupert Harrison, and John Van Reenen, "How Special Is the Special Relationship? Using the Impact of U.S. R&D Spillovers on U.K. Firms as a Test of Technology Sourcing," *American Economic Review* 96, no. 5 (December 2006): 1859–75.

42. Richard Lester and Michael Piore, *Innovation: The Missing Dimension* (Cambridge, MA: Harvard University Press, 2004); and William Kerr, "Ethnic Scientific Communities and International Technology Diffusion," *Review of Economics and Statistics* 90, no. 3 (August 2008): 518–37.

43. Ufuk Akcigit, William Kerr, and Tom Nicholas, "The Mechanics of Endogenous Innovation and Growth: Evidence from Historical U.S. Patents" (unpublished manuscript, 2017); and Hyejin Youn, Luis Bettencourt, Deborah Strumsky, and Jose Lobo, "Invention as a Combinatorial Process: Evidence from US Patents," *Journal of the Royal Society Interface* 12, no. 106 (May 2015): https://doi.org/10.1098/rsif.2015.0272.

44. CIC occupies three large buildings in the Boston area, as well as labs and community gathering spaces. Basic amenities include printing (regular and 3-D), legal advice, phone and Internet service, on-demand conference spaces, fully stocked kitchens, and month-to-month leases. Its weekly Venture Cafe attracts more than 250 entrepreneurs and tech workers. CIC is currently expanding to other cities globally. See William Kerr, Sari Kerr, and Alexis Brownell, "CIC: Catalyzing Entrepreneurial Ecosystems (A)," Harvard Business School Case 817-126 (Boston: Harvard Business Publishing, 2017).

45. Jeff John Roberts, "Tech Workers Will Get Average of $5,770 Under Final Anti-Poaching Settlement," *Fortune,* September 3, 2015, http://fortune.com/2015/09/03/koh-anti-poach-order/; and Kartikay Mehrohta, "Samsung, LG Accused of Silicon Valley Anti-Poaching Deal," *Bloomberg,* September 12, 2016, https://www.bloomberg.com/news/articles/2016-09-12/samsung-lg-accused-of-silicon-valley-anti-poaching-agreement.

46. Augustin Landier, Vinay Nair, and Julie Wulf, "Trade-offs in Staying Close: Corporate Decision Making and Geographic Dispersion," *Review of Financial Studies* 22, no. 3 (March 2009): 1119–48.

47. Charles Murray, *Coming Apart: The State of White America, 1960-2010* (New York: Crown Forum, 2012).

Chapter 7

1. The material on Rakuten draws from Tsedal Neeley, "Language and Globalization: 'Englishnization' at Rakuten (A)," Harvard Business School Case 412-002 (Boston: Harvard Business Publishing, 2012); Tsedal Neeley, "Global Business Speaks English: Why You Need a Language Strategy Now," *Harvard Business Review* 90, no. 5 (May 2012): 116–24; Tsedal Neeley and Robert Kaplan, "What's Your Language Strategy?" *Harvard Business Review* 92, no. 9 (September 2014): 70–76; and Tsedal Neeley, *The Language of Global Success: How a Common Tongue Transforms Multinational Organizations* (Princeton, NJ: Princeton University Press, 2017). All quotes in the Rakuten account are sourced from Neeley (2012).

2. "Our Strengths," About Us, Rakuten, https://global.rakuten.com/corp/about/strength.html.

3. British Council, "The Shape of Things to Come: Higher Education Global Trends and Emerging Opportunities to 2020," *Going Global Report*, 2012, https://www.britishcouncil.org/sites/default/files/the_shape_of_things _to_come_-_higher_education_global_trends_and_emerging_opportunities_to _2020.pdf.

4. PwC, "20th CEO Survey: US Key Findings," http://www.pwc.com/gx/en/ceo-agenda/ceosurvey/2017/us.

5. Luc Minguet, Eduardo Caride, Takeo Yamaguchi, and Shane Tedjarati, "Voices from the Front Lines," *Harvard Business Review* 92, no. 9 (September 2014): 77–82; Honeywell (2018), Form 10-K, http://investor.honeywell.com/Cache/392131729.pdf.

6. "Starwood Hotels and Resorts to Relocate Global Headquarters to India in March 2015 for Month-Long Immersion," *BusinessWire*, September 30, 2014, http://www.businesswire.com/news/home/20140930005330/en/Starwood -Hotels-Resorts-Relocate-Global-Headquarters-India.

7. Boris Groysberg, Nitin Nohria, and Kerry Herman, "Solvay Group: International Mobility and Managing Expatriates," Harvard Business School Case 409-079 (Boston: Harvard Business Publishing, 2011).

8. Tarun Khanna, Krishna Palepu, and Phillip Andrews, "Haier: Taking a Chinese Company Global in 2011," Harvard Business School Case 712-408 (Boston: Harvard Business Publishing, 2012).

9. In 2016, Haier acquired GE's appliance division. Patti Waldmeir, "China's Haier Pays $5.4bn for GE Appliance Unit," *Financial Times*, January 15, 2016, https://www.ft.com/content/12cea338-bb64-11e5-b151-8e15c9a029fb ?mhq5j=e6.

10. Rebecca Fannin, "China's Tech Giants Are Pouring Billions into US Start-Ups," CNBC, March 9, 2017, http://www.cnbc.com/2017/03/08/chinas -tech-giants-are-pouring-billions-into-us-start-ups.html.

11. Liza Lin, "Tencent Opens U.S. Data Center as American Rivals Face Hurdles in China," *Wall Street Journal,* April 26, 2017, https://www.wsj.com/articles/tencent-expands-its-cloud-computing-services-in-u-s-1493205244; and Michael Hiltzik, "Suspicions Keep Chinese Telecom Firm Huawei Out of U.S. Market," *Los Angeles Times,* December 5, 2014, http://www.latimes.com/business/hiltzik/la-fi-hiltzik-20141207-column.html.

12. Antoine Gara, "M&A Flashback: Rockefeller Center's Japanese Take-over," *Forbes,* July 18, 2017, https://www.forbes.com/sites/antoinegara/2017/07/18/ma-flashback-the-takeover-of-rockefeller-center-capped-a-1980s-frenzy-now-a-new-mania-is-afoot/#630804166331.

13. While knowing how industries perform in the U.S. is useful for Canada, the predictive power is much weaker for less-similar markets. Tarun Khanna, "Contextual Intelligence," *Harvard Business Review* 92, no. 9 (September 2014): 58–68; and Tarun Khanna and Jan Rivkin, "How Well Correlated Is Industry Profitability Across Countries?" *Harvard Business Review* 92, no. 9 (September 2014): 63.

14. Italics in the original. Khanna, Palepu, and Andrews, "Haier."

15. Paul Grol and Christopher Schoch, "IKEA: Culture as Competitive Advantage" (ECCH Collection No. 398-173-1, Chamber of Commerce and Industry, Paris, 1998).

16. Foreign direct investment averaged less than 0.5 percent of world gross domestic product in the early 1990s; over the past decade it fluctuated between 2 percent and 5 percent. World Bank Open Data, "Foreign Direct Investment, Net Inflows (% of GDP)," http://data.worldbank.org/indicator/BX.KLT.DINV.WD.GD.ZS.

17. Tim Hardwick, "Apple Reportedly Running Secret Car Lab in German Capital," MacRumors, April 18, 2014, https://www.macrumors.com/2016/04/18/apple-secret-car-lab-in-german-capital/.

18. In 2013, U.S. companies conducted about 18 percent of their R&D overseas, up from less than 5 percent in the 1980s. The U.S.-based R&D of foreign companies is about the same. Brandon Shackelford and Raymond Wolfe, "U.S. Companies Performed $73 Billion in R&D Outside the United States in 2013" (InfoBrief No. 17-317, National Science Foundation, Arlington, VA, 2017).

19. "Microsoft Research Lab—Asia Site," Microsoft, https://www.microsoft.com/en-us/research/lab/microsoft-research-asia/#.

20. Vijay Govindarajan, Gunjan Bagla, and Avinash Agrawal, "Which U.S. Companies Are Doing the Most R&D in China and India?" *Harvard Business Review Digital,* March 26, 2015, https://hbr.org/2015/03/which-u-s-companies-are-doing-the-most-rd-in-china-and-india.

21. OECD, "How Is the Global Talent Pool Changing (2013, 2030)?" *Education Indicators in Focus* no. 31 (Paris: OECD Publishing, 2015).

22. Chapter 3 used USPTO patents to quantify the ethnic composition of U.S. inventors. These calculations used only inventors residing in America at the time of their work, but the data also record foreign-based inventors. Many USPTO patents only have foreign inventors, such as a team working for Samsung in Korea. The calculations in this section focus on patents where at least one inventor is working in America. "Large companies" are those that filed one thousand or more patents from 1975 to 2014. For smaller companies, the share of patents with a foreign inventor rises from 0.6 percent in 1975 to 7 percent in 2014, and 16 percent of teams are now global.

23. Sari Kerr and William Kerr, "Global Collaborative Patents" (Working Paper No. 21735, National Bureau of Economic Research, Cambridge, MA, 2015).

24. American multinationals use global teams for half of the early work in Europe or Japan, in contrast to 75 percent for developing and emerging economies. These differences dissipate after about seven years of experience. In settings where intellectual property rights are especially weak, the collaborative share remains high for much longer. See Kerr and Kerr, "Global Collaborative Patents"; Lee Branstetter, Guangwei Li, and Francisco Veloso, "The Rise of International Coinvention," in *The Changing Frontier: Rethinking Science and Innovation Policy*, ed. Adam Jaffe and Benjamin Jones (Chicago: University of Chicago Press, 2015), 135–68; and Ernest Miguelez, "Inventor Diasporas and the Internationalization of Technology" (Discussion Paper Series No. 25/14, Centre for Research & Analysis of Migration, London, 2014).

25. C. Fritz Foley and William Kerr, "Ethnic Innovation and U.S. Multinational Firm Activity," *Management Science* 59, no. 7 (July 2013): 1529–44; Prithwiraj Choudhury, "Innovation Outcomes in a Distributed Organization: Intrafirm Mobility and Access to Resources," *Organization Science* 28, no. 2 (March–April 2017): 339–54; Prithwiraj Choudhury, "Return Migration and Geography of Innovation in MNEs: A Natural Experiment of Knowledge Production by Local Workers Reporting to Return Migrants," *Journal of Economic Geography* 16, no. 3 (May 2016): 585–610.

26. This strategy is discussed in William Kerr, "Entrepreneurship Reading: Launching Global Ventures," Core Curriculum Readings Series, Harvard Business Publishing 5277 (Boston: Harvard Business Publishing, 2015); William Kerr and Alexis Brownell, "EverTrue: Mobile Technology Development (A)," Harvard Business School Case 813-122 (Boston: Harvard Business Publishing, 2013).

27. Beam website, at https://suitabletech.com.

28. A resource for managers is Tsedal Neeley, "Global Teams That Work," *Harvard Business Review* 93, no. 10 (October 2015): 74–81.

29. The firm-employee relationship is better at preventing idea theft than external collaborations. Thomas Hellmann and Enrico Perotti, "The Circulation of Ideas in Firms and Markets," *Management Science* 57, no. 10 (October 2011): 1813–26.

30. Larry Huston and Nabil Sakkab, "Connect and Develop: Inside Procter & Gamble's New Model for Innovation," *Harvard Business Review* 84, no. 3 (March 2006): 58–66. Stefan Lindegaard, *The Open Innovation Revolution* (New York: Wiley, 2010).

31. This discussion and case examples draws heavily from Kevin Boudreau, Karim Lakhani, Hila Lifshitz-Assaf, and Michael Tushman. Kevin Boudreau and Karim Lakhani, "Using the Crowd as an Innovation Partner," *Harvard Business Review* 91, no. 4 (April 2013): 61–69.

32. Karim Lakhani, Hila Lifshitz-Assaf, and Michael Tushman, "Open Innovation and Organizational Boundaries: Task Decomposition, Knowledge Distribution and the Locus of Innovation," in *Handbook of Economic Organization: Integrating Economic and Organization Theory,* ed. Anna Grandori (Northampton, MA: Edward Elgar Publishing, 2013), 355–82.

33. Maria Krisette Capati, "10 Indispensable Open Innovation Platforms for Global Corporations," Crowdsourcing Week, December 29, 2015, http://crowdsourcingweek.com/blog/10-indispensable-open-innovation-platforms-global-corporations/.

34. This section draws from William Kerr, "Reaching Beyond Your Organization: Empowering Innovation," Harvard Business School Background Note 817-044 (Boston: Harvard Business Publishing, 2016).

35. Some ATAP projects in 2015: "A look inside Google's secretive ATAP group," YouTube video, posted by The Verge, June 26, 2014, https://www.youtube.com/watch?v=L31JmmjjnEw. Dugan left Google in April 2016, and this account draws from interviews with Dugan while she was leading ATAP. See also Regina Dugan and Kaigham Gabriel, "'Special Forces' Innovation: How DARPA Attacks Problems," *Harvard Business Review* 91, no. 10 (October 2013): 74–84.

36. Accelerators provide intensive instruction, seed funding, networking, and rapid development of ideas for founders, with Y Combinator being a famous example. The large company typically takes a small equity stake.

Chapter 8

1. William Kerr and Alexis Brownell, "NetDragon," Harvard Business School Case 818-042 (Boston: Harvard Business Publishing, 2017).

2. America is rather rare in its taxation of overseas citizens. See Mihir Desai, Devesh Kapur, and John McHale, "Sharing the Spoils: Taxing International Human Capital Flows," *International Tax and Public Finance* 11, no. 5 (September 2004): 663–93.

3. Shulamit Kahn and Megan MacGarvie, "How Important Is U.S. Location for Research in Science?," *Review of Economics and Statistics* 98, no. 2 (May 2016): 397–414.

4. This concept is captured in endogenous growth theory, starting with Paul Romer, "Endogenous Technical Change," *Journal of Political Economy* 98, no. 5 (October 1990): S71–S102; and Phillipe Aghion and Peter Howitt, "A Model of Growth Through Creative Destruction," *Econometrica* 60, no. 2 (March 1992): 323–51.

5. Although this link to global prosperity is impossible to prove empirically, as we can't rerun history with global migration turned off or doubled to see what would happen, the simulations built to make these types of calculations usually find quite large and globally beneficial effects. See Julian di Giovanni, Andrei Levchenko, and Francesc Ortega, "A Global View of Cross-Border Migration," *Journal of the European Economic Association* 31, no. 1 (February 2015): 168–202.

6. Nicholas Bloom, Benn Eifert, Aprajit Mahajan, David McKenzie, and John Roberts, "Does Management Matter? Evidence from India," *Quarterly Journal of Economics* 128, no. 1 (February 2013): 1–51. The many forces pushing the world closer to a global frontier are emphasized by Thomas Friedman, *The World Is Flat: A Brief History of the Twenty-First Century* (New York: Farrar, Straus & Giroux, 2005).

7. A review of this literature is Gerald Carlino and William Kerr, "Agglomeration and Innovation," *Handbook of Regional and Urban Economics*, ed. Gilles Duranton, J. Vernon Henderson, and William Strange (Oxford: North-Holland, 2015), 5:349–404.

8. Daron Acemoglu and Fabrizio Zilibotti, "Productivity Differences," *Quarterly Journal of Economics* 116, no. 2 (May 2001): 563–606; and Ben Jones, "The Human Capital Stock: A Generalized Approach," *American Economic Review* 104, no. 11 (November 2014): 3572–77.

9. GDP per capita levels from 2015: America, $55,837; Korea, $27,221; Mexico, $9,009; and India, $1,581.

10. María Eugenia Aubet, *The Phoenicians and the West: Politics, Colonies and Trade* (Cambridge: Cambridge University Press, 2001).

11. James Rauch, "Business and Social Networks in International Trade," *Journal of Economic Literature* 39, no. 4 (December 2001): 1177–203; James Rauch, "Networks Versus Markets in International Trade," *Journal of International Economics* 48, no. 1 (June 1999): 7–35; and William Kerr and Dan Isenberg, "Take

Advantage of Your Diaspora Network," Harvard Business School Background Note 808-029 (Boston: Harvard Business Publishing, 2008).

12. AnnaLee Saxenian, with Yasuyuki Motoyama and Xiaohong Quan, *Local and Global Networks of Immigrant Professionals in Silicon Valley* (San Francisco: Public Policy Institute of California, 2002); and AnnaLee Saxenian, *The New Argonauts: Regional Advantage in a Global Economy* (Cambridge, MA: Harvard University Press, 2006).

13. William Kerr, "Ethnic Scientific Communities and International Technology Diffusion," *Review of Economics and Statistics* 90, no. 3 (August 2008): 518–37; Ajay Agrawal, Devesh Kapur, John McHale, and Alex Oettl, "Brain Drain or Brain Bank? The Impact of Skilled Emigration on Poor-Country Innovation," *Journal of Urban Economics* 69, no. 1 (January 2011): 43–55; and Ernest Miguelez, "Inventor Diasporas and the Internationalization of Technology" (Discussion Paper Series 25/14, Centre for Research & Analysis of Migration, London, 2014).

14. Integration with the American tech frontier is visible in the exports of a nation. William Kerr, "Heterogeneous Technology Diffusion and Ricardian Trade Patterns," *World Bank Economic Review* 32, no. 1 (February 2018): 163–82. See also Richard Freeman, "One Ring to Rule Them All? Globalization of Knowledge and Knowledge Creation," in *Nordic Economic Policy Review: Globalization, Labor Market Institutions and Wage Structure*, ed. Erling Barth and Kalle Moene (Copenhagen: Nordic Council of Ministers, 2013), 11–33.

15. Antonio Spilimbergo, "Democracy and Foreign Education," *American Economic Review* 99, no. 1 (March 2009): 528–43.

16. This section draws from William Kerr, "Entrepreneurship Reading: Launching Global Ventures," Core Curriculum Readings Series, Harvard Business Publishing 5277 (Boston: Harvard Business Publishing, 2015); and William Kerr, "Harnessing the Best of Globalization," *MIT Sloan Management Review* 58, no. 1 (Fall 2016): 59–67.

17. Rocket Internet exploits these diffusion lags, efficiently matching ideas from talent clusters with the best spots in the world to implement them. Rocket has frequently sold its cloned businesses to the companies it originally copied them from, as the acquirer decides it is better purchasing the clone than rebuilding the localized elements from scratch.

18. A powerful example from a traditional sector is Alvogen, a generic pharmaceutical company based in Iceland. Founder Robert Wessman designed Alvogen from its start in 2009 to be a global company that capitalized on the absence of leading drugs in many countries. Alvogen now spans thirty-five nations. Dan Isenberg and William Kerr, "Alvogen," Harvard Business School Case 816-064 (Boston: Harvard Business Publishing, 2017).

19. Ian Thomsen, "Show Time! Is Kobe Bryant the Second Coming of Magic or Michael? The Playoffs Are the Place to Find Out If He's Truly a Prodigy or Merely a Creature of Hype," *Sports Illustrated*, April 27, 1998, 43–50, https://www.si.com/vault/issue/703053/49/2; and AZ Quotes, January 12, 2018, http://www.azquotes.com/quote/561497.

20. John Gibson and David McKenzie, "The Microeconomic Determinants of Emigration and Return Migration of the Best and Brightest: Evidence from the Pacific," *Journal of Development Economics* 95, no. 1 (May 2011): 18–29.

21. Satish Chand and Michael Clemens, "Skilled Emigration and Skill Creation: A Quasi-Experiment" (Working Paper No. 152, Center for Global Development, Washington, DC, 2008).

22. The biggest gains accrue to countries with low average education levels and initial migration rates. Although many African and Central American countries do not benefit, positive gains in key emerging countries like China, India, Indonesia, and Brazil result in an overall gain for the developing world. Frederic Docquier and Hillel Rapoport, "Globalization, Brain Drain, and Development," *Journal of Economic Literature* 50, no. 3 (September 2012): 681–730.

23. Howard Stevenson and Shirley Spence, "Paresh Patel: Building a Life in the Context of Global Business—October 2007," Harvard Business School Case 809-045 (Boston: Harvard Business Publishing, 2009).

24. "In Fintech, China Shows the Way," *The Economist*, February 25, 2017, https://www.economist.com/news/finance-and-economics/21717393 -advanced-technology-backward-banks-and-soaring-wealth-make-china-leader.

25. Chang-Tai Hsieh, Erik Hurst, Chad Jones, and Pete Klenow, "The Allocation of Talent and U.S. Economic Growth" (Working Paper No. 18693, National Bureau of Economics Research, Cambridge, MA, 2013).

26. Richard Florida has strongly emphasized these features in his work on the creative class, connecting innovation to local diversity, bohemian cultures, and openness to sexual orientations, in *Cities and the Creative Class* (New York: Routledge, 2005). Recent tabulations of U.S. gaps are in Paul Gompers and Sophie Wang, "Diversity in Innovation" (Working Paper No. 17-067, Harvard Business School, Boston, MA, 2017).

27. John Kao, "Tapping the World's Innovation Hot Spots," *Harvard Business Review* 87, no. 3 (March 2009): 109–14.

28. Sari Kerr, William Kerr, Çaglar Özden, and Christopher Parsons, "Global Talent Flows," *Journal of Economic Perspectives* 30, no. 4 (Fall 2016): 83–106.

29. The employer-based immigration systems used in many developing countries make the migration of talent outside of firms difficult to accomplish, just as in America. Another important factor is whether a country provides a

reasonable pathway to permanent residency and possibly citizenship, which is exceptionally hard in many nations.

30. Dan Wang, "Activating Cross-Border Brokerage: Inter-Organizational Knowledge Transfer Through Skilled Return Migration," *Administrative Science Quarterly* 60, no. 1 (March 2015): 133–76.

31. Martin Kenney, Dan Breznitz, and Michael Murphree, "Coming Back Home After the Sun Rises: Returnee Entrepreneurs and Growth of High Tech Industries," *Research Policy* 42, no. 2 (March 2013): 391–407.

32. Interview with Holmström on December 11, 2017.

33. "About Us," Aaltoes, https://aaltoes.com/#about.

34. Malaysia's efforts in this regard are described in William Kerr, Danielle Li, Mathis Wagner, and Alexis Brownell, "TalentCorp Malaysia and the Returning Expert Programme," Harvard Business School Case 817-092 (Boston: Harvard Business Publishing, 2017).

35. Sources include Agence France-Presse, "Narendra Modi Unveils Bid to Make India the HR Capital of the World," *The Guardian,* July 6, 2015, https://www.theguardian.com/world/2015/jul/16/narendra-modi-unveils-bid-to-make-india-the-hr-capital-of-the-world; Narendra Modi, PM's Address at the Inauguration of the 14th Pravasi Bharatiya Divas Convention in Bengaluru, January 8, 2017, PMIndia, transcript and video, 39:58, http://www.pmindia.gov.in/en/news_updates/pms-address-at-the-inauguration-of-the-14th-pravasi-bharatiya-divas-convention-in-bengaluru; and Indo-Asian News Service, "PM Narendra Modi Asks Diaspora To First Develop India," NDTV, January 8, 2017, https://www.ndtv.com/india-news/pm-modi-asks-diaspora-to-first-develop-india-1646376. Earlier, India reviewed in detail in its connection and strategy toward diaspora: High Level Committee on the Indian Diaspora, *The Indian Diaspora,* December 19, 2001, http://indiandiaspora.nic.in/contents.htm.

36. Deep and lively accounts of these linkages for China and India are included in Robert Guest, *Borderless Economics: Chinese Sea Turtles, Indian Fridges and the New Fruits of Global Capitalism* (New York: St. Martin's Griffin, 2011).

37. Docquier and Rapoport, "Globalization, Brain Drain, and Development." See also the measures of global inequality in Branko Milanovic, *Global Inequality: A New Approach for the Age of Globalization* (Cambridge, MA: Harvard University Press, 2016).

Chapter 9

1. The quotes used in the accounts of the Google bus protests draw from Clayton Rose, Allison Ciechanover, and Kunai Modi, "San Francisco, 2015 #tech #inequality," Harvard Business School Case 315-076 (Boston: Harvard Business Publishing, 2015); and Nicholas Bloom, "Corporations in the Age of

Inequality," *Harvard Business Review* 95, no. 2 (March 2017): https://hbr.org/cover-story/2017/03/corporations-in-the-age-of-inequality.

2. "The Boom Interview: Rebecca Solnit," *Boom California* 4, no. 2 (Summer 2014): https://boomcalifornia.com/2014/06/19/the-boom-interview-rebecca-solnit/.

3. Raj Chetty, Nathaniel Hendren, Patrick Kline, and Emmanuel Saez, "Where Is the Land of Economic Opportunity? The Geography of Intergenerational Mobility in the United States," *Quarterly Journal of Economics* 129, no. 4 (November 2014): 1553–1623. See also Richard Florida, *The New Urban Crisis: How Our Cities Are Increasing Inequality, Deepening Segregation, and Failing the Middle Class and What We Can Do About It* (New York: Perseus Books, 2017). Florida considers the connection of U.S. talent clusters with inequality and the formation of global cities of great wealth.

4. Philip Bump, "The 25 Top Hedge Fund Managers Earn More Than All Kindergarten Teachers Combined," *Washington Post*, May 10, 2016, https://www.washingtonpost.com/news/the-fix/wp/2015/05/12/the-top-25-hedge-fund-managers-earn-more-than-all-kindergarten-teachers-combined/?utm_term=.aba0e43d0971.

5. Alexander Bell, Raj Chetty, Xavier Jaravel, Neviana Petkova, and John van Reenen, "Who Becomes an Inventor in America? The Importance of Exposure to Innovation" (Working Paper No. 24062, National Bureau of Economic Research, Cambridge, MA, 2017).

6. Inequality may be necessary for the U.S. to hold its leading edge for innovation, as in Daron Acemoglu, James Robinson, and Thierry Verdier, "Asymmetric Growth and Institutions in an Interdependent World," *Journal of Political Economy* 125, no. 5 (October 2017): 1245–1305. A broader literature is inconclusive on how inequality relates to innovation and economic growth. At the state level, the link is better established: Philippe Aghion, Ufuk Akcigit, Antonin Bergeaud, Richard Blundell, and David Hémous, "Top Income Inequality" (Working Paper No. 21247, National Bureau of Economic Research, Cambridge, MA, 2015).

7. Calculations from the 2016 American Community Survey. Measures of inequality like the Gini index or the 90th/50th percentile earnings ratio only slightly change when removing college-educated immigrants from the sample.

8. John Bound, Gaurav Khanna, and Nicolas Morales, "Understanding the Economic Impact of the H-1B Program on the U.S." (Working Paper No. 23153, National Bureau of Economic Research, Cambridge, MA, 2017).

9. One study estimates each robot replaces six human workers. Daron Acemoglu and Pascual Restrepo, "Robots and Jobs: Evidence from US Labor Market" (Working Paper No. 23285, National Bureau of Economic Research, Cambridge, MA, 2017); International Federation of Robotics, "World Robot-

ics Report 2016," press release, September 29, 2016, https://ifr.org/ifr-press -releases/news/world-robotics-report-2016; and PwC, "20th CEO Survey: US Key Findings," http://www.pwc.com/gx/en/ceo-agenda/ceosurvey/2017/us.

10. Founded in 1862, Long-Stanton originally produced private currency and has continually reinvented itself toward new product areas, ranging from precision valves to brake parts for Boeing and Airbus. They got back into pseudocurrency with their "Indecision 2016" coin, featuring Trump and Clinton on opposing sides for those having trouble on election eve.

11. David Autor, "Why Are There Still So Many Jobs? The History and Future of Workplace Automation," *Journal of Economic Perspectives* 29, no. 3 (Summer 2015): 3–30.

12. Enrico Moretti, *The New Geography of Jobs* (Boston: Houghton Mifflin Harcourt, 2012).

13. Nir Jaimovich and Henry Siu, "High-Skilled Immigration, STEM Employment, and Non-Routine-Biased Technical Change," in *High-Skilled Migration to the United States and Its Economic Consequences*, ed. Gordon Hanson, William Kerr, and Sarah Turner (Chicago: University of Chicago Press, 2018); and Michael Waugh, "Firm Dynamics and Immigration: The Case of High-Skilled Immigration," in *High-Skilled Migration to the United States and Its Economic Consequences*, ed. Gordon Hanson, William Kerr, and Sarah Turner (Chicago: University of Chicago Press, 2018).

14. China's share of U.S. imports grew from 5 percent in 1991 to 23 percent in 2011. Daron Acemoglu, David Autor, David Dorn, Gordon Hanson, and Brendan Price, "Import Competition and the Great U.S. Employment Sag of the 2000s," *Journal of Labor Economics* 34, no. S1 (pt. 2, January 2016): 141–98.

15. James Rauch and Vitor Trindade, "Ethnic Chinese Networks in International Trade," *Review of Economics and Statistics* 84, no. 1 (February 2002): 116–30.

16. This section draws from *Hearing on The Impact of High-Skilled Immigration on U.S. Workers, Before the Subcommittee on Immigration and the National Interest,* 114th Cong. (2016) (testimony of Leo Perrero, former Disney IT engineer), https:// www.judiciary.senate.gov/imo/media/doc/02-25-16%20Perrero%20Testimony .pdf and https://www.judiciary.senate.gov/meetings/the-impact-of-high-skilled -immigration-on-us-workers; Julia Preston, "Pink Slips at Disney: But First, Training Foreign Replacements," *New York Times,* June 3, 2015, https://www .nytimes.com/2015/06/04/us/last-task-after-layoff-at-disney-train-foreign -replacements.html?mcubz=2; along with related news articles.

17. "H-1B Visa: Won't Allow US Workers to be Replaced, says Donald Trump," Livemint, http://www.livemint.com/Politics/w7hBow997FO1RKLFC l8z2N/H1B-visa-Wont-allow-US-workers-to-be-replaced-says-Donal.html.

18. Ron Hira has led this criticism, as in Ron Hira and Anil Hira, *Outsourcing America* (New York: AMACOM, 2005); and Ron Hira, "The H-1B and L-1 Visa

Programs: Out of Control," (Briefing Paper, Economic Policy Institute, Washington, DC, 2010).

19. Sari Kerr and William Kerr, "Immigration and Employer Transitions for STEM Workers," *American Economic Review* 103, no. 3 (May 2013): 193–97.

20. Matthew Slaughter, "IT Services, Immigration and American Economic Strength" (ACAlliance White Paper, Washington, DC, 2015).

21. If dividends are issued, shareholders may spend their distributions and thereby generate employment demand, but the high savings rates of many wealthy investors slow this process.

22. Pew Research Center, "The State of American Jobs," October 6, 2016, http://www.pewsocialtrends.org/2016/10/06/the-state-of-american-jobs/. The phrasing of the reported poll question is biased because it isolates outbound outsourcing from its inbound counterpart, but any form of the question would measure deep worries.

23. Alan Blinder and Alan Krueger, "Alternative Measures of Offshorability: A Survey Approach," *Journal of Labor Economics* 31, no. S1 (pt. 2, April 2013): S97–S127.

24. Karthik Ramanna and Sugata Roychowdhury, "Elections and Discretionary Accruals: Evidence from 2004," *Journal of Accounting Research* 48, no. 2 (May 2010): 445–75.

25. Caroline Davies, "Software Developer Bob Outsources Own Job and Whiles Away Shifts on Cat Videos," *The Guardian,* January 16, 2013, https://www.theguardian.com/world/2013/jan/16/software-developer-outsources-own-job; and Steven Poole, "Programmer Bob Was a Model Modern Employee," *Sydney Morning Herald,* January 18, 2013, http://www.smh.com.au/technology/technology-news/programmer-bob-was-a-model-modern-employee-20130117-2cx2x.html.

26. A strong piece describing these challenges is Steven Pearlstein, "Outsourcing: What's the True Impact? Counting Jobs Is Only Part of the Answer," *Washington Post,* July 1, 2012, https://www.washingtonpost.com/business/economy/outsourcings-net-effect-on-us-jobs-still-an-open-ended-question/2012/07/01/gJQAs1szGW_story.html?utm_term=.39e4390e49b3.

27. Avraham Ebenstein, Ann Harrison, and Margaret McMillan, "Why Are American Workers Getting Poorer? China, Trade and Offshoring" (Working Paper No. 21027, National Bureau of Economic Research, Cambridge, MA, 2015); Runjuan Liu and Daniel Trefler, "A Sorted Tale of Globalization: White Collar Jobs and the Rise of Service Offshoring" (Working Paper No. 17559, National Bureau of Economic Research, Cambridge, MA, 2011). A longer review is David Hummels, Jakob Munch, and Chong Xiang, "Offshoring and Labor Markets" (Working Paper No. 22041, National Bureau of Economic Research, Cambridge, MA, 2016). Further inquiry may find the results understated, as

economists keep revising upward their estimations of consequences, with some initial predictions even arguing no employment impacts.

28. Gary Pisano and Willy Shih, *Producing Prosperity: Why America Needs a Manufacturing Renaissance* (Boston: Harvard Business Publishing, 2012). See also Andy Grove's op-ed "How America Can Create Jobs," *Bloomberg Businessweek,* July 1, 2010, https://www.bloomberg.com/news/articles/2010-07-01/andy -grove-how-america-can-create-jobs.

29. Moretti, *New Geography of Jobs.*

30. Much of the historical narrative around the evolving social contract pulls from Rick Wartzman, *The End of Loyalty: The Rise and Fall of Good Jobs in America* (New York: Public Affairs, 2017), which follows Coca-Cola, General Electric, General Motors, and Kodak in rich historical detail.

31. Andrei Shleifer and Lawrence Summers, "Breaches of Trust in Hostile Takeovers," in *Corporate Takeovers: Causes and Consequences*, ed. Alan Auerbach (Chicago: University of Chicago Press, 1988), 33–56.

32. David Floyd, "CEO-to-Worker Pay Ratio Just 276 to One Last Year," Investopedia, August 15, 2016, http://www.investopedia.com/news/ceotoworker-pay-ratio-just-276-one-last-year/. Although America's ratio is quite high, it exceeds 100 in many other nations as well: Wei Lu and Anders Melin, "The Best and Worst Countries to Be a Rich CEO," *Bloomberg*, November 16, 2016, https://www.bloomberg.com/news/articles/2016-11-16/ranking-where -to-work-to-be-a-rich-ceo-or-richer-than-neighbors.

33. Marianne Bertrand and Sendhil Mullainathan, "Are CEOs Rewarded for Luck? The Ones Without Principles Are," *Quarterly Journal of Economics* 116, no. 3 (August 2001): 901–32.

34. Nathaniel Cahners Hindman, "The 10 Highest-Paid CEOs Who Laid Off the Most Workers: Institute for Policy Studies," *Huffington Post,* September 1, 2010, http://www.huffingtonpost.com/2010/09/01/ceo-pay-layoffs_n_701908 .html; Kevin Hallock, "CEO Pay and Layoffs," *Worldatwork Workspan,* June 2013, https://www.ilr.cornell.edu/sites/ilr.cornell.edu/files/workspan/June -2013-Research-for-the-Real-World_0.pdf; and Roger Martin, "We Can't Talk About Inequality Without Talking About Talent," *Harvard Business Review Digital*, September 23, 2014, https://hbr.org/2014/09/we-cant-talk-about-inequality -without-talking-about-talent.

35. Sebastian Blanco, "Elon Musk: At Tesla, 'You're Choosing to Be the Equivalent of Special Forces,'" *Autoblog*, September 6, 2012, http://www .autoblog.com/2012/09/06/elon-musk-at-tesla-youre-choosing-to-be-the -equivalent-of-sp/.

36. Brad Stone, "Why Facebook Needs Sheryl Sandberg," *Bloomberg Businessweek,* May 12, 2011, https://www.bloomberg.com/news/articles/2011-05 -12/why-facebook-needs-sheryl-sandberg.

37. Jae Song, David Price, Fatih Guvenen, Nicholas Bloom, and Till von Wachter, "Firming Up Inequality" (Working Paper No. 21199, National Bureau of Economic Research, Cambridge, MA, 2015); Bloom, "Corporations in the Age of Inequality"; David Autor, David Dorn, Lawrence Katz, Christina Patterson, and John Van Reenen, "The Fall of the Labor Share and the Rise of Superstar Firms" (Working Paper No. 23396, National Bureau of Economic Research, Cambridge, MA, 2017).

38. Termed "smart creatives" by Google. Eric Schmidt and Jonathan Rosenberg, with Alan Eagle, *How Google Works,* with a foreword by Larry Page (New York: Grand Central Publishing, 2014); and Laszlo Bock, *Work Rules! Insights from Inside Google That Will Transform How You Live and Lead* (New York: Twelve, 2015).

39. William Kerr, Ben Jones, and Alexis Brownell, "Supercell," Harvard Business School Case 817-052 (Boston: Harvard Business Publishing, 2016).

40. Neil Irwin, "To Understand Rising Inequality, Consider the Janitors at Two Top Companies, Then and Now," *New York Times,* September 3, 2017, https://www.nytimes.com/2017/09/03/upshot/to-understand-rising -inequality-consider-the-janitors-at-two-top-companies-then-and-now.html; and Walter Frick, "Big Companies Don't Pay as Well as They Used To," *Harvard Business Review Digital,* February 13, 2017, https://hbr.org/2017/02/big-companies -dont-pay-as-well-as-they-used-to.

41. Moretti, *New Geography of Jobs.*

42. Silicon Valley and Columbus had seventeen and fifteen H-1B requests per thousand workers, respectively. Neil Ruiz, Jill Wilson, and Shyamali Choudhury, "Geography of H-1B Workers: Demand for High-Skilled Foreign Labor in U.S. Metropolitan Areas" (Brookings Report, Brookings Institution, Washington, DC, 2012).

43. These rural investments can be subverted, with a ski resort being a more attractive target than an old mining town, but the government's intention toward rural areas is genuine.

44. In one measurement, half the growth in U.S. income inequality during 1994–2006 is explained by five counties: New York County (NY), Santa Clara (CA), San Francisco (CA), San Mateo (CA), and King County (WA). James Kenneth Galbraith, *Inequality and Instability: A Study of the World Economy Just Before the Great Crisis* (Oxford: Oxford University Press, 2012).

45. Matthew 25:29 (New International Version).

46. Jennifer Hunt and Marjolaine Gauthier-Loiselle, "How Much Does Immigration Boost Innovation?" *American Economic Journal: Macroeconomics* 2, no. 2 (April 2010): 31–56; William Kerr and William Lincoln, "The Supply Side of Innovation: H-1B Visa Reforms and U.S. Ethnic Invention," *Journal of Labor Economics* 28, no. 3 (July 2010): 473–508; Giovanni Peri, Kevin Shih, and Chad

Sparber, "STEM Workers, H-1B Visas and Productivity in US Cities," *Journal of Labor Economics* 33, no. S1 (pt. 2, July 2015): S225–S255; and Chad Jones, "Sources of U.S. Economic Growth in a World of Ideas," *American Economic Review* 92, no. 1 (March 2002): 220–39.

47. Robert Ward, "Downstate Pays More, Upstate Gets More: Does It Matter?" *RIG Blog, Rockefeller Institute of Government, State University of New York,* December 2011, http://www.rockinst.org/observations/wardr/2011-12-giving_getting .aspx.

48. Five of the six states making the most H-1B requests are net fiscal contributors: California, Massachusetts, New York, New Jersey, and Illinois, with Texas as the one exception. John Tierney, "Which States Are Givers and Which Are Takers?" *Atlantic Monthly,* May 5, 2014, https://www.theatlantic.com/ business/archive/2014/05/which-states-are-givers-and-which-are-takers/ 361668/.

49. Fareed Zakaria, "Why Trump Won," *CNN,* August 25, 2017, http:// www.cnn.com/2017/07/31/opinions/why-trump-won-zakaria/index.html.

Conclusion

1. Depictions of the travel ban are from the first January 2017 action. As of December 2017, the Trump administration was continuing to adjust the travel ban and argue its merits in court. See Joanna Walters, Edward Helmore, and Saeed Kamali Dehghan, "US Airports on Frontline as Donald Trump's Travel Ban Causes Chaos and Protests," *The Guardian,* January 28, 2017, https://www .theguardian.com/us-news/2017/jan/28/airports-us-immigration-ban-muslim -countries-trump; Alexander Schroeder and Maria Sacchetti, "Warren Criticizes Trump's Immigration Order at Logan," *Boston Globe,* January 29, 2017, https://www.bostonglobe.com/metro/2017/01/28/elizabeth-warren-decries -donald-trump-immigration-order-logan/YwrOLjoOtgskLFS78PU6dN/story .html; Maryam Saleh, "Thousands Protest Donald Trump's Travel Ban," *U.S. News & World Report,* January 29, 2017, https://www.usnews.com/news/national -news/articles/2017-01-29/thousands-protest-donald-trumps-travel-ban; Associated Press, "Hundreds of Comcast Workers Protest Trump Travel Ban," *Washington Times,* February 2, 2017, http://www.washingtontimes.com/news/ 2017/feb/2/hundreds-of-comcast-workers-protest-trump-travel-b/; Sapna Maheshwari, "Super Bowl Commercials Feature Political Undertones and Celebrity Cameos," *New York Times,* February 5, 2017, https://www.nytimes.com/2017/ 02/05/business/media/commercials-super-bowl-51.html?_r=0; Charles Ornstein, "Hours after Landing in U.S., Cleveland Clinic Doctor Forced to Leave by Trump's Order," *ProPublica,* January 29, 2017, https://www.propublica.org/ article/cleveland-clinic-doctor-forced-to-leave-country-after-trump-order; Ford

Vox, "Trump's Travel Ban Hits Hospitals Hard," CNN, January 30, 2017, http://www.cnn.com/2017/01/29/opinions/trump-ban-impact-on-health-care-vox/index.html; Steve Almasy and Darran Simon, "A Timeline of President Trump's Travel Bans," CNN, March 30, 2017, http://www.cnn.com/2017/02/10/us/trump-travel-ban-timeline/index.html; Azadeh Ansari, Nic Robertson, and Angela Dewan, "World Leaders React to Trump's Travel Ban," CNN, January 30, 2017, http://www.cnn.com/2017/01/30/politics/trump-travel-ban-world-reaction/index.html; and Reuters, "Canada PM Tweets Welcome to Refugees as Trump Puts Hold on Arrivals," January 28, 2017.

2. Scott Suttell, "Cleveland Clinic Doctor Suha Abushamma Returns Home," *Crain's Cleveland Business*, February 7, 2017, http://www.crainscleveland.com/article/20170207/NEWS/170209856/cleveland-clinic-doctor-suha-abushamma-returns-home.

3. A review is in Branko Milanovic, *Global Inequality: A New Approach for the Age of Globalization* (Cambridge, MA: Harvard University Press, 2016).

4. The skills and experiences from an overseas education are becoming more common, and some hiring managers note that the increased number of overseas Chinese students has diluted the quality of those skills. Workers who stayed behind in China have local knowledge and contacts to compete with these "sea turtles." Colin Shek, "Homeward Bound: Chinese Sea Turtles Return to a New Reality," Cheung Kong Graduate School of Business Knowledge, May 5, 2015, http://knowledge.ckgsb.edu.cn/2015/05/05/globalization/homeward-bound-chinese-sea-turtles-return-to-a-new-reality/.

5. Tito Boeri, Herbert Bruecker, Frederic Docquier, and Hillel Rapoport, eds., *Brain Drain and Brain Gain: The Global Competition to Attract High-Skilled Migrants* (Oxford: Oxford University Press, 2012).

6. Japan is a powerful example of a country struggling to harness immigration within a society that has not been very open: Enda Curran and Connor Cislo, "Japan Opens Up to Foreign Workers (Just Don't Call it Immigration)," *Bloomberg*, October 25, 2016, https://www.bloomberg.com/news/articles/2016-10-25/a-wary-japan-quietly-opens-its-back-door-for-foreign-workers.

7. Robert Guest, *Borderless Economics: Chinese Sea Turtles, Indian Fridges and the New Fruits of Global Capitalism* (New York: St. Martin's Griffin, 2011).

8. An example of a broad-based playbook is Darrell West, Allan Friedman, and Walter Valdivia, "Building an Innovation-Based Economy" (Brookings Report, Brookings Institution, Washington, DC, 2012).

9. Economists use the term "Pareto improvement" to describe when a reallocation of resources can make at least one individual better off and no one worse off. This condition rarely, if ever, holds with immigration. See also George Borjas, *We Wanted Workers: Unraveling the Immigration Narrative* (New York: W. W. Norton & Company, 2016).

10. U.S. Department of Labor website, visited on January 10, 2017, https://www.doleta.gov/business/.

11. Politico & Morning Consult, "National Tracking Poll #170208 February 24–26, 2017: Crosstabulation Results," February 2017, http://www.politico.com/f/?id=0000015a-81a1-d487-a37e-edb1a8f30001. The February poll is the most recent comprehensive tabulation at the time of writing. An August 2017 poll provides similar support for high-skilled immigration but lacks the H-1B-specific questions.

12. Jens Hainmueller and Daniel Hopkins, "The Hidden American Immigration Consensus: A Conjoint Analysis of Attitudes toward Immigrants," *American Journal of Political Science* 59, no. 3 (July 2015): 529–48.

13. One study estimates a $27 billion gain over six years from this simple change, which would be further magnified to the extent that better talent became more likely to apply. Chad Sparber, "Choosing Skilled Foreign-Born Workers: Evaluating Alternative Methods for Allocating H-1B Work Permits," *Industrial Relations* 57, no. 1 (2018): 3–34.

14. Vivek Wadhwa, "Boost Visas for Foreign Entrepreneurs," *Nature* 543, no. 7643 (March 2, 2017): 29–31; and Heather Kelly, "Canada Wants to Be the Next Silicon Valley," CNN Money, June 22, 2017, http://money.cnn.com/2017/06/14/technology/business/canada-silicon-valley/index.html.

15. "Six Degrees and Separation: Immigrants to America Are Better Educated Than Ever Before," *The Economist*, June 8, 2017, https://www.economist.com/news/united-states/21723108-far-being-low-skilled-half-all-legal-migrants-have-college-degrees-immigrants; and Binyamin Appelbaum, "Fewer Immigrants Mean More Jobs? Not So, Economists Say," *New York Times*, August 3, 2017, https://www.nytimes.com/2017/08/03/us/politics/legal-immigration-jobs-economy.html?_r=0.

16. In parallel settings, "diploma mills" have been a problem: "UK Rolls Out New Service to Help Fight Diploma Mills and Degree Fraud," ICEF Monitor, June 15, 2015, http://monitor.icef.com/2015/06/uk-rolls-out-new-service-to-help-fight-diploma-mills-and-degree-fraud/.

17. This guaranteed work period after schooling also helps ensure that a revised system with wage ranking doesn't crowd out recent graduates with lower starting salaries until they gain employment footing.

18. Sari Kerr, William Kerr, and William Lincoln, "Firms and the Economics of Skilled Immigration," *Innovation Policy and the Economy* 15, no. 1 (2015): 115–52. This report provides examples of information housed in separate government agencies that would be very valuable when connected. For example, the LEHD data set used in this book identifies immigrants but does not include their visa status. Adding that detail would unlock tremendous research opportunities.

19. The 2018 first-quarter ranking is Apple, Alphabet/Google, Amazon, Microsoft, Tencent, Facebook, Berkshire Hathaway, Alibaba, JPMorgan Chase, and Johnson & Johnson. ExxonMobil and Wells Fargo also appeared in the top ten during 2017. The 1997 ranking is General Electric, Royal Dutch Shell, Microsoft, ExxonMobil, Coca-Cola, Intel, Nippon Telegraph and Telephone, Merck, Toyota, and Novartis. "List of Public Corporations By Market Capitalization," Wikipedia, last modified December 21, 2017, 15:40, https:// en.wikipedia.org/wiki/List_of_public_corporations_by_market_capitalization #1996.E2.80.931999.

20. The origin of this quote is debated, with some linking it back to a Canadian politician in the 1930s. Garson O'Toole, "If You Want Jobs Then Give These Workers Spoons Instead of Shovels," Quote Investigator, http:// quoteinvestigator.com/2011/10/10/spoons-shovels/.

INDEX

Page numbers followed by f indicate material in figures.